TERRIBLE BEAUTY

TERRIBLE

Reckoning with Climate Complicity and Rediscovering Our Soul

BEAUTY

Auden Schendler

HARVARD BUSINESS REVIEW PRESS

BOSTON, MASSACHUSETTS

The web addresses referenced in this book were live and correct at the time of the book's publication but may be subject to change.

Library of Congress Cataloging-in-Publication Data
Names: Schendler, Auden, author.
Title: Terrible beauty : reckoning with climate complicity and rediscovering our
    soul / Auden Schendler.
Description: Boston, Massachusetts : Harvard Business Review Press, [2024] |
    Includes bibliographical references and index.
Identifiers: LCCN 2024016080 (print) | LCCN 2024016081 (ebook) |
    ISBN 9781647829759 (hardcover) | ISBN 9781647829766 (epub)
Subjects: LCSH: Sustainable development. | Environmentalism. | Climatic
    changes.
Classification: LCC HC79.E5 S28264 2024 (print) | LCC HC79.E5 (ebook) |
    DDC 338.9/27--dc23/eng/20240517
LC record available at https://lccn.loc.gov/2024016080
LC ebook record available at https://lccn.loc.gov/2024016081

ISBN: 978-1-64782-975-9
eISBN: 978-1-64782-976-6

For Ellen, Willa, Elias, and their counterparts.

From this day to the ending of the world,
. . . we in it shall be remembered.

—St. Crispin's Day speech, Shakespeare,
Henry V, act 4, scene 3

CONTENTS

TERRIBLE BEAUTY

Devils of Dust and Spirit, and a New Climate Journey

I'm on fire, but I'm trying not to show it.

—Florence and the Machine, "Free"

My old friends Matt, Stu, and I spotted a dust devil from the truck. A spinning pillar, twisting and dancing through the red and brown landscape of the Utah desert, building power and color, dissipating, and then building again.

As a boy spending summers in North Dakota visiting my grandparents, I had always been obsessed with tornadoes. That landscape—flat to the horizon—with a giant sky prone to epic electrical storms, had a haunting and desolate beauty. And the notion that some vast force of awe and destruction could boil out of the black thunderclouds was as thrilling and terrifying an experience as I could imagine—just the stuff of boyhood. As Michael Herr, the great Vietnam War reporter, said, "You know how it is, you want to look and you don't want to look."[1] I never caught sight of a twister.

But here was a miniversion right in front of me, all those years later, more than half a lifetime ago. Matt started filming, of course. And as we drove on, we got closer and closer to it, and it to us, as it spun toward our very dirt road.

"It's coming toward us!" Matt said.

"Let's get it!" Stu bellowed.

"Let me out!" I yelled.

Matt pulled over as the devil spun almost to the road, and I opened the door and jumped out, in a Taco Bell T-shirt my daughter got me from Target, filthy Patagonia shorts, red Crocs. Holding my nose and closing my eyes, I ran into the center of the dust devil, Matt and Stu cackling, as it spun around me and dissipated almost as soon as I arrived. "Like our youth," Matt said.

But I had been there: inside the very center of, well, of the universe.

Over the next month, Matt said he looked at that video over and over and showed it to anyone he crossed paths with. Why?

Well, first, it was funny as hell. And weird and crazy, the stuff of viral TikTok. But there was more to it. It was an expression of unbridled freedom and pure joy. It displayed a level of total carefree existence and euphoria that is as ethereal and hard to nail down as love, as elusive as the good dream you can't remember.

Considering that feeling, I thought of the word *chrysopoeia*, a term from alchemy. In Greek it means "gold making," specifically the artificial production of gold, by transmuting base metals like lead. Kind of like manufacturing joy out of a short little trip to the desert with three middle-aged guys in a big truck-like SUV. But the word has more, almost uncanny depth. The slightly different spelling, *Chrysopelea*, is the genus of . . . a flying snake found in Asia—much like, in meteorological form, the dust devil featured in Matt's video. And the term *chrysopoeia* was first used in a book about alchemy by the awesomely named Cleopatra the Alchemist (not the more famous Queen Cleopatra). The volume features an image of an Ouroboros— a snake eating its own tail—containing the words "the all is one." The all is one—without getting ahead of my skis here, that's nothing much, just the essential tenet of all religion—the idea of the unity of everything and, therefore, of the divine presence in all things. Which was, you might say, the sort of transcendence Stu, Matt, and I felt in our moment in the desert. All that from a dust devil! Thank you, dust devil!

And what had brought us to this epiphanic place? Well, Matt's enormous SUV, of course. It was truly giant: a black Toyota Sequoia TRD Pro. Twenty-two miles per gallon. Huge mud tires that brought the mileage down further but which were perfect for this trip. Enough horsepower to tow a camper and big enough for Matt to sleep in, which he did, to escape the desert dust and wind.

"This truck is the ultimate badass thing," I commented at one point in the trip, as we overcame rock obstacles worthy of mythology. "It's the ideal apocalypse vehicle."

"Yeah," Matt said. "You'll be the baddest thing out there. Until you run out of gas."

And there it was, the zeitgeist encroaching.

The big truck—specifically its fossil fuel provenance—haunts us even in our ecstasy. As it does any caring, sentient citizen. Because the thing we had staked our civilization on contradicted, simply, everything we care about as parents, neighbors, and citizens. The stuff that brought us transcendence was also an essential—perhaps the essential—component, maybe even the soul, of a societal Ouroboros, a fossil fuel economy that we now know threatens the very existence of civilization. And so we all felt guilty in our euphoria.

But why?

The truth of the matter is that Matt, Stu, and I hadn't ever said, "Hey, auto industry. Can you provide me with mobility, please? But a favor: Could you do so in a way that will threaten and eventually destroy civilization? And everything we love out here? And our kids' future?"

Similarly, Americans and other global citizens never particularly asked for cold sodas, hot baths, heat in their homes, transportation, or illumination delivered in the most damaging possible way to the planet.

That may be true, one might argue back, but people did ask for those services delivered at the lowest possible cost, and coal and oil did that—magnificently, in fact. Alchemically, even. A dark, smelly, filthy substance, or a dirty rock that burns, was converted over the last century and a half into both the greatest antipoverty program in the history of humanity and the engine of near-religious opportunities at transcendence, like Jack Kerouac's jazz-inspired road trips or Neil Armstrong's steps on the moon.

But what is missing in that analysis is information. In the 1950s, scientists knew what fossil fuel extraction would do. In fact, by 1977, using whatever awesome supercomputers or models or physics they had at the time, Exxon scientists accurately predicted that the continued combustion of fossil fuels on a business-as-usual path would warm the Earth by about 1.2°C above preindustrial times by . . . about right now.[2] They were exactly right.

They were right, but they buried the information. And so in the country that burned the most fossil fuels, had the largest economy, and enjoyed a position of global leadership, the citizens of the world's greatest democracy had to make electoral and even policy decisions absent absolutely essential information. We did not know, or were intentionally confused about the fact, that our own policy decisions could unleash some vast force of awe and destruction that would boil out of the atmosphere in the form of systemic overheating, a tornado of our own manufacture. But the fossil fuel industry knew, and it funded science obfuscation and contributed buckets of money to the politicians who opposed regulation—the one thing that could solve the climate problem but cost them money—as they continue to do today.[3] (Historian Naomi Oreskes has said, "The reason we are confused is that people are trying to confuse us.")

What would we have done had there not been decades of misinformation campaigns and the corporate capture of government? One might imagine we would have said, "Hey, this fossil fuel stuff, it's amazing. It's powering an agricultural and economic revolution that is literally saving lives. Refrigeration, air-conditioning, mobility, fertilizers, it's all incredible. But I wonder if we *ought to slowly, deliberately, carefully, without moving too fast or causing too much damage*, evolve toward cleaner forms of energy." After all, we mostly knew how to do it even then—the first electrified cities in the United States were hydroelectric powered. Windmills blew in Holland before people ever dug up rocks that burn.[4]

Indeed, Jimmy Carter suggested the United States ought to get 20 percent of its electricity from renewable sources by the year 2000. Imagine if we had judiciously proceeded along that path—gently supporting technology development and deployment so that we would have more quickly gotten to the place we are today, where solar and wind are simply cheaper sources of power than coal or gas.

But it didn't happen. And instead, something occurred that is almost hard to believe in retrospect.

Encouraged by propaganda from the fossil fuel industry like the "Crying Indian" ad that put the blame for litter on us, not the makers of the plastic bottles, and abetted by Americans' unique sense of personal agency, we not only went along with the fossil fuel dream and nightmare but also felt guilty about it. We were emasculated and unable to act, because we were convinced of our own complicity, and therefore hypocrisy. As a friend said to me once, "Auden, I can't serve on that environmental foundation board. I drive an SUV, so I'm part of the problem." But he hadn't asked for an internal combustion engine; he had asked for affordable mobility.

As it turned out, Americans *were* at least partly complicit, not because they drove gas cars and not so much because of their silence, though over time they better understood the science. Instead, they were guilty of unquestioningly buying into a theory of environmentalism that specifically avoided meaningful change, swapping revolution for sorting plastic bottles that never actually got recycled, and righteously thinking modifying one's life with Priuses and LED light bulbs was enough to solve a global problem. We implemented a series of solutions that we very well knew, or should have known, had no chance at all of fixing the problem they were meant to address. We were guilty of not thinking things through. For the average American, the internal colloquy goes something like this: "What do I love? Family, community, faith. What am I doing in the face of climate change, which threatens to destroy those things? Uh . . . sometimes I remember my canvas bags at the supermarket."

Could a problem of global industrial scale really be solved by a Prius and a recycle bin? It was either magical thinking or willful blindness. Either way, it added up to a planet on fire.

Simultaneously, in my own world of business, an immense field called *corporate sustainability* evolved to use the powerful, influential, and nimble engines of capitalism—corporations—to help drive solutions to climate change and to implement those solutions themselves. But that movement was also complicit and co-opted. Instead of using the political tools (e.g., trade groups, direct lobbying, and cash contributions) that business had deployed for generations to effectively move public policy, corporate America seemingly decided that if enough companies cut their emissions significantly, the practice could catch on (because lots of those emissions cuts made through energy efficiency came at a profit). In this way, the thinking went, business could lead—even show government the way—in the climate fix. It was a technocratic fantasy, but it was also an intentional dodge of meaningful action, akin to responding to racism in America by asking people to *just be nicer*, instead of passing the Voting Rights Act. Corporate leaders took this path in part because by the time the climate threat was a clear and present danger, business had locked into the idea that industries should never, ever advocate for regulation in any way.

But the corporate climate fix didn't play out the way it was promised by sustainability gurus, CEOs, and think tanks. Over decades, business spiraled deeper and deeper into carbon navel-gazing, overly fixated on their own carbon footprints and their own impact, despite the fact that large societal change never happens at the firm or individual level. Trying to look good, businesses created environmental and social governance (ESG) systems (each of which was different and none of which could be easily pinned down). Academics wrote papers arguing that ESG boosted revenues. It took decades to show those papers were wrong.[5] Businesses created acronyms like CSR (corporate social responsibility) to make it seem like they knew something the public didn't, even though CSR meant really anything anyone decided it should mean.

An example of the absurdity is the current corporate obsession with scope 1, 2, and 3 emissions, a complicated system of understanding all emissions, ranging from those related to electricity purchases to those caused by employee plane travel. Thinking they were doing good work, even the Securities and Exchange Commission (SEC) got into the game, passing a new rule that will require rigorous carbon accounting by corporations. The law will take years to comply with and occupy time that could be spent on real change; it is a law that could have been written by the fossil fuel industry.

What has been happening in the world while business and even regulators focused on the wrong thing—an analysis paralysis driven by some level of good intention, a major dose of cluelessness, and a dollop of intentional distraction? We all know the answer: CO_2 emissions continued to tick upward, and global temperatures set records year after year.

As it turns out, the only problem with the American approach to sustainable business and environmentalism more broadly was that the entire thesis simply supported the status quo fossil fuel economy. It was the climate equivalent of asking for prayer in response to school shootings. In other words, the sustainable-business movement—indeed, the bulk of American environmentalism after the Clean Air Act and Clean Water Act revisions—functioned in ways that never had any oomph, never pushed remotely hard enough to change anything. And the fossil fuel industry itself made sure of it by implanting notions of personal responsibility, personal action (BP popularized the idea of a carbon footprint, which could just as easily have been called your "carbon fault"), and free-market theology into the very fabric of the nation. We were all susceptible to these ideas because of our (also manufactured) notion of an individualistic frontier heritage.[6]

The result was a booming corporate sustainability movement that operates by its own invisible hand: anything that might move the needle and change fossil capitalism for the better is off the table. Movements, revolution, protest, hardball environmental politics, even CEOs writing op-eds demanding climate action from Congress—they are all verboten.

At the same time, overtly duplicitous actions like paying dues to giant trade groups—like the US Chamber of Commerce, which opposes all climate legislation—that's just something you do, because change comes from within, and you can't just take your ball and go home. And if you suggest more radical stuff, like, say, dropping out, you're a crank, which I have been called many times. "That's not how business works," a friend of mine who works in a major corporation pursuing an admirable sustainability strategy told me. His firm was also paying dues to the Chamber. "You work for change from within. You don't just quit." But this isn't a football game, where quitters are shamed. The literal future of civilization depends on rapid change, not glacial nudging from within, an approach that has demonstrably failed for decades. The result has been that corporate sustainability professionals are rewarded for doing the conventional things that don't move the needle. And if you choose another path, trying to be better, you are asked, "Why is everyone else doing this stuff and you're not?" Or worse: "Oh, Schendler. He's a bomb-thrower."

Meanwhile, the fossil fuel industry and the Chamber of Commerce did just the thing I was being told not to do. They fostered change from the outside, capturing government, owning elections, and dominating the policy landscape to the point that legacy subsidies of fossil fuels in the United States amount to more than $20 billion a year even today.[7] This, well over a century after commercial oil development began and when a carbon tax has become a political impossibility.

So climate-concerned businesspeople like me were told not to take our ball and go home—that's just not how big boys and girls play—while the fossil fuel industry took *our* ball. And now, because of it, in a burning and melting and flooding and baking land, we can never go back to the thing we remembered as home.

This book isn't so much about how that happened. Rather, it's about what is happening now—what our complicity looks like, how we've bought into a system that ensures it. It's about the puzzling gap between what we care about as parents and neighbors and citizens and the actions we take to address the glaring problem of climate change that threatens everything we profess to love.

Most importantly, this book is about how to break that system down, to cleave through the Ouroboros of our fossil fuel economy, and emerge into a world in which the heedless jubilance of a dust devil adventure is available to the great masses of humanity. In this world, people are living lives of thriving abundance and joy, not permanently beset with issues of survival and terror, basement sumping, and rebuilding from fire and flood. In this world, we live in comfort and stability, not in a hellscape where society is forced to spend disproportionate and historically unprecedented dollars on road reconstruction and other climate-induced disasters instead of the things that make us thrive, like art and education and music and song.

What will motivate us to get there, ironically, is the very threat itself or, rather, the juxtaposition of that threat with the things we love, care about, and aspire to. Those two ideas, put together, constitute terrible beauty. Anything—any person, any idea, any dream, any *thing*—you truly love comes accompanied with visceral terror, because that thing is, by definition, ephemeral, mortal. Terrible beauty is your neighbor's two-year-old child, who you deliver a kid-sized snow shovel to on a winter night. He opens the door crying; it's the witching hour, close to bedtime. "We're going to need your help shoveling out tomorrow, dude . . ." He takes the shovel, says, "I like this one." And stops crying. His parents, and I, love him so much in this moment that they want to protect him forever, and the very nature of our dangerous and unpredictable life on earth makes us tremble.

Terrible beauty is your life partner, without whom you would be incomplete. It's your teenage son, days out from having destroyed his knee in a basketball game, a season-wrecking injury in a year when he was putting up all-state numbers, who walks out onto the porch at 6 a.m. on the day of surgery, looks at the violet clouds to the west, and says, "The light is so pretty." It's hugging your daughter going off to college and not being able to let go.

The idea of terrible beauty is also about opportunity and presence, the joy to be had in the midst of crisis, if one has been able to cultivate a present mind and the associated serious tackling of the moment. Nothing better exemplifies that idea than the Zen koan about the tiger and the strawberry, as translated by Paul Reps:

> A man traveling across a field encountered a tiger. He fled, the tiger after him. Coming to a precipice, he caught hold of the root of a wild vine and swung himself down over the edge. The tiger sniffed at him from above. Trembling, the man looked down to where, far below, another tiger was waiting to eat him. Only the vine sustained him. Two mice, one white and one black, little by little started to gnaw away at the vine. The man saw a luscious strawberry near him. Grasping the vine with one hand, he plucked the strawberry with the other. How sweet it tasted![8]

All the solutions to climate feature an element of this joy in crisis, an ability to appreciate beauty and exhibit humor in the midst of chaos. And yet in many ways, the solutions laid out in the latter part of the book—which are meant to help readers think through their own solutions at scale—are tastier than the man's strawberry. Because those victories are steps along the road to a civilizational cure. How deliciously wonderful!

And terrible beauty is also closely tied to what we care about most.

I don't think I understood the visceral nature of our love for our children, the thing humans care about above all else, until I developed a recurring dream after 9/11 in New York City. In it, I am high in the first tower, which is on fire below me. I am with my two small children. This place has been part of my consciousness since I was born. I grew up in New Jersey, five minutes from the city, and could see the Twin Towers from a spot a block from my house. But I was also a rural spirit—at eight, I asked my mom if I could tell people I was from North Dakota. At sixteen, I started rock climbing, and that passion began my migration away from the city. My dream of the tower on fire merges urban life and rural inclinations. I look out the window and see the unique vertical exterior columns of the World Trade Center on an undamaged face. A climber could brace himself between these columns, with feet on one wall of a chimney, and his back on the other. In this way, I could, conceivably, Batman out the window and into the chimney, and although it would be hard, I could probably make my way down eighty stories.

But I could not do it with my children.

The dream ends in this state of nauseating realization. That feeling is so limbic, so sickening, and so powerful because it evokes a great human truth. I see it as a parable of the greatest human fear: the inability to take care of our children. Inverted, it is also the greatest human hope: that we should be able to ensure a long and prosperous and meaningful life for all children, not just our own.

This book is about finding a way to turn that oldest and greatest aspiration to use: to weaponize our deep love by ensuring that it meets the moment in the scope and scale of our actions.

Because of that, the stories you'll read here are optimistic at their very core, a secular form of the Good News. You'll learn about a small business that helped change forestry practices at a giant multinational by using a form of asymmetric warfare. About how a new climate movement from the outdoor industry would, if realized to its full potential, represent a political force ten times the size of the National Rifle Association. And you'll also come to understand why fighting battles like this—impossible fights against great odds—are the very thing humans were created to do.

This book is not "ten ways to solve climate change." Nor is it cluelessly optimistic. It's something more powerful and more practical: it's a path to help you understand and then realize your own power and your own aspirations and maximize your abilities. It is a way to wed our dreams and our aspirations to action worthy of those dreams. It is, fundamentally, what Barry Lopez described in *Arctic Dreams,* his book about human desire and its relation to the landscape: "The continuous work of the imagination . . . to bring what is actual together with what is dreamed, is an expression of human evolution. The conscious desire is to achieve a state, even momentarily, that like light is unbounded, nurturing, suffused with wisdom and creation, a state in which one has absorbed that very darkness which before was the perpetual sign of defeat."[9]

The first half of the book traces my evolution from a New Jersey environmentalist (all environmentalists come from New Jersey; the locale forces it on you) to a corporate sustainability practitioner. It also lays out the original thesis of the movement and the basis of modern environmentalism. And then it examines what went wrong.

The second half of the book is about how to think about change and one's own abilities to maximize power. And it uses real stories to demonstrate how to do it.

Importantly, this book is based in lived experience, from a world where some fairy tales of climate repair actually came true, even at significant scale. For our own sanity, this is *not* another claxon signaling the imminent end-time (most of us already got that missive). It describes a path forward unique from other prescriptions in that it offers a way to think and to be, instead of a particular thing to do. As such, it enables each reader to find their own unique levers to drive disproportionate change.

This book includes some level of memoir, not because I'm an important person, but because I represent an important time. I was born in 1970, just as the most significant environmental laws in the history of the world were being enacted or passed: the Clean Air Act and the Clean Water Act. And this was happening as part of a massive governmental response to unacceptable environmental degradation.

I was born in the epicenter of this response. I grew up in an urban hellscape that reflected the need for those laws: New Jersey in the

1970s. My memories of that place are the ruined world of apocalyptic mythology; half-built apartment buildings on Hudson River Road; the epic wetlands of the Meadowlands turned into a garbage dump; the air itself purple at night from pollution; antique and beautiful piers on the Hudson burning from arson; fumes billowing up past the baseball field atop the Lincoln Tunnel where I played first base. And a culture to reflect that collapse. Gangs of boys chased me after school in third grade because my haircut made me look like a girl; a friend's father was shot and killed in his liquor store in Jersey City, which I always thought was the model for *Blade Runner*'s cityscape. My father was repeatedly mugged as he wandered through Manhattan. (They didn't know that mugging a guy whose mission was to wander into and out of bookstores and thrift shops was not worth robbing.)[10]

I also came of age in the era of corporate sustainability, learning at the feet of some of the founders of the field, and so I have been able to track the movement from my initial enthusiasm to my eventual disillusionment.

. . .

When I left for college, I was on fire with ideas of possibility, adventure, freedom, and wildness. What hooked me first was, of all things, a 1985 Banana Republic catalog. It featured a leather jacket that I coveted. The copywriter had channeled Jack Kerouac's *On the Road*, a book whose author I had never heard of: "In gray chilly light of Frisco dawn, torso-hugging coat zipped up tight against spectral fog, disembodied legs of the orange bridge descending . . ."[11] My lab partner and I later read Kerouac secretly held under the desk in our advanced placement biology class. Bruce Springsteen, a descendant of Kerouac and a fellow New Jerseyite, spoke to me with his visions of kinetic movement toward great, unrealized possibilities.

"The dogs on Main Street howl," Bruce wrote in "The Promised Land," "'cause they understand. If I could take this moment into my hands."[12]

As it turned out in our lives, in this time, climate was the thing to take into our hands, not just for me, but for all of us. It was no big deal really, *just a chance to save civilization.*

Today, in my midfifties, I am not tired. I wake up every day with that same amount of fire, abetted by several cups of espresso-strength pour-over dark roast. My old favorite quote, a Charles Bukowski observation that I put on business cards, was "What matters most is how well you walk through the fire." I still believe that, but I'm getting older, and I realized I needed something fresh. My new business-card motto is from Florence and the Machine: "I'm on fire, but I'm trying not to show it."[13]

I try, but at my desk, my knees are bouncing, and at night, my thoughts are racing, because of this great thing we have the chance to be part of. A chance to enact one of the oldest and best ideas in human thought, consistent among religions: the Golden Rule. What gets bigger than that? What a time to be alive! As Kerouac's Dean Moriarty would have said, "We gotta go!"

Our motivations and our aspirations, when connected to meaningful action, can't help but play out as a good kind of fairy tale that will stand for the ages. We, as citizens of the world, are writing a fable with an open ending. In one version of our story, we fail to stop the climate locomotive, and it runs us over. It is an epic tragedy.

But the story you'll read here, and the one that I think will play out, is truer, more likely, and more worthy of a species that created "Ode to Joy" and Notre-Dame de Paris and the Mars Rover and *Les Demoiselles d'Avignon* and Emmylou Harris and a guy who walked across a tightrope between the Twin Towers. A species that weathered the Black Death and World War II and ended smallpox. A species capable of both magic and epic grunt work.

This is a story in which a people struggle mightily against great odds to achieve momentous things, transmuting the leaden bleakness of current climate forecasts into a golden future of our own making. Want to come along?

1

The Axe

The Human Dimensions of Climate Change

*The miracle is not to fly in the air, or to walk
on the water, but to walk on the earth.*

—Chinese proverb

I have a slow-motion video of my son, Elias, in our backyard in Basalt, Colorado. He is probably eight, wearing his go-to outfit of gray sweatpants and a camouflage jacket, one blue glove and one black. His haircut is my handiwork, done on our back porch, to save money until he is old enough to care. And he's swinging an axe, which I had remounted onto a yellow polyethylene handle after the old hickory one shattered.

He brings the axe down onto a round perched on a stump, and glancingly cleaves off a portion. It's not a clean split, but it achieves the same, satisfying effect known to wood splitters over the millennia: the grain-assisted, effortless calving. The axe continues its arc to the ground and just misses a garden hose. He also avoids chopping off a toe, because his stance is wide and he's far enough away from the strike point, as I had taught him.

Behind Elias, early snow blankets the yard, and behind that Basalt Mountain looms, a volcanic pile of cheese-grater rocks, and the piercing royal blue sky of Colorado September. Our backyard is a wild montane ecosystem that reflects our location in the world: there are juniper and pinion but also sage and cactus, here at six thousand feet in the Rockies. We live between the desert of Moab, Utah, and the alpine of Aspen, Colorado. (Not perceiving we were in high desert, Elias's sister, Willa, as a two-year-old, once sat down on a cactus, leading to a delicate afternoon of tweezer work by her dad.) The climate here has been remarkably stable for 10,000 years, as it has been worldwide. During that time, agriculture and later nation-states flourished, and global population grew from a few million people at the end of the last ice age to 1.2 billion in 1850 and 8 billion today.[1]

The act Elias is engaged in is not just a skill that has been practiced for millennia—the first hand axes showed up about 1.5 million years ago, the first hafted, or handled, axes 6,000 years ago—but something he had to learn from his parents, like children throughout time. Socketed axes in the Bronze Age were both the main tool of the period and likely used to store value.

After the successful split, he looks up, straight at the camera, and flashes the smile all parents of young children know: "Can you believe that? Did you see that? How great is this?" I have seen the same from Elias and Willa when they first rode a carousel, ate Frosted Flakes, or saw baby robins hatch in our spruce tree.

Elias walks away, past the camera, still grinning.

In my life, I have seen no greater expression of human thriving, or what Aristotle called *eudaimonia*, than this. Elias is healthy, young, happy, learning, outside in a beautiful landscape, practicing a skill and task that reaches back through time, not just culturally, but physically. He is operating in a stable landscape, a functional society, and in a climate that produces seasons and enables the success of the flora and fauna living here, Elias included. The axe head he is using is certainly 150 years old, salvaged from my grandfather's garage. It is Elias's great-grandfather's axe.

This is, as best as I can frame it, the definition of sustainability, the idea of being able to stay in business forever. For Elias, his business is boyhood. For me, it's fatherhood. For the land, it's the continuity of the cycles of ecology and the seasons.

Our axe is a way to store value, a tool—a machine, actually, since it uses an inclined plane, or wedge, to do work—that represents the value of a life lived with certain constants assumed, like the idea that wood chopping, and fatherhood as we understand it, and boyhood, and the nature around us, will endure more or less as we've known it for days and years and centuries forward. Cormac McCarthy: "And he said if he were God he would have made the world just so and no different."[2]

There is another image I look at often. It's a color-coded map developed by the National Aeronautics and Space Administration (NASA) showing the predicted climate in North America in 2095 under a business-as-usual scenario. Shades of brown indicate relative drought. All of Mexico and Central America and much of the West around Elias's home, including Colorado, Utah, Arizona, Wyoming, Texas, and Kansas, are the darkest, almost black, indicating soil moisture content equivalent to the dust bowl of the 1930s.

Indeed, if I were to take a new video of Elias, who is now seventeen and able to dunk a basketball, it would show that Basalt Mountain had entirely burned. In the summer of 2018, a catastrophic wildfire nearly took out our whole town and was only avoided by lucky wind patterns, astounding heroics by local firefighters, and $40 million worth of air tanker drops. When we rushed to evacuate our home, we dropped Elias off on my friend Matt's porch to wait for us to return. They were not home, and Elias was crying, but he had asked us to do it. He didn't want to see his hometown burn down.

Grabbing a stick from the yard as a cane and walking hunched over, Elias used to describe how one day he'd be an "old little man." In 2095, if he is lucky, Elias will be eighty-eight, his old little man-ness realized in that parched landscape. The axe, I'm certain, will have lasted. Perhaps there will also be wood for him to chop, even if it is juniper, not aspen. Those are the things that will endure. But virtu-ally everything else around him, both physically and societally, will be different, the result of warming between 3°C and 6°C over prein-dustrial times.

It will be different, but it will not be better.

Kevin Anderson, a climate scientist who used to run the Tyndall Centre for Climate Change Research, has famously said that "a 4 de-grees C future is incompatible with an organized global community." That amount of warming is "likely [to be] beyond adaptation . . . is devastating for the majority of ecosystems . . . [and has] a high prob-ability of not being stable."[3]

"Incompatible with an organized global community" is a master-ful example of obfuscatory scientific bureaucratese. But the concept is simple: he's describing the society depicted in *Mad Max*.

Meanwhile, each successive report from the United Nations gets bleaker. As reported in the *Guardian*, "Emissions must fall by about half by 2030 to meet the internationally agreed target of 1.5C of heating but are still rising, the reports showed—at a time when oil giants are making astronomical amounts of money."[4] And yet the planet touched on 1.8°C in 2023.

The climate crisis has reached a "really bleak moment," said a leading climate scientist after a slew of major reports laid bare how close the planet is to catastrophe.

The *Guardian* piece continued: "Collective action is needed by the world's nations more now than at any point since the Second World War to avoid climate tipping points, Prof Johan Rockström said, but geopolitical tensions are at a high. He said the world was coming 'very, very close to irreversible changes . . . time is really running out very, very fast.'"

That kind of news makes you think about your family.

Elias's sister Willa has always been a badass. A black belt in Soo Bahk Do, an ace student who at twelve traveled to Washington, DC, to meet with the head of the US Environmental Protection Agency (EPA), she plays the baddest of all instruments: the saxophone. Elias, a different creature, spent years obsessed with gnomes, writing letters to them in the yard, and building them elaborate homes. When he took a sixth-grade aptitude test to determine what future careers he might be suited to, high on the list was "Airline Baggage Handling Supervisor."

"At least he's a supervisor," my wife Ellen said.

When he entered high school, Elias said, "I'm not going to work all the time like Willa. I'm going to do well, but I'm also going to have fun."

And Elias's light touch on life has led to success too, just different from that of his sister. A journalist reporting on people who collect weird things found out about him, and his gnome story came out in *Parade*, the ubiquitous national newspaper insert. Overnight, with no effort, Elias had become a celebrity. He began receiving letters—and packages of gnomes—from all over the country, with notes of friendship and loneliness, kinship and admiration, from California and Virginia, from older women whose husbands had died long ago. A gnome carver from Ohio sent a bespoke figurine; Eunice from South Carolina became a pen pal. Willa observed his fame with frustration and disbelief.

The story of Elias and Willa is not special, and it is no different from the stories we all have of our children and spouses or partners, family, and friends. But this stuff, this silliness, these dust devils, and the ability to pursue them as part of a life unencumbered by questions of survival and continued existence, is what we care about as humans. And such things of grace and beauty—such stories of human thriving—are not possible in a climate-changed world.

Regardless of our political backgrounds, our ethnicities, our relative wealth, our class or creeds, we all universally care about Elias and Willa. We want them and their fellow citizens and fellow humans to live in a world somewhat similar to what we know, to have at least close to the same chance of thriving that we had. The same shot at silliness, fun, and humanity.

And yet despite a seemingly obvious universal consensus about the need to sustain our lives and families, our approach to ensuring that future has been flawed across the board. It has, with few exceptions, consisted of token actions not remotely equal to the task. Sustainable-business strategies that tweak operations but are voluntary and don't move systems. Measures based more on hope than on effect, like biodegradable packing peanuts. Obviously false solutions presented as real ones, like most carbon offsets and renewable energy certificates. Magical thinking, like the notion that free markets will naturally drive sustainable solutions at a profit. And flagrant lies like plastics recycling, which never actually worked or occurred, though we still diligently "recycle" to this day. Each of us has, to some extent, bought into this false narrative that misses the bigger picture and the need to change whole systems, not tweak small dials.

In some cases, the best of us even knew the solutions didn't work, but we thought we had no better ideas. (As an employee of a leading environmental nonprofit said to me once when I explained that the measures he suggested could never solve the problem, "I know that. But we have to do *something*!")

And yet. Solving climate change—ensuring a stable future for Elias's and Willa's goofy lives and their equivalent throughout the world—is perhaps the greatest opportunity ever presented to humanity. Because, in fact, those of us alive today have a chance to save civilization from untold suffering and calamity.

And such an opportunity is hard to turn down. As writer Barry Lopez explains, "One of the oldest dreams of mankind is to find a dignity that might include all living things. And one of the greatest of human longings must be to bring such dignity to one's own dreams, for each to find his or her own life exemplary in some way."[5]

What the climate crisis asks of us is that we save the world as we know it.

An appropriate response would be, "I agree, but you've got the wrong guy. I am just a person. I feel cripplingly depressed when I wake up at 4 a.m. to pee (for the third time). I can barely get out of the house in the morning. I find it hard enough just to engage people at the supermarket, let alone save the world. I'm not Jackie Robinson,

Susan B. Anthony, Gandhi, Martin Luther King Jr., Rosa Parks, Franklin D. Roosevelt. I'm just a person who half the time doesn't even know where the car keys are."

And in response to that, I'd say that history is full of people without power driving enormous change. An example of one such person is Mohamed Bouazizi, the Tunisian vegetable vendor who, frustrated with his treatment by the police, set himself on fire and triggered the Arab Spring. We do not know how the revolution he gave his life for will play out, even if hopes have now dimmed. But the change he created is undeniable. And Bouazizi was perhaps the least powerful person in the world at the time.

I am not saying you should set yourself on fire. But I *am* saying you should be on fire for the fix, burning, as Allen Ginsberg put it, "for the ancient heavenly connection" to what matters as a human being.

Kurt Vonnegut has written beautifully about the Genesis story of Lot's exile from the burning cities on the plain. God had decided to punish the residents of Sodom for their sins. He sent an angel down to warn Lot, a good man. "Take your family and run from the city," the angel said. "But there's one condition: you must not look back."

Vonnegut writes, "And Lot's wife, of course, was told not to look back where all those people and their homes had been. But she did look back, and I love her for that, because it was so human. So she was turned into a pillar of salt. So it goes."[6]

Of course she looked back. Behind her in the distance, in the flames, was the place she dropped her children off to school for the first time. The place she had her first kiss. The kitchen where she baked her first pie. Of course she looked back: it was the most human thing to do.

The opportunity to solve climate change would seem similar. When presented with the chance to grapple with a great and epic problem and, in the process, to endow our lives with some of the oldest human aspirations—ideas like dignity, grace, and justice—*you would think we couldn't help but do it.*

But as it turns out, Lot's wife was exceptional. (She is, after all, a character in Genesis, so probably has some chops.) Most of us, though, take the exact opposite lesson from this story. We don't look back. Indeed, this is arguably direction we're taking from the fossil fuel industry: never mind that your home is burning—keep going with your life, and don't look back. Leonardo DiCaprio's film *Don't Look Up*, about two astronomers warning about a deadly comet threatening Earth, and which is also about climate change, has eerie modern similarities. The world's response is . . . "Whatever, dude." Somehow, the human impulse to look up, to look back, to think, and to care has been suppressed.

Our great opportunity as a society is straightforward: to relearn what Lot's wife already knew.

. . .

The climate crisis will not be solved by one solution or one approach and not with a silver bullet, as environmentalist Bill McKibben has noted, but with silver buckshot. Much of this book is about the technical or political reality of climate action or inaction. But there's one human element of the struggle that is essential. In fact, if we're unable to recruit people on a moral and even a spiritual journey into why it matters to engage on climate with force and energy, we won't win this fight. To get to critical mass, their motivation will have to go beyond national security and energy savings. It will need to come from their heart and soul, their values and their faith.

All the great societal changes of our time—from women's suffrage to civil rights to marriage equality—have had a human or moral component; rarely have they been technocratic or purely political.

There are skills and qualities we will need, demons to wrestle with, models to learn and follow. We must develop resilience and hope, perseverance and respect; we need to grapple with possibility and regret, to fight our lesser angels, and take at least a few moments to stand in awe. We also need to remember what we're fighting for: the humanity that grounds us; the neighbors we want to treat, but have forgotten how to treat, as if they were ourselves; our crippling love for our spouses and children; the moments of grace that not only make life worth living but also reveal the numinous, incandescent, divine quality of existence.

Throughout this book, we'll take breaks, or interludes, to consider the human dimensions of a life lived in the midst of climate crisis and to consider the things we stand to lose and to gain. Many of these stories feature my children, Willa and Elias, and my wife, Ellen, and take place across the kids' entire childhood. As of this writing, Willa was twenty and Elias seventeen.

A seminal experience for all of us involved turtles.

 ## On Hatteras, Putting the World, and Ourselves, Back Together

Like summer, turtle hatching season is coming to a close on Hatteras Island, North Carolina, and all along the coast, sunbathers incubate themselves in late-summer heat under strategically planted umbrellas that skirt dozens of fenced nesting areas. Only feet away, just under the surface, the eggs of five turtle species slowly mature, a process that has endured since the dinosaurs.

That cycle almost came to a crashing halt. In humanity's short reign, overfishing drove sea turtles almost to extinction—Winston Churchill's favorite meal was sea turtle soup—and today ocean gyres of plastic kill still more. These protected nesting sites are an attempt to bring them back.

Bobbing in the waves, my daughter Willa wondered why. "What does it matter if a turtle goes extinct?" she asked. I defaulted to the old saws: the value to humans, medicine, ecology. I told her we're using the psychedelic-colored blue blood of an even older animal, the horseshoe crab, in medicine. Who knows how we might use turtles? I mentioned the risk to the food chain, the role of *indicator species* that act as barometers for broader ecosystem health. But those arguments seemed weak and embarrassingly self-serving, and they reeked of rationalization. In the end, for all our flaws as humans, I told her, we just can't bear to see these animals go away after thriving for a hundred million years. That instinct, I say, has to be the most remarkable thing about us: it is a miracle that we care.

But we do. News about turtle activity spreads like a storm surge across the beaches of North Carolina, an underground network, a black market in turtle intel. Near our s'mores fire one night, my wife learned of an unannounced excavation the next day. When we arrived at what we thought was a secret event, we found forty others.

A ponytailed National Park Service biologist with his fly charmingly undone sweated through his uniform describing turtle biology— they swim out to sea to catch the Gulf Stream ("Just like in *Finding Nemo*!" a kid yells). The males never return, but the females come back thirty years later to lay their eggs. We learned that a nearby nest was likely to "boil" in the next few days. That night, we visited the site, Willa, Elias, Ellen, and me. There too, we found throngs.

Turtle mania had hit the beaches! Info on excavations spread not through Twitter or Instagram but though the oldest form of human contact—schmoozing—and it went viral like the latest sex tape or reality show. (Though, I admit, this too is a reality show and a sex tape, of sorts.) One Ohio couple spent six nights up until midnight waiting for the eggs to hatch.

The biologist explained that other causes of turtle mortality are massive beach rebuilding projects that pump sand off the continental shelf. These efforts to at least forestall the impact of another human screwup—the changing climate—also kill turtles even while beach nourishment restores some of the nesting sites eroded by sea-level rise and superstorms. We can't win for losing, it seems.

Perhaps turtle mania is a sign we've had enough. Despite our society's obsession with the inane and vapid, when offered something utterly and beautifully important, something that fulfills the ancient Hebrew notion of *tikkun olam*, the obligation to repair God's creation, we can't resist. Donald Trump and the Kardashians are interesting, I guess, but loggerheads and leatherbacks have soul. On the night of the boil, Elias refused to go to bed, insisting we stay late, his own instincts as inexplicable and deeply rooted as the internal compass that pulls hatchlings into the sea.

From 8:30 to 10 p.m., a group of about fifteen milled around, fighting the occasional mosquito and, for the Ohioans, at least, the sense that their vacation would end with nothing to show for their waiting. And then the ground broke. A silver-dollar-sized hatchling groveled out of the earth in the dull red of an infrared light. And then another, and then eighty-eight more. Guided by the moonlight and the helpful flashlight of a volunteer, they crawled slowly into the ocean to face the longest of possible odds—only one in a thousand will survive.

Their odds are low, but they couldn't be much lower than the chance that we'd care about them at all. And they are higher than the likelihood we'd put down our devices and, for a waning summer moment, focus on our species' earnest, halting, and late efforts to put one part of the world back together.

2

A Hole and a Door

The Problem with the
Sustainable-Business Thesis

I went down to the bowels of the five-star Little Nell Hotel in Aspen to visit chief engineer Mark. On my way, I passed catering trays stocked with foie gras, black-jacketed waitstaff moving out flutes of champagne on silver trays, and three or four accountants buried in low-ceilinged rooms with looks of creeping desperation. I don't think Mark—past middle age, white-haired, sardonic—was ever eager to see me, the sustainability guy at Aspen Skiing Company, then the parent company that owns the Nell.[1] We environmentalists are notoriously pains in the ass, especially for an understaffed, near-retirement Irishman like Mark who's just trying to keep the lights on for incredibly high-maintenance guests. But Mark instead always accepted my visits genially, if perhaps out of obligation, the way anyone with real work deals with management muckety-mucks. My job—energy efficiency, clean energy, carbon-footprint reduction, public policy—must have seemed ancillary to him because, well, it was.

If you don't know the five-star-hotel world, you can't fathom it. The level of attention required to maintain those stars is mind-boggling: 24-7 room service, multiple sommeliers to ensure that the right prosecco pairs with your prosciutto and cantaloupe. Mark's job, first and foremost, was to make sure the place ran—heat and air-conditioning for guests, hot showers on demand, functional plumbing. ("Code brown" = a clogged toilet.)

That responsibility alone wasn't easy: hotels are complex systems, and a lot can go wrong. If they do—and the guest without hot water is maybe the sultan of Brunei paying tens of thousands of dollars for a week's visit in the Paepcke Suite overlooking Aspen Mountain, well, you've got a problem. So, when I came down unannounced with another distraction of an energy project—another lighting retrofit, computerized building controls, improved boilers—he might understandably feel put-upon.

At the same time, though, Mark was a funny guy who enjoyed life. The place I found him most often outside the office was the Tipsy Trout Bar and Grill in the town of Basalt, a watering hole on his way home. Drinking Coors Banquet beer. That's where his Buddha nature was revealed, an old-school-pub guy, unwinding with the boys after work almost anytime I happened to pass through.

Once, when I asked him for a headshot I could use in our internal environmental newsletter, he sent me a picture of himself sitting at his cramped basement desk, apparently holding a pencil and working away on some purchase order.

"Looks like you're working, for a change," I offered.

"Take a look at the hand I'm writing with," he said. I looked. There was no pencil in it.

After fifteen years of energy work, I was visiting Mark again to probe him for any new projects he could possibly think of that might save us a bit more energy. The Nell was by far the biggest energy hog in our company's fleet of buildings. And the more we could save on heat, light, pumping, and ventilation, the more money we could drop to the bottom line, the more carbon pollution we could keep out of the air, and the more we could tell a semipositive story of sustainable business to guests, the media, and the world. But we had already done a lot—in fact, we'd done more than most businesses. We changed out every light bulb in the place, from hallways to the garage, even finding efficient versions of the little flame-shaped bulbs for the weird candelabras in the ballroom, switching from incandescents and even fluorescents to LEDs. We had replaced the boilers, ancient gas units running at 60 percent efficiency, with modern condensing boilers that can run at higher than 95 percent efficiency. We had installed a new roof, and a $250,000 computerized building automation system that helped Mark, as he liked to say, "turn shit off and down," the most effective way to save energy. And we had even put a few solar panels on the roof and tied it to the fanciest room, so people could see how much energy was being produced each day.

A Door

"Mark," I said, "what are we missing? Are there ways you could save energy here that we haven't thought of? What stuff have you always wanted to do that you need funding for?"

He paused, leaned back in his chair, put his hands behind his head, and said, "Yeah. You could put a door on the garage."

A door. It was outrageous. In the absurd simplicity and unexpectedness of his answer, I thought of the ship captain in *Apocalypse Now*. When hit with a spear, he grabs it and says, quizzically, semi-understandingly, "A spear."

The Nell has an underground heated garage. It's where valets park the Porsches and Bentleys. It has two levels, and it was the site of one of our first sustainability triumphs, a lighting retrofit that annually saved $10,000 on a $20,000 investment. The project improved light quality while cutting wattage 75 percent and even more later as bulb technology improved.

That project was the great vision of sustainable business realized, a measure that saved money, cut carbon emissions, and improved performance. It was the sort of project that drove the entire nascent sustainability movement in the early 1990s, when I began this work. The idea: if projects like that exist—that save money while protecting the climate—then business is going to lead the charge on the climate fix. Because, after all, businesspeople are hugely motivated by that kind of profit opportunity. Aren't they?

Still . . . a door . . . after fifteen years, we hadn't thought of a door.

In fact, it gets better. The place you'd put a door would be at the *top* of the garage. That meant that for the history of the hotel—which had been built in 1989—heated air had been venting out a de facto chimney, as if you'd simply left your kitchen window open year-round and compensated for it by cranking the oven. The hot air represented energy, and carbon pollution, since the heat came from natural gas. It also represented money—as we reheated incoming air and then let it leak out again into the often-subzero nights in eight-thousand-foot Aspen, Colorado. The practice was costing us money. Not an astounding amount, but every day and every night for decades.

For all the tech involved with energy efficiency, what Mark was proposing was decidedly low-tech: he was fixing a building failure known as a *hole* with an energy-saving technology known as a *door*.

It took a while, but we eventually installed a sweet insulated overhead door. And you could look at this story as a victory. Years of energy-efficiency work, plus a developing (Mark might say *blossoming*) relationship between the sustainability guy and the hotel engineer, led to even more savings. And who knows what other big opportunities remain?

But it's not a victory. It's an illustration of the essential problem with the sustainable-business thesis, the notion that without regulation, free-market forces will drive businesses to be key actors in solving the climate crisis.

Here's the problem: we live in an economy where hotel management, and me, the energy guy at the company, didn't notice that the front door was open . . . for more than twenty years. And the reason we didn't notice was that the energy cost of not having a door was irrelevant. It has just been so cheap to burn natural gas that it doesn't matter at all. Indeed, energy costs at hotels tend to be approximately 5 percent of revenue. When you can sell a bottle of wine for a week's worth of energy costs, who cares about conserving energy? The reality is that a business will always make more money selling the thing it provides rather than trying to find dollars elsewhere, and the time it takes to find those dollars can be spent selling the thing the business makes.

Unless, of course, you care about the climate. Which business typically doesn't. And the only way to make it care is to force it to, through regulation or taxation. Which is the opposite of the sustainable-business thesis.

Why Even Turn Off the Lights?

Because the historically cheap price of carbon-based energy is one of the essential barriers to solving climate change—since the vast bulk of the climate problem comes from combusting fossil fuels—we need to understand just how cheap energy has always been in the United States.

Thirty-five years ago, when I was a teenager, I visited my cousin in Seattle. (I was idealistic then, not the jaded wreck of a man I've become.) When we went out for dinner, I told him he ought to turn off his porch light.

"Why?" he asked. "Do you know how much it costs me to leave that thing on?"

"No," I said, "actually, I don't."

He said, "About two cents. I pay four cents for a kilowatt-hour, or the equivalent of a thousand-watt bulb running for one hour. That's a hundred-watt bulb, and it will run for a couple of hours. So being conservative, I might be out a penny or two. It's not worth it to turn it off."

My cousin isn't depraved; he was just being honest. Electricity prices in Seattle have gone up over the years, but they're still cheap.[2] Right now, the cost of a kilowatt-hour of energy is about twelve cents.

The fact of the thing—that we are being delivered magic through a wire, for almost free—is hard to grasp until you ponder it a bit. A good way to understand it is to think of me, in my kitchen, dealing with my teenagers and their dishes.

When I come home from work, typically tired, I often find the double sink full to the brim with dishes. Often, Ellen or I will launch into the pile and, half an hour or so later, complete the task. It's hard work. Harder without wine. In this economy, if I were going to hire a dishwasher to do that work for me (or pay my kids a fair wage)—let's say the worker would come in every morning and evening for half an hour—I'd have to pay them twenty bucks. That's a low estimate of the market value of having the dishes done.

But you know what? I'm not going to hire that person. I have a dishwashing machine. And so instead of all that work, I'm just going to take a few minutes to load the dishes. And then I'm going to push a button that will run the dishwasher for one hour, drawing about a thousand watts. In other words, I will buy a kilowatt-hour of electricity from my utility. For how much? About nine cents. What the heck: I will do the same at breakfast.

But I just showed that *conservatively*, the market value to clean my dishes is about $20. I'm getting at least $20 worth of labor—of work done, as physicists call it—for about eighteen cents. There's only one word for something like that: magic. What's magic worth? Could it possibly be so cheap as to be almost free?

There's more. Fifteen years ago, where I live, when I turned on that dishwasher, it required that the utility burn about a pound of coal. That flammable rock, when combusted, would release two pounds of carbon dioxide (CO_2) into the atmosphere. In turn, that CO_2 would go on to change the climate, leading to costly impacts like floods, fire, crop failure, drought, and more-powerful storms. It will require me to spend money on an air conditioner one day, cut brush around my house to avoid wildfire, pay higher insurance premiums, and incur a host of other expenses. The coal also emits pollutants like mercury (a neurotoxin that bioaccumulates in fish), nitrogen oxides (which causes smog that harms people), and sulfur dioxide, which causes acid rain and erodes buildings (and their gargoyles). Air pollution from coal, among other dirty sources, is one of the leading causes of mortality globally—studies show that one in five deaths are related to air pollution, some nine million deaths a year. The costs of the impacts created by the release of CO_2 are calculable: the US government's interim "social cost of carbon," meaning an estimate of those impacts combined and monetized, is $51 per ton. (That number is without question on the low side: economists have argued the true cost is closer to $200.) That means the cost per pound of CO_2 is very conservatively about 2.5 cents. Which means that the power I used to buy fifteen years ago, mostly from coal, was at least 25 percent underpriced, even ignoring my dishwashing labor comparison. And even then, it would have been the bargain of the century.[3]

And it doesn't matter what carbon-emitting fuel you pick, it's all cheap. Take gasoline. A gallon of gasoline, which is incredibly *energy dense*, meaning it holds a whole lot of power in a small package, contains about thirty-three kilowatt-hours of energy. Even at five bucks a gallon, that's fifteen cents for a dishwasher load . . . which means it would make sense economically, at least in many parts of the country, to convert your dishwasher to gasoline because it's even cheaper than electricity![4]

And another thing . . .

Just kidding. I'm done talking about how cheap, and how magical, electricity is. I'm here to make a point, and here it is: there is simply no way that business, or society as a whole, will implement enough energy-saving measures fast enough (combined with renewable energy deployment) to stabilize the climate if the price of carbon-based energy is effectively free. That's because the savings simply don't matter at the prices we're paying. And for new power, even though clean energy is cheaper than fossil fuels, the cost is still not *enough* cheaper to drive the radical change we need in a short time frame to stabilize the climate at a couple of degrees Celsius above preindustrial conditions. The price of energy is too low to enable us to do what we need to do, which is convert the power system, all transportation, and all buildings to zero-carbon electricity by 2050.[5]

And the idea that business is going to capitalize on energy efficiency like lighting and boiler retrofits and other sustainability measures around energy at the speed and scale required and at current market prices is simply a pipe dream. We know for sure it's a false hope, because the sustainable-business movement has failed to do it over three decades. Emissions keep going up. The thesis failed.

What we need, instead, are commonsense guardrails on capitalism. Today, businesses can pollute the atmosphere with damaging CO_2 for free. This lack of consequences is absurd given what we just learned about the costs and impacts of CO_2. Putting a price on those emissions is not a radical idea. We don't dump our trash on the street; we pay for it to be disposed of properly. There are many other ways to boost implementation of climate solutions using government policy: the Inflation Reduction Act, which is full of tax credits and other incentives, is one such way. It's an effective mechanism that doesn't even touch tax reform.

Business cares about these policies—how they're done, whether they're durable, what they prioritize—and could, if it wanted, play a role in establishing legislation, but it has universally avoided doing so. In fact, the approach business has taken over decades has ensured that almost no regulatory policy, whatever the form, sees the light of day.

Changing that situation will require that we think very differently about environmentalism, sustainability, and climate solutions. It will require a revolution.

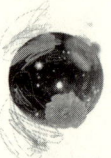 ## Stop Talking and Start Caulking

My customer Royce Green and his wife were eating dinner by the kitchen window during a storm when the wind blew their new roof into the air, opening the tin trailer like a can opener. Royce's wife thought the whole place was going to go, just like Dorothy's house in *The Wizard of Oz*.

I built that roof when I worked for an energy center. Did I forget the nails?

In my early twenties, I had one of the unhealthiest and most disgusting jobs in Western Colorado: energy technician. It sounds fancy, but it meant this: I crawled under trailers through mud and animal carcasses into spaces so small you couldn't turn your head.

I poked holes in the floor and blew boric-acid-coated cellulose insulation into crevices. I breathed in fiberglass—the next asbestos—while wrapping water heaters. I fought hordes of children while sheet-rocking attics filled with dust. I fell through the ceiling while blowing insulation, landing close to a seventy-year-old man sucking on oxygen.

Working for the Energy Center in Carbondale, my partner and I inhaled fiberglass in trailers in the Colorado towns of Rifle, Meeker, Maybell, Craig, and Silt. "Silt happens" is the unofficial town motto. "Stop talking and start caulking" was ours.

Royce Green's yard in Rifle was a sea of car parts inherited from his father-in-law. "When he died, we took five truckloads of carburetors and differentials from his garage," Royce said.

I only found that out later. The first time we drove into his yard and said, "Morning," we got no response, even though he was no more than twenty feet away. That's the "trailer park hello," a common form of nongreeting, no malice intended.

We had to repair his sieve of a roof. The night before, it had rained, and the sea moved indoors, dumping forty gallons of water in the living room. True, the roof we built eventually blew off, I told myself, but it also got Royce through the winter.

It was hard to set up appointments for weatherization. Often, phones didn't work, unpaid bills having led to disconnections. Sometimes even a trip to the address was worthless. The client might have moved on, employing trailer park rule number one: if your credit is bad and you haven't paid the rent, skip town. If a potential client was home, we had to overcome trailer park rule number two: keep three huge dogs to discourage visitors.

Giving out applications for free weatherization was never a breeze.

"She's not here. They stole a moving truck. Now they're somewhere in Texas."

"She's in Peru."

"He's in jail."

And from an older woman in a threadbare pink nightgown: "Yes. How about yesterday?"

At Royce's house, we patched holes in the heating registers and vacuumed them clean. Vents in kitchens are usually covered with a combination of hair, mud, honey, and unidentifiable brown pastes. In every trailer, there's at least one room so full of junk that human activities like motion or sight, let alone finding ducts, are impossible. Walmart, beyond extinguishing Main Street, can claim credit for this: it is now possible to have the money of a peasant but the possessions of a king. Inflatable neck cushions for the tub. See-through telephones. Juicers. Stuffed animals that squeak when you step on them. Soft-soap dispensers.

Working for the Energy Center, I got an intimate look at old boomtowns on Colorado's Western Slope. Towns not located near ski resorts have little economic base beyond hunting season, but "near" can mean within a hundred miles. I picked up a hitchhiker who told me he takes the bus from Rifle every morning to Snowmass Village, some sixty miles, and then hitchhikes home.

"I meet interesting people and save wear and tear on my truck," he said. When I dropped him off, he said as if it were a recitation, "Thanks for the ride. Wonder who I'll get next?"

We coated a trailer roof in Cottonwood Springs with liquid white rubberized paint. The renter, Luke, was very accommodating. He took his speakers out into the yard and, with the volume as high as it could go, blasted music by Boston and Journey. Then he started mowing the lawn, so no one could hear the music. Then the speakers blew. Though his house could have been a Superfund site, he complained that we had dripped paint down the sides. Then he went fishing.

I wondered what Luke's plan was. I wondered about all our clients. When I allowed myself to think he was lazy, I feared I might be turning into a Republican, channeling my grandfather. I asked my writer friend, Randy. He pointed out that Luke was paying sky-high rent for a trailer that was overpriced and underinsulated. Rent, the great American tapeworm. Utility bills are outrageous, my friend added. Luke has three kids. Once he accounts for clothes, food, and medical expenses, plus a $100 medication cost for beer, the family's already in hock.

Many dreams in Rifle went bust when Exxon's Colony oil shale plant dissolved in 1982. Town borders are peppered with trailers that are falling apart. The scene would look natural if the trailers were old farmhouses, but their fiberglass, vinyl, and plastic wheels won't return to the earth. Trailers punctuate the West with nonbiodegradable periods.

The big dream that fueled a trailer's journey westward is still around, but now it's spent on Lotto. Gambling is the new buffalo, some Indigenous tribes say.

Royce Green said he knew a week in advance that Exxon was going to lay off two thousand workers. He felt it in the air. More than a decade later, his fencing business is floundering, undercut by cheaper work based in Grand Junction, Colorado.

After repairing his doomed roof, we patched holes in the trailer underbelly. Under a trailer, wearing a respirator and a Tyvek suit made of the material used in air-mail envelopes, everyone becomes a spider expert, and all spiders become black widows. We stuffed insulation into the floor cavities and stapled aluminum-coated cloth over the holes as fiberglass settled in our eyes.

Every job was like that: dirty, unhealthy, and tinged with desperation. And yet that work formed the basis of my philosophy around solving climate change and gave me a lifetime of credibility since it framed me as a practitioner, not just a theorist. As my friend Randy Udall said to me once about a consultant, "That guy has never baked a pie, built a shed, sweated a pipe." Thanks to that job, I would never be accused of such crimes of omission. And philosophically, I began to understand that the solutions to climate change would look more like trailer insulation than TED Talks. Though I left the job for something (slightly) cushier (teaching high school), I still think about the lives I walked into and insulated, and the broader problems we were trying to solve. Like some of the amateur roofing we did, the answers were never obvious. Try caulk. Try solder. Try duct tape. Try roofing tar. And if nothing works, pull the whole thing off and rebuild it from the start. But don't call the roofer; it costs too much. Better to obey trailer park rule number three: you can always figure things out yourself. Improvise.

3

"Terlets" and Trauma

A Brief Personal History of American Environmentalism

I grew up thinking I hated New Jersey. Raised in Weehawken, the lesser-known town adjacent to Hoboken, I played one half-season of Little League on a field above the Lincoln Tunnel. High foul balls would fly up into the purple night sky through plumes of diesel pollution and plummet down into traffic. It's a wonder nobody was killed. Maybe they were. But given that it was New Jersey in the 1970s and 1980s, maybe their reaction, when the ball hit, was, "Thank God. Relief at last."[1]

It was a hell of a time. Inflation was in the double digits, the South Bronx was on fire, and Vietnam had just ended catastrophically. Only recently, students had been burning down ROTC buildings on campuses and B-52s were dropping five-hundred-pound bombs on Cambodian villages; American infrastructure was in collapse; a home mortgage was 16.63 percent in 1981. If you leaned on the neighbor's Chevy Nova, the dad, who had captained a landing craft on D-Day and had carried a tommy gun to shoot anyone who didn't get off the boat, would yell, "Get off the caaaah!" We got off the car. John Schwartz, the neighbor directly across the street from the Nova owner and next door to my house, had climbed out of a crashing B-24, parachuted *on fire* into the ocean, was rescued by the Germans, and spent the rest of the war in a prisoner of war camp. His face, entirely burned, was just the way he was, and we thought nothing of it. We played Nerf football in the one-lane streets, occasionally colliding with a rearview mirror while extending for a pass. If you hit it with your sternum, the mirror would come clean off and hang by a wire. It was good that cars weren't built that well back then.

There were grandmas who would lean out their second-floor windows all day and observe the neighborhood. Usually they too would yell at us for various infractions, but occasionally, they would beckon us over and lower a basket on a clothesline filled with, among other treats, circus peanuts, the legendary puffy orange peanut-shaped candies that tasted like *banana* and were as good an icon or mascot for the 1970s as anything.

Today, I still have in my garage a watercolor I painted when I was about ten. It's a destroyed suburban landscape with what looks like a tenement building spewing smoke from a stack, windows cracked and shattered. There's what looks like a storage building with wire-covered windows, also spewing smoke, a trash can chained to a hitching post, an antenna sticking up off the roof. And in the upper right, where the sun should be, there's a green field surrounded by a fence, a vision of walled-off escape. I often wonder, as I'm doing laundry and looking at that picture I hung behind the washer, what was going on. And I think I wasn't painting a destroyed landscape per se, but rather I was depicting the world as it was. My father was an unreconstructed New Yorker, a flaneur, walking the streets and visiting thrift shops, spending hours at the Strand Bookstore and Barnes & Noble. Sometimes he drove into the city in our red Ford Fairlane, and twice, he returned to the parked car and turned the key, only to find a mugger in the back seat. The stress triggered a heart attack in one case.[2]

When my bike pump stopped working, the D-Day dad came out with a jug and dumped its contents into the opening around the piston. "What was that?" I asked. "Olive erl." For him, and everyone else native to the region, "toilet" was "terlet." Neighborhood kids and I would play cops and robbers, zooming around on our Huffys and Schwinns. My friend from across the street was always the brutal cop, inclined to use a bit too much force. "I'm anti-Jew," he casually told me once as we sat on a car together before being chased off. Later, he became an antiterrorism officer for the Port Authority, embezzled $700,000, and ended up in jail. Once, a thug from two blocks over told me he'd beat me up if I left my street. I lived in fear for weeks, sneaking around the neighborhood.

In Jersey in the 1970s and 1980s, people were always yelling at us. At Roosevelt Public School, the principal would occasionally show up in class and yell at us in tonsil-revealing, spittle-projecting acts of terrorism. I found it absolutely terrifying. The oddness of that time: Why should I deserve a beating for leaving my street? Why all the damn yelling? What was the deal about leaning on a car? What happened to language to turn a toilet into a terlet? That was Jersey, where, the saying goes, "only the strong survive."

The social depravity and decadence of that moment was one thing. But what I really didn't like was the filth. Beyond rampant litter and grime, one of my most striking memories of childhood was the purpleness of the sky at night—it was beautiful, but it was filthy. Manhattan, which I could see in its entirety from a few blocks from my house, was often covered in smog. Nearby, the Meadowlands, which later became a sports complex, was a dumping ground. When I would visit my grandparents in North Dakota in the summers, it was as if I could finally exhale. The beauty, the clean air, the pink sunset, they made me feel that that world, this place of prairie and sky, was where I was from—so much so that I asked my mom if I could tell people I was from North Dakota. And it was there that the seeds of some vague environmentalist vision were planted. How do you fix the bad places? New Jersey, for all its neglect, was a breeding ground for environmentalists.

Years later, I realized it wasn't Jersey I hated so much as America before environmental regulation. I hated pollution, not the Garden

State. I had this epiphany when I found a collection of pictures called "America Before the Clean Air Act" on the internet. As *Popular Science* reported:

> In 1970, Republican President Richard Nixon signed an executive order creating the United States Environmental Protection Agency (EPA). It was a time when pollution made many of our nation's rivers and streams unsafe for fishing or swimming. Back then, New York City's air pollution was so thick that you often couldn't see the city's iconic bridges . . . .
>
> From 1971 to 1977 [the exact years I was hanging out on the streets], the nascent agency, in an act of prescience, enlisted the services of freelance photographers to help us remember. These photographers captured images of America's environmental problems before we'd cleaned them up. In 2011, the US National Archives digitized more than 15,000 pictures from the series "Documerica."[3]

Many of those pictures were from New Jersey: trash dumped along the turnpike with the Twin Towers in the background, the New York skyline lost in smog, the George Washington Bridge clouded in haze. My mother would drive my sister and me out to North Dakota in the summer in the red Fairlane. One year, we stopped at a town in Illinois along the Mississippi, and my sister and I went swimming in that legendary river. It was shallow, and we emerged with a greasy sheen. I have no idea what that was, and I often wonder when that pollution will come back to get us. Polychlorinated biphenyls (PCBs), one of the gnarliest, carcinogenic human-made chemicals used widely at that time in electrical transformers, are very greasy feeling. Indeed, while retrofitting light fixtures as part of my job, I once unwired a ballast and felt an oily substance on my hands, and with a sick, haunting feeling, I washed my hands over and over. PCBs weren't banned until 1979, and by that time, they were pervasive in the environment.[4]

The EPA pictures are stunning now—it's almost unfathomable that an advanced society not beset by vast structural poverty (at least, not everywhere) could allow such desecration. But the pictures too are a testament to what we are capable of as a society—the very big changes we can put in place when required to. The collective sacrifice—and gain—we can choose to make together.[5]

But.

What happened next—*after* the United States did the hard and necessary thing to protect itself, its economy, and the natural world—is telling.

For the most part, the American approach to environmentalism changed. The last revision to the Clean Air Act occurred under George H. W. Bush in 1990, when I was halfway through college. The Energy Policy Act, which set standards for appliances, toilets, and motor efficiency, among other things, passed in 1992 and was enacted in 1997. Minor progress continued, but ultimately those bills started to look like last glimmers of meaningful bipartisan environmental legislation in Congress.[6]

Environmentalism became more focused on individual- or firm-level actions. And to some degree, this is because business saw what happened after the Clean Air and Clean Water Acts and decided, Never again. Never again will we let the people so severely regulate us. Never again will we take the blame for pollution the way we just did.

That was certainly part of it. But what abetted that approach was the final entrenchment of a profound and dominant corporate-sponsored ideology long in the making. That ideology, Naomi Oreskes and Erik Conway explain in their excellent book on the origins and consequences of free-market fundamentalism, *The Big Myth: How American Business Taught Us to Loathe Government and Love the Free Market*, "insists on limiting the power and reach of the federal government and relying on markets to solve our problems. Most damagingly the market-oriented framework of recent decades has resisted any facts—scientific, historical, sociological, or otherwise—that suggest a need for a strong centralized or otherwise coordinated governmental response."[7] By the time I finished high school, the notion that government was bad and markets were God-like in their efficiency and virtue had a hammerlock on American politics.[8]

As it turned out, this intense faith in the market was a problem, since unfettered capitalism—the so-called free market—was in the process of destroying the climate, and "big government," the only entity capable of solving giant international problems (like climate change or . . . pandemics), was not seen as an acceptable solution.

This was the world I entered as I began my career.

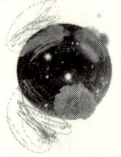 ## Maryland: Journeys We Take at Home

Every day, I hear the same thing from parents of grown children.

"Enjoy it while you can, it goes so fast."

When my son Elias was three, he consistently woke up in the middle of the night "needing sumfin'." His then six-year-old sister, Willa, would also wake up frequently, saying, "I just can't get back to sleep." Our house was so colossally messy, I would tell Ellen it looked like wild animals lived there. Extreme time poverty made even taking a shower difficult, let alone arriving at work on time or weeding the front yard. So I found those parents' advice baffling. How can you enjoy something when you can barely function, especially when the thing you are supposed to enjoy is the cause of your dysfunction?

When I came home one windy day, a day when a porta-potty had blown over in the park, Elias asked me if I had blown away. At work that day after a two-week vacation and an exceptionally sleepless night, I had forgotten the combination to the door, forgotten my intern's name, put on two pairs of underwear by accident, and entirely spaced on an important meeting in a room adjacent to my office. "No," I said, "I'm here. I'm OK," thinking maybe I *had* blown away.

Of course, children are gems that decorate and inform our lives with running, miraculous commentary, and there's an unending supply. Staying at a crappy Comfort Inn, Willa says, "And we get to stay in these incredibly fancy hotels!" Elias, on a road trip: "When do we get here?" (A metaquestion I ask myself, in other forms, all the time.) On the counter in the morning, a note from Willa: "peder pan will you pleys leev mee a mesij." Elias: "A song is not a thing. It is a sound."

But the reality is that one is often too harried, tired, or overwhelmed to fully appreciate it all. So sadly, disengagement sometimes becomes the holy grail of parenting, like when a child gets in a rhythm and plays alone. When they're in the zone, it can go on for hours, and it's a miraculous deliverance, a time when one can clear the detritus from the kitchen floor and deal with the piles of papers on every surface. When it happens, it's crucial not to break the spell.

Elias had started playing cars on the living room rug, moving two Jeeps around and narrating the story, always a journey. "OK, I'll see you when we get there. Do we have our things? OK, let's go." To me, who in dazed exhaustion finds meaning and metaphor in everything, Elias was narrating the only human story, a quest for something yet undefined, and he will continue to do so, if he is lucky, for four score years or more.

One day, with a second to spare from work and the bathroom remodel and temporarily ignoring the sink full of dishes, I sat down on the rug and started playing cars with Elias. It wasn't absent-minded on my part; I did it consciously, trying to heed the advice "Enjoy it while you can."

"OK, get in the car, Dada. You are with Willa and I am with Momma." I like that Elias speaks in formal English, without contractions. I ask, "Where are we going?"

"Maryland."

Moving the cars around on the rug, I realized what I had done: Now, playing cars is a two-person activity, no longer a break for me. Now, I've blown my chance to get anything done around the house. "All for the cause," I think. And we pretend that the patterns are roads.

Funny that he should choose Maryland, I think, pushing my Jeep and mumbling, "Babababroom, broom, broom, broom!" It's where I met Ellen. We were at a friend's wedding, and we had breakfast at a diner whose motto was "Love at First Bite." As Ellen recalls, I took her leftover omelet, wrapped it in a napkin, and put it in my pocket. Unbelievable. How could any person have been so cheap? It reminded me: I used to cook at the Charburger, and one of the servers came in one day from the laundromat where she worked as well. She had six pairs of tighty-whities someone had left. They were probably my size. Did I want them? Yes, I did. And I wore them for years. Was I really that person?

Elias shakes me from my reverie: "Dada! Dada! Listen to me! You have to come with me." Crawling behind his Jeep, he looks up and into my eyes quizzically, as if to say, "Dude, get it together!" Grasping for the present, I had found myself touching the unfathomable past.

He says, "We need to get some gas! You are driving Willa and I am driving Mama. We are going to Maryland."

I am happy to go.

4

The Flawed Vision

Why Environmentalism Lost Its Way, and How to Bring It Back

Everyone has a plan until they get punched in the mouth.

—apocryphal quote typically attributed to Mike Tyson

After getting out of college with a degree in biology and environmental studies in the early 1990s, I worked in a closet next to the bathroom at Rocky Mountain Institute, a sustainability think tank in Colorado. My partner in crime was an intellectually ravenous Yale MBA named Chris. He was a brilliantly eccentric guy, prone to riffing—at great length and with incandescent enthusiasm—on wide-ranging topics like special forces operations, the paranormal, search and rescue training, and emergency medicine and then breaking to give you an awkward foot massage at a dinner party. Once, after getting stoned and talking for, I'm not kidding, two straight hours about UFOs during a long car drive to a conference in Santa Fe, Chris handed me a Maglite flashlight held like a microphone and said, "Now you go. Here's the talking stick." I didn't know what to say. I couldn't follow his bravura performance that was like Neal Cassady on crack.

Crammed in beneath towering stacks of energy reports, to-be-read copies of the *New York Times*, and Chris's own crazed drafts of novels and journal entries, we cowrote brochures and consulting papers with phrases that suggested the nascence of our field and the optimism of the time: "Corporations are the only entities large enough, nimble enough, and motivated, by profit, to solve the climate problem," we wrote. The idea was that doing good by the environment—cutting energy use with better light bulbs and boilers, reducing waste and pollution through design and engineering, and adding renewable energy supply—was not only environmentally responsible but also profitable. And, importantly, it could become a key part of the global climate solution.

Cream First

In the early 1990s, this new vision captured the imagination of progressive businesses and the environmental community, both of which were beginning to grapple with climate change, the overreaching challenge needing to be addressed if humans were to achieve a sustainable way of life on planet Earth. It was, essentially, the idea of adding cream to your coffee first, and business was the entity to realize it.

Imagine you're in a Starbucks, waiting for coffee.

The barista hands you an Americano with a little room left, and you pour in some cream. But because you're adding the cream second, you now need a stir stick—a piece of wood harvested from forests, milled and manufactured, then packaged in plastic and paper, and transported using fossil fuels. If you could add the cream first, you suddenly don't need a stir stick at all. That's what's called a design solution. You've replaced a material thing with intelligence; you've eliminated waste through thought. How cool is that?

The thinking was that of all the organizations trying to solve the climate problem—government, nonprofits, citizens—the most likely to actually lead was business. And the reason was that corporations could save (or, put differently, make) a boatload of money by slashing CO_2 emissions through energy savings and cutting material waste just by implementing new technologies or rethinking operations. Your coffee cup was just a vanilla macchiato taste of the opportunities that were everywhere.

For example, if you looked up to the ceiling after tossing your stir stick in the trash, you might see an older halogen light bulb, which gives off mostly heat—light is just a by-product. That means it's wasteful, and in the summer, the business has to pay more for air-conditioning to battle the heat from the bulb. But replace that halogen with an LED—which gives off mostly light, not heat—and you save energy in lighting *and* air-conditioning. That kind of story is catnip for TEDx.

This seductive approach, known as corporate sustainability but with analogs in communities and the broader environmental movement—with action focused on profit at the level of the individual or firm, not society—became the dominant response to climate change in America, not just from the private sector but also as encouraged by governments and nongovernmental organizations (NGOs), even academia. It got traction because stories like the preceding ones made for amazing Silicon Valley hero talks but also because it was easy. The approach absolved business of the need to answer to regulation; excused government from lawmaking responsibility; and meant individuals didn't have to engage in the increasingly nasty politics of energy. The green business consultants called the approach win-win. You make money, and you protect the environment.

We were surrounded, in person and intellectually, by the originators of the movement, energy efficiency guru Amory Lovins; *Ecology of Commerce* author Paul Hawken; Ray Anderson, whose environmental epiphany transformed Interface; and visionary engineers like Eng Lock Lee, who treated systems design like Chinese cooking, where you use everything, even the chicken feet. In our overreaching thesis was nothing short of the salvation of the world, the cure for climate change, and the end of pollution and waste. All of it, naturally, driven by business profits and strategic motivation. A piece of the logic was that if a business could make, say, even as low as 10 percent on an energy investment, then that investment would *have* to be made, partly because you could borrow money at a lower rate to fund the efficiency and therefore make money out of nothing.[1]

That vision got people like me into the field, made for great inspirational talks, and excited customers, employees, and investors. And corporate sustainability as practiced in that fashion does have value: good design can, at no cost, accomplish great things. The Starbucks example—replacing energy with design—is an unbelievably compelling way to view our problems! But other examples abound. Just by orienting a new house so that the long axis faces south, you can save 10 to 40 percent on energy use for the life of the home.[2] Imagine the glory of retrofitting light bulbs in a public parking garage—as I did early in my career—so that the total fixture wattage dropped from 400 to 30 watts while providing better light with longer-lasting bulbs that were cheaper to replace. Bonus: valets were no longer crashing cars in the dark garage. It was safer down there. The maintenance staff could do other things like replace filters and tune the heating system instead of changing light bulbs all the time, saving more energy. Often just by showing people how much energy their home or office is using, you can get them to save energy. Better labeling of appliances like refrigerators, to showcase energy savings, could sell many more of the good ones. You don't have to be a quant to find that kind of thing inspiring. (OK, maybe you do.)

The opportunities are endless. Imagine installing odor-free, waterless urinals in skyscrapers because water pumping accounts for a significant percentage of total building energy, saving water *and* saving energy. Are you kidding me? Sign me up!

Twenty-Five Years Burning Down the Road

That stuff—we called it cascading benefits—actually happened. But thirty years or more in, even as the sustainable-business movement flourished, climate change, the single most important barometer for the possibility of a sustainable future—marched on. And a planet on fire, deluged in flood, and disrupted by drought and famine, warfare, and heat waves—where governments and citizens are preoccupied with disaster response instead of stability and thriving—is nobody's picture of sustainability. Over the course of the corporate sustainability "revolution," climate change evolved from a concern to a certainty, with catastrophic warming beyond 2°C more or less baked in. The ten hottest years on record were the last ten. When I started in this field, total human-caused warming since the Industrial Revolution was about 0.5°C. In 2023, we were at 1.3°C and headed toward 1.5°C, even though the Paris Accords said, "You'd better not go past 1.5°C, or shit's going to get rough." We hit 1.8°C above preindustrial times in 2023, though that is a spike, not an average.[3]

As the world was warming fast, corporate sustainability became a thing: a really big thing. When I started work, there were virtually no jobs in the field, and few people even had a name for it. Now, between the field of environmental, social, and governance (ESG); corporate social responsibility (CSR); carbon tracking, carbon targets, and carbon footprinting; sustainability reporting; third-party management standards like ISO 14001; green building certifications like LEED; B Corp certification; and a host of other related work, the internet is swarming with these positions. Corporations have sustainability departments, and colleges teach to the field.[4]

Not Enough

Still, in the face of the climate change reality, even a major triumph like a large corporation cutting its carbon footprint by 30 percent—the stuff of *Shazam*-level superheroism and incredibly difficult to pull off—wouldn't even dent the climate problem. There are just too many people and too many governments, and most don't care. And since these efforts are all voluntary, they stop with the select few who want to lead. But that's not enough: our society is so carbon infused that even people who are experiencing homelessness have unsustainably large carbon footprints.[5]

So even if all the willing companies and individuals took the most radical action, it wouldn't come close to the scale of change required. (We know, because the sustainability movement has effectively tested that theory for thirty years. If it hasn't taken off yet, how long should we wait?)

Meanwhile, even within businesses that get it and care (and such unicorns exist), there are structural barriers to implementing carbon-reducing measures. For example, it might seem like a no-brainer to retrofit lights in the garage of a five-star hotel, at a cost of $20,000 and an annual payback of $10,000. But while such a move makes obvious sense to an energy nerd, it might not happen. The hotel manager could take the $20,000, buy five expensive bottles of wine, sell them the next week, and double that money. In that context, the energy retrofit would be bad business . . . a distraction from core business, a missed customer service opportunity, a missed revenue opportunity, and a use of labor in a direction entirely at odds with the mission of the hotel.[6] If the return on investment were 50 percent, wouldn't a smart business simply borrow the money to do it—at, say, 8 percent—because you can't afford not to? No. It's hard to get a loan. It takes time and energy. Better to just keep selling wine.

Such challenges led me to believe that all this work was important, but that it just wasn't enough.

Little did I know how inside the box I was.

A Well-Intentioned Distraction

The next level in my increasingly pessimistic take: the issue wasn't only that sustainable-business practices are hard to scale or that they're insufficient, though both points are true. The problem was, I started to think, that they displace or distract from meaningful action.

In fact, I recently brought up this idea with a colleague who was likely going to come under pressure to create carbon targets within their company. "Be careful," I said. "You're just one person. Once you embark on that path, it's all you're going to do . . . . You may never get to cutting emissions."

The reality is, even if carbon footprints and targets and then plans to reduce emissions don't *do* anything, they're hard work. Developing a carbon footprint, then replicating it every year, can be either mind-numbingly complicated (in my company, we still analyze bills from archaic natural gas companies like chad-hunting election reviewers) or, if you hire it out, expensive. Making targets or goals isn't too hard, but developing (never mind implementing) the energy reduction plan sure is. And if you report on your work, you're booked up permanently. The groundwork isn't the setup for eventual emissions reduction; it's the destination, and an end in itself.

Dodgeball

Sinking deeper into cynicism, not because I'm a cynic but because of my experience and reflection, I started to think that conventional sustainability, even coupled with some level of emissions-cutting action, may actually be worse than a distraction. A business that pursues sustainability as it is conventionally understood (and all the accounting, reporting, and standards meeting that moves paper and displays commitment) becomes, in the media's eye and in customer perception, a green company, absolved of doing anything else. Hell, a business wouldn't even need to cut its emissions to be labeled a leader. It would just need to aspire to it. When I started in this field, the unquestionable leaders even I admired were doing several key things: publishing sustainability reports, setting carbon targets, signing up for third-party certifications, and calculating their carbon footprints. That was state of the art. It was an optics win and therefore a no-brainer. But none of those actions did anything to cut emissions, and even if they had, it was never at a meaningful scale.

Yet firms deploying these techniques have a major lifestyle advantage: they don't have to undertake the hard, unpleasant, and nasty work of political activism that might truly drive down global emissions. They can skip tough things like advocacy; writing op-eds in major newspapers; flying the CEO to Washington to give testimony to Congress or to lobby senators; noisy, messy, uncomfortable coalition building; applying peer pressure that annoys allies; controversial divestment; or publicly calling out bad behavior. They can appear to be good and righteous without having to do the good and righteous work that is messy and controversial.

The Supermarket Problem

All of the aforementioned steps that do matter and that do drive change are hard as hell. And it leads inevitably to what I call the *supermarket problem*. If you give an average CEO a moral balance scale, the exec will weigh the pros and cons of activism like that just described. On the one hand, they'll say, my actions will likely make me a material part of solving the climate problem, the greatest threat ever to face civilization, because I'm leveraging the greatest power we have as a business and because people will listen. On the other hand, if I do that unpleasant stuff, showing up at public meetings, talking honestly about climate science, taking no prisoners on climate policy, I absolutely guarantee I'm going to run into someone in the cereal aisle at Costco—a climate denier dad, an ultraconservative mom— and it's going to ruin my day. So, while I do want to save civilization on the one hand, on the other, I'm going to have a really bad day in the supermarket aisle. In the end, weighing those two things—saving civilization or having an awkward encounter near the Cheerios or getting totally flamed on social media . . . Eh, I'd rather not be an activist.

Anyway, why bother? A CEO could simply roll out corporate sustainability as conventionally practiced and garner the imprimatur of greenness without demanding the hard work of power-wielding and political activism. The public doesn't know the difference between real and token work, and the media doesn't help. Vail Resorts, for example, has made reputational hay by aggressively recycling plastic, which doesn't actually get recycled. The point is, the more meaningful work, in addition to all the unsavory consequences already described, also risks irritating shareholders and possibly triggering regulation and the anger of elected officials from whom managers want other favors, anyway.[7]

Also, don't forget rule 1A of business: for all the lionizing of outside-the-box innovators who "think differently" and break stuff, being a boat rocker is not a path to success in the corporate world.

This dodge played out in spades. In the early stages of the climate fight, businesses avoided even *acknowledging climate science*, because talking about it brought out the haters and ticked off politicians at a time when many more of them were climate deniers. Better to dodge that unpleasantness, criticism, claims of hypocrisy, and general difficulty of taking a public position on a "controversial" issue with what became (and remains) a common refrain: "This stuff is so profitable, we should do it regardless of what the science says!" You can see in that construction the beginnings of moral decay. Imagine: "Racism aside, we should treat people equally because it's good for the bottom line! Plus, our customers demand it."

But it did matter very much that business acknowledged the science, because policy was then, and even is today, being made on the basis of science denial. Many awkward stances are difficult because they are also moral stances. In fact, they all are. And yet despite some nascent efforts in Barack Obama's second term to frame climate change as the moral issue that it is, we have mostly missed that opportunity, despite the necessity of solving the climate crisis to preserve our humanity and honor our responsibility to each other.[8]

Elias and the Crucifix

But I still struggled to understand exactly what was going on—exactly why conventional corporate sustainability practice was tragically flawed and how to explain it to others. To this day, people regularly ask me, "I understand conventional practices like changing light bulbs is a distraction. But why can't we do both that *and* the bigger stuff?" We can, of course, but most businesses don't. And the pressure to stop at convention is enormous, and doing so comes without consequence. Double down on plastic recycling. Declare victory. Ignore the reality of climate. Dunzo.

To really understand the essential conflict, I had to go to a church in Santa Fe, New Mexico. I was on vacation there with my family when then eight-year-old Elias and I walked into one of the many beautiful adobe churches in the city. Walking toward the back, Elias saw a crucifix—Jesus on the cross. "What's that?" he asked.

"That's Jesus, being crucified."

"Why did they kill him?" Elias asked.

I paused as my natural dad-answer syndrome kicked in. I looked up at Jesus, and I thought for a bit. And then I realized that I had absolutely no idea and that there was a big gap in my understanding of history, religion, and society. Why did they kill Jesus? I resolved to find out.

My digging led me to a *Medium* post that explained the rationale behind the crucifixion: "The problem with Jesus [from Rome's perspective] was that he didn't just preach loving kindness. He also preached justice—and it wasn't Rome's justice; it was God's justice . . . . *Preaching compassion often gets you canonized. Preaching justice often gets you crucified.*"[9]

Changing light bulbs and otherwise cutting carbon footprints—all the conventional practices of sustainable business—that approach is loving kindness; there is nothing *not* to like about it. Tackling the systemic climate problem head-on and therefore overturning a very moneyed, and very entrenched, fossil fuel power structure—that approach is ultimately about justice. And that will get you in trouble.

In fact, it got *me* in trouble.

Businessweek Blows the Whistle

It was about a decade into my tenure at Aspen Skiing Company that the seeds of my cynical realization began to take hold. And that change led to some problems.

In 2007, *Businessweek* published a cover story by Ben Elgin, an absolute bulldog of a reporter. The piece blew up the idea of sustainable business as a meaningful path to climate solutions. It featured an executive who argued that corporate environmentalism, as practiced, was never going to solve large, systemic problems like climate and therefore had little to do with the idea of sustainability. The title of the piece was "Little Green Lies." The executive was me.[10]

When the piece went live, I was coming home from giving a talk in Estes Park, Colorado, a beautiful mountain town at the south end of Rocky Mountain National Park. My pretty drive was quickly ruined when the phone rang: it was the CEO of Aspen Skiing Company, where I had been head of sustainability for a decade. He wasn't happy. "What was that about?" he asked. "You seem to be attacking your own colleagues and even our own work . . . . You're going to need to apologize to Don, to Eric, and probably to the senior team." Next, I got a spine-chilling message from our vice president of human resources: "Will you come see me Monday morning, please?"

When I arrived back at my office, all my personal items had been removed.

In the corporate sector, that only means one thing: you've been fired. But emerging from my vacant office with a heavy feeling in my gut, I ran into our chief financial officer, my friend Matt, from the dust devil trip. He was cackling. The office move and the HR call had been an elaborate joke, orchestrated, in part, by him.

And yet, as with all jokes, there was an element of truth to the mock firing. In fact, I did get grilled in front of senior management for what I had done. And there *was* a problem in the world.

Sustainable business had been praying to a false god.

Duplicity

What had begun to dawn on me during the *Businessweek* interview was that in so many cases, the operational corporate sustainability dodge of the hard work becomes open duplicity: like Penelope, corporations learned to weave the funeral shroud of their carbon credits and waste reduction by day and undo it at night with their corporate contributions and lobbyists. "Leaders" in the corporate sustainability movement are more or less silent on policy. Meanwhile, with the vast bulk of their action and messaging focused on how they are greening their own operations, they give money to politicians like Mitch McConnell or other climate deniers like David Perdue (as Microsoft, Bank of America, and vocal climate leaders Google and Walmart did before the 2020 election). As just one historical example, had Perdue won, climate action in the Senate would have been impossible, undoing all the other climate aspirations those businesses may have pretended to care about.

But this kind of thing is going on all the time. Green-talking businesses, we find, may also design and sell cloud-hosting services, custom artificial intelligence software, and machine learning tools that are used to better find and distribute fossil fuels while claiming to care about climate change. (I won't name names, but, uh, Microsoft, Amazon, and until recently, Google.) In some cases, they directly lobby against their professed environmental goals, as GM had done on automobile standards under Trump, despite its membership in the corporate sustainability group Ceres. And while GM nominally supported the Inflation Reduction Act at the last minute, the automaker's CEO, Mary Barra, served as chair of the Business Roundtable that opposed the legislation. Given this conflict, what do you think lawmakers thought of GM's "support?" It was wink-wink, nod-nod.

As Rhode Island senator Sheldon Whitehouse has pointed out, you have corporations taking big action internally and sharing that story but unleashing their lobbyists to do the opposite.[11]

The duplicity often extends beyond climate into social responsibility and justice, causes that are intrinsic to the climate movement, as we'll see later in the book. As journalist Osita Nwanevu has observed, many self-declared responsible corporations also fund anti-democratic practices by supporting groups like the Republican State Leadership Committee's Redistricting Majority Project: "Coca-Cola, for example, whose CEO declared it would be putting its 'resources and energy toward helping end the cycle of systemic racism' in June (2020) should probably stop putting its resources toward the reelection of Republican state legislators—including in states like Georgia where it is based and where the Republican Party has been particularly dogged in its efforts to disenfranchise African Americans."[12]

And the next shoe dropped for Coke: it took no action to stop an egregiously restrictive voter suppression law from passing in Georgia and then vocally criticized it once it was in place. The company got the cake it wanted from the law (protection of the status quo) and then ate it too by donning the cloak of righteous indignation only after the law had passed.

As another example, Procter & Gamble has sustainability reports all the way back to 1999 and released an ad on racial justice in 2020. But during the 2016 election cycle, P&G donated almost twice as much to House and Senate Republicans as they did to Democrats. This imbalance seems difficult to square, given the GOP's positions on climate and racial equity policy in recent times.[13]

Playing into the Fossil Fuel Industry's Hands

Over the years, these sorts of dismal discoveries led me to an even unhappier place: the actions businesses take under the banner of win-win, profitable, and good-for-the-planet corporate sustainability were exactly and precisely what the fossil fuel industry would want them to do. These moves ensure that businesses take responsibility for the climate problem only in terms of the challenge of their own individual emissions, instead of seeing it as a systemic issue. Their actions create a focus on actions so pathetic and small ball that they could never and would never disrupt the fossil fuel industry's hammerlock on governance. This approach is, in part, what climate scientist Michael Mann calls "the new climate war."

Think about it. Fossil fuel companies *like* net-zero homes and offices. They love carbon-neutral companies. And carbon offsets. Any talk of the circular economy, where things get reused and recycled, is music to their ears. They embrace the idea of science-based targets, where businesses determine their "fair share" of the globe's carbon reduction burden (which may not even make sense—what is your fair share in putting out the forest fire threatening your neighborhood?). They like citizens and corporations to "do their part," and talk about how "every little bit helps." Most of all, they like it when individuals and corporations focus on themselves, not the system.

Fossil fuel companies like these things because they distract business and citizens from actions that would actually hurt the industry, dangerous stuff the fossil fuel industry fears. What are those hobgoblins?

The fears are many: Removing money from politics, or assaults on fossil fuel companies' social license to operate. Public shaming. Divestment. Public policy that eliminates subsidies and encourages renewable energy and electrification. Boycotts and protests against pipelines or business operations. Public shaming by peers. Occupation of their main offices by activists. EPA regulation, right-sized carbon taxes, media that actually digs in on what *green* means (e.g., major US banks loudly proclaiming bans on funding for arctic drilling that at the time was not happening and is risky and expensive anyway), and powerful CEOs who declare the need for aggressive climate policy in major media. They hate free and fair elections that empower the vast majority of Americans who care about aggressive climate action.

How Did We Get Here?

When an arm of the fossil fuels business—the plastics industry—realized in the late 1960s that soda pop bottles and yogurt containers were clogging highways and rivers, they knew they needed to get the blame off themselves and onto citizens. They did it masterfully, with the famous "Crying Indian" ad, in which an actor (of Sicilian heritage) played a Native American shedding a tear over trash-chunking by inconsiderate Americans. It worked. Instead of coming after the plastics industry with pitchforks, Americans took responsibility for the problem on their own, even though they had no more demanded plastic bottles than they had insisted on mobility or cold beer delivered in a way that would destroy civilization.

Later, the rest of the fossil fuel industry embraced the same strategy, just as it had previously adopted Big Tobacco's cancer denial. As journalist and science editor Mark Kaufman puts it, "British Petroleum . . . hired the public relations professionals Ogilvy & Mather to promote the slant that climate change is not the fault of an oil giant, but that of individuals."[14] A result was the ingenious carbon footprint calculator: a tool for determining just how guilty we all are, neatly shifting blame from the architects of the problem to the pawns of the systems. Remember: American citizens did not create the carbon-friendly laws and infrastructure that govern our world. Industry influence did.[15]

Thoreau and Personal Responsibility

But it's not entirely fair to just blame the plastics and fossil fuel crowd. The carbon footprint—first coined as the "ecological footprint"—originally came out of the environmental community and was fully embraced by the environmentalists and green NGOs before, and after, BP decided to push the idea.[16] And Americans have long viewed environmentalism through the lens of individual action, and so industry was tapping into something real about the American character. Indeed, at least in our own myth of ourselves, we see Americans as rugged individualists.[17]

Nonetheless, this worldview goes all the way back to the origins of American environmentalism and Thoreau. As biographer Jeffrey S. Cramer explained in an interview about his book *Solid Seasons: The Friendship of Henry David Thoreau and Ralph Waldo Emerson*:

> Thoreau, had no love for the political system . . . . So . . . he stayed out of it as much as possible. For Thoreau, the idea of changing the world was through self-reformation. That we change ourselves, change how we live, we change what we're doing that affects other people or the world . . . . And, so, he's throwing the responsibility for what is happening directly back to the individual. So Thoreau and Emerson would take that sense of we as individuals have to reform our lives. And, that's the way to change the world.[18]

Even Thoreau's famous essay "On the Duty of Civil Disobedience" was about his own resistance, not movement building.[19] But in a way, Thoreau was right. In his time, all environmental problems were local and individual. There were no PCBs, no PFAS (per- and polyfluoroalkyl substances, the "forever chemicals") in Inuit mothers' milk, no ozone-depleting chemicals, no climate change. And you could, in fact, protect the environment through your own personal actions. Americans were predisposed to the sort of thinking laid out in the "Crying Indian" ad well before the ad was created. But by the time of US industrialization after the Cold War, individual action was no longer a plausible fix. Was corporate action?

Complicity

As it turns out, the great vision that business could, through its own operations, drive the solutions to climate change played directly into the hands of the purveyors of a warming world. I would even put it more strongly: Sustainable-business practices haven't just been inadequate to the task (unfortunate) or a distraction (bad). Nor are they simply a dodge of hard, controversial work (sinister) or even just intentionally duplicitous (corrupt). The approach has been borderline *evil* because it represents *complicity*. Complicity with the fossil fuel industry and the structure it created—its capture of government; its ownership of the economy; its buried but enduring subsidies; its support, by political proxy, of antidemocratic practices that would restrict regulation; its construction of a world in which citizens exist in a fossil economy not of their creation but nonetheless blame themselves for it.

Importantly, while the system that functions today may be evil, and while it makes agents of that system complicit, the vast majority of the practitioners are good people. Indeed, they are some of the most well-intentioned humans I've met, dedicating their lives to change from within, earnestly trying to do their job and do it well. The point of this book is to enable these extremely high-quality people to step back, reassess, and better understand their landscape.

In short, corporate sustainability, as currently practiced, researched, taught, and reported on, remains the best way to enable the success of the fossil fuel industry in accelerating climate catastrophe.[20]

Indeed, a useful exercise is to make two parallel lists. On the left, lay out all the measures that currently constitute corporate sustainability best practice. On the right, list all the actions the fossil fuel industry, if given godlike powers, would want the powerful business world to take. These actions would make businesses appear to be taking action on climate but would actually not even remotely affect the fossil fuel status quo. Most importantly, these activities would enable the fossil fuel industry to continue to monetize all its proven reserves. Here's a hint: those two lists are the same. Table 4-1 compares these two lists and adds a third category: actions that could threaten the fossil fuel industry.

The sad reality? Fifty years after the "Crying Indian" ad, we're still dinking around, trying to figure out how our businesses can go carbon-neutral, how we can work "within the system" and through "market forces" to solve the climate problem. When some businesses make slight progress outside the policy realm—say, by announcing their own carbon neutrality or the goal to achieve it— academics, the public, and the media praise them up and down. Meanwhile, the people who criticize these businesses—people like Joe Romm, whose deep research at the University of Pennsylvania has shown that carbon-neutral claims are fraudulent and even legal

TABLE 4-1

Complicity versus change making

CSR/ESG best practice	What the fossil fuel industry would want corporations to do	Meaningful, dangerous actions
Carbon targets	Carbon targets	Op-eds demanding climate action
Carbon footprint reduction	Carbon footprint reduction	Movement building
Offset purchases	Offset purchases	Customer mobilization
Reporting	Reporting	Pressuring trade groups
Emissions tracking	Emissions tracking	Calling peers to account
Third-party certifications	Third-party certifications	Radical transparency and honesty
Operational greening	Operational greening	Political action committees funding for good
Measuring waste and water	Measuring waste and water	Resigning from misaligned trade groups and partnerships
Carbon targets and neutrality goals	Carbon targets and neutrality goals	Crafting and supporting legislation
Production of elaborate sustainability reports	Production of elaborate sustainability reports	Backing climate-forward candidates
Blame-taking for emissions	Blame-taking for emissions	Freaking out the fossil fuel industry

liabilities—are typically called cranks, radicals, and Marxists who just don't understand capitalism.[21] They're the sorts of people who fit the bill of purported extremists: George Monbiot. Amy Westervelt. Sheldon Whitehouse. Bill Moyers. Bernie Sanders. Naomi Klein. Bill McKibben. Emily Atkin.

If you were paranoid, you might even think all this was intentional. How can it be, you have to ask, that the consistent response to accelerating climate change is to double down on the same strategies that have failed over many decades? In fact, the environmental community clearly recognizes the failure of climate strategy. But its approach has been to try to make existing failed strategies more rigorous. Standard targets for corporate emissions reduction aren't working, so make a new, better standard—let's call those new targets *science based*. Unregulated offsets are bogus, so let's develop a new, more robust certification system but one that is still voluntary, and therefore just as ineffective.

As an example of this failed approach, a recent *Harvard Business Review* piece describes what business can do to address climate change now: "Set an emissions reduction target. And if they have already done that, set milestones on the road to that target. And if they have already done that, make sure that the company is clearly on track to meet these milestones. And if they have already done that, explore what can be done within their industry to reduce emissions together."[22] These steps are certainly part of it, but why stop short of the really effective, dangerous things a corporation *could* do? Even the big ask—that businesses work within the industry while moving in the right direction—misses the really meaningful action, like banding together to drop out of trade groups that block climate action and forming new ones that advocate for climate policy. Why not include the really big measures that would drive real change, not small-ball adjustments?

I can hear the frequent response I get to this critique from businesspeople: "Auden, you can't just take your ball and go home. That's not how business works."

Allow me to reiterate: the practitioners and advocates of an operational and management-based approach to corporate sustainability are not bad people. I know many, many of them, and they are attempting to live out ideas of dignity and grace and respect. As much as any group I know, sustainable-business practitioners are trying to live to the Golden Rule and do good in the world. What I call *complicity* has been an evolution, resulting from good ideas—like the ability of corporations to lead, to move fast, to cut carbon at a profit—that were not reexamined or course-corrected over time. The failure of the initial idea doesn't mean it was ill intentioned. And yet we are where we are. We have been repeating the same actions and ideas that have failed over decades, violating the old dictum, "Never try the same thing over and over and expect different results," and positioning those actions as thought leadership. This approach is dominant and pervasive and has me rubbing my head and mumbling like Marlon Brando as the insane Colonel Kurtz in *Apocalypse Now*.

Fortunately, there is a growing cadre of apostates fighting back. One of them is Ken Pucker, who was chief operating officer at Timberland when that company was pioneering new thinking in sustainable business. Now, he's a lecturer at Tufts University. He quoted ecological economist Herman Daly to me in response to my concerns about the trends toward doubling down on operational greening and associated measurement: "If you jump out of an airplane, what you really need is a parachute, not an altimeter."[23]

The Problem with Environmental, Social, and Governance Approaches

The sort of operational tweaks described previously in this book are commonly known as environmental, social, and governance (ESG), which has become a white-hot buzzword in the sustainability movement. As it gained in popularity, the term lost any specific meaning and became hopeful pabulum, the multitool of sustainable business. For some, it refers to a style of management—meaning that a company takes into consideration the environment and society when making decisions and has the governance in place to stay out of trouble. For money managers, ESG is an investing strategy—one that uses ESG data when picking stocks for an investment portfolio. For corporate environmentalists, it is a stand-in for the belief that voluntary action will solve social and environmental problems. For politicians like Mike Pence, it's the devil's mischief, signifying the arrogant misuse of funds by "woke" managers.

The originators of the ESG term deserve some of the blame for this confusion. The original idea was that data about a firm's ESG performance would help the stockholder pick better stocks, so ESG was intended to measure the effect of the planet on the corporation, not the corporation on the planet. According to Bloomberg, "[ESG] ratings don't measure a company's impact on the Earth and society. In fact, they gauge the opposite: the potential impact of the world on the company and its shareholders." So, if a DDT manufacturer used this approach, it would be less concerned about the extinction of bald eagles than with how the extinction of bald eagles affected the company. The manufacturer could even get a high ESG score if it looked like it could safely dodge DDT's environmental impacts.[24]

Recognizing the absurdity of this situation, boosters tried to salvage the ESG idea by claiming it would do both: raise profits and save the planet. But this just meant that ESG lost all meaning and became a stand-in for whatever was desired. Higher stockholder returns . . . improved planetary health . . . all with reduced regulation. And this malleable meaning turned out to be a great strength. Separated from any ground truth or logic, the term could be used to signify a magic potion that enabled anything desirable.

One might have hoped that serious academics would have bridled at such wishful thinking and abuse of logic, but that's not what happened. With power and resources, and big money flowing toward ESG, academics began to "find" evidence that ESG really did have marvelous powers. ESG data could double stockholder returns, ease access to capital, and leverage the profit motive to solve grand challenges! Trillions of dollars flowed into ESG investments. Wall Street moguls announced the dawn of a new era in which profit and purpose ran together.[25]

But when things seem too good to be true, they often are. Not all academics jumped on the bandwagon, and when they took a second look at the evidence, they uncovered a lot of problems. They pointed out confused logic and misleading marketing. They replicated influential empirical studies and found math errors, invalid logic, exaggerated claims, and brittle findings. In some cases, understanding these problems requires headache-inducing deciphering of statistics. In other cases, they are evident to anyone who cares to look. Andrew King of Boston University pointed out one such case to me, where a study from New York University's Center for Sustainable Business is used to make opposing claims within the same document. A press release for the center claims the study reviewed 1,000-plus research reports and concluded that "sustainable business is good business." The final academic report considered only 238 reports and makes the opposite claim: there was "no financial return for ESG strategies." Personally, I have my own concerns about ESG.[26]

ESG management in companies is just a more bureaucratic way to talk about sustainability. In that sense, it adds a layer of jargon that makes the field even more obscure and therefore less assailable and auditable. But even this quality doesn't make ESG *management* the devil's work.

ESG investing, however, is a problem. It's a complicated field, but there are several essential challenges. One is that the screens used to determine what's in a fund are often so broad that the result is a basket of companies that just looks like the S&P 500. Indeed, many years ago, I inquired of the managers of a low-carbon index fund why Berkshire Hathaway was included. After all, Berkshire had invested in Suncor, a developer of the dirtiest oil reserves on the planet, the Canadian tar sands. "Well, Berkshire is *mostly* low carbon," the fund manager told me, as I melted into my chair on the other end of the phone.[27]

ESG is now being criticized from all sides. The Milton Friedman market fundamentalists don't like it, because they believe that the role of business is to do business, nothing more, and that anything additional distracts the firm from its societal role of providing jobs for workers, services or products for consumers, and revenue for investors. But progressives also criticize ESG. They attack ESG rankings, management, and investing for several reasons:

1. ESG hasn't worked over the decades. Society keeps pressing up against sustainability thresholds, and even the notion that these firms perform better has been debunked.[28]

2. As a management practice, ESG means the conventional sustainability I've criticized in this book. As such, it allows firms to avoid the hard work of meaningful change making (i.e., engaging in the political process, using voice and power, or being part of a broad movement to address climate change). Meanwhile, firms can appear to be working diligently to fix societal problems, even when the actions they take are just basic business management.

3. Because ESG is a formal and seemingly rigorous way to ensure the status quo, it is supported and disseminated by status quo institutions in academia and beyond. If the fossil fuel industry wanted to design a way to avoid ever being called to account on the carbon economy, that approach would be called ESG management, ranking, and investment. That's because ESG creates an excuse not to undertake actions that might alter the status quo, particularly political engagement. If political engagement is included in ESG rankings, it's a tiny percentage of the whole. That's a way to nod to the issue but, by deemphasizing it, structurally diminish its importance.[29]

4. When ESG is shown to have failed, the answer is always "We
   need better metrics, goals, measurement," which naturally
   takes time and therefore ensures delay. That seems to be the
   response to critiques today.[30]

As a practitioner of sustainable business, I can say there is enormous pressure to set goals, file reports, create "science-based targets," measure, marginally tweak emissions, and show progress,
even if that progress is fake. There is almost no pressure to engage
in systemic change, wield power, influence politics, or participate
in movements. In fact, there are numerous barriers. And, thanks to
the ESG cloak of invisibility—the fact that it seems serious—there
is no punishment for not doing meaningful work, even when the
lack of that work becomes absurd (e.g., remaining a member of the
US Chamber of Commerce while announcing your carbon footprint
reduction efforts). You can think of ESG management as a more rigorous way of doing very little. Use a big word or a bunch of words,
and people think you're legit. For example, the idea of science-based
targets, which sounds impressive to many people, is just another
operational greening goal.[31]

Happily, there is a way to fix the problem. Change what ESG
means. In ranking systems or governance structures, heavily weight
the things that matter (climate lobbying; political engagement,
whether environmentally positive or negative; the use of voice;
and power-wielding in other forms). And then put less weight on
the things that are simply business management (energy efficiency,
carbon-reduction targets, goal setting) and that do not of themselves
reduce emissions or achieve goals that improve society. Massively
overweight a company's influence on politics, the political system,
and climate. So, if you're a member of the US Chamber of Commerce
and are not taking action far beyond the damage this group is doing,
you get a bad ranking. If you have enormous investments in fossil
fuels (e.g., as a bank or a fossil fuel firm), you should do terribly
in these rankings, not better than a company that is building, say,

electric cars. You could categorize things that matter as *leadership*, whereas operational tweaks, measurement, and accounting could be considered "management."

Is It Really That Bad?

From one perspective, business has arguably been all over the climate crisis. Most *Fortune* 500 companies have dedicated sustainability staff and spend tens of millions of dollars on greening up their businesses and supply chains. So far so good. But as we've seen, virtually all the climate work stops there. Pepsi's climate strategy is a great surrogate for all of corporate America. Its web page speaks volumes: "PepsiCo's climate action strategy is centered around two pillars. Mitigation: reducing GHG [greenhouse gas] emissions to decarbonize our operations and supply chain; and adaptation."[32] Nothing on policy or politics. True, many large businesses have joined sign-on letters in support of legislation like the Inflation Reduction Act, but this action has proven to be more performative than effective. Moreover, corporations like Pepsi (and many, many others) continue to fund trade groups that, like the Business Roundtable and the US Chamber of Commerce, actively oppose *all* climate legislation. Not only is this decades-old approach to "green business" hypocritical, but it has also been an effective prescription for climate inaction.[33]

Google, for example, consistently posts self-congratulatory notices on social media about its greening progress. Here's a 2022 LinkedIn post from Kate Brandt, Google's chief sustainability officer: "Accelerating the transition to a clean energy future is at the core of Google's sustainability work. Today we're honored to receive an award from the US Environmental Protection Agency (EPA) that recognizes our commitment and collaboration in this space. Thank you to EPA for this honor and onward!"[34]

Bill Weihl, founder of ClimateVoice, former director of sustainability at Facebook, and the green energy czar at Google itself, had this to say in the run-up to the Inflation Reduction Act: "Google's consistent and energetic leadership makes it all the more puzzling that Google has been silent on the Inflation Reduction Act now in front of the House of Representatives. Salesforce, Walmart, and Constellation have been vocal supporters of the bill (and Microsoft just added their voice). Meanwhile, your big trade associations continue to spend money (your money, in your name) to kill or weaken the bill."[35]

Brandt was also chief sustainability officer at the White House, so she certainly knows what Weihl is talking about. But she and Google never respond to challenges to their thinking. Corporate America remains captive to a sort of anti-zeitgeist, a narrow-thinking reflexivity born of long-standing antiregulatory bias, even though new, young customers want the opposite. In the bulk of corporate America, responding to the climate crisis means doing all the things Google does—buying clean power, cutting operational energy use, improving supply chain efficiency, investing in sketchy voluntary market offsets, and humble-bragging about it all—while at the same time ignoring policy. These common responses are so accepted that businesses receive almost no criticism from the media, the public, or the NGO community when they take seemingly duplicitous action.[36]

Systemic change is the only path to climate stability. But what the well-intentioned corporate sustainability movement has truly succeeded at is ensuring that everyone works within a narrowly defined playing field that leaves the one thing we need to upend—the fossil-fuel-based economy—intact and unthreatened. Meanwhile, the practitioners who have mastered the accepted path are lionized, made famous, and therefore made unassailable. "If (fill-in-the-blank corporate sustainability leader) says it's OK to pay trade groups to block climate policy, it must be the right path." Again, this is not to shake a fist at corporate sustainability professionals—I am one of them. We have all been shaped by a late twentieth-century business and governance philosophy that emphasized shareholder profit and Milton Friedmanesque market fundamentalism. It must seem unlikely to many experienced businesspeople that corporate leaders would advocate for policies that may reduce profitability or restrain commerce. So instead, we work within the system, thinking it's all we *can* do.

Why Bother?

A good question would be, if the corporate Buddha nature is never likely to care about an issue like climate—if even the concept of caring is not expected of corporations—then why should we bother to try to move them? Wouldn't it be better to spend our time, energy, dollars, and angst in other places? The short answer is that we don't have a whole hell of a lot of levers when it comes to climate. There's government, civil society (movements and voters), the legal system, environmental nonprofits, the faith community, foundations. That's about it. Business is an incredibly powerful and influential component of society. As we battle an all-encompassing civilizational threat like climate change, business *must* be part of the solution. It would be a tragic oversight, and a consequential mistake, to leave that hammer on the table.

Academia's Role

The truth is, academics, researchers, and sustainability gurus are the ones who helped steer people in the wrong direction. Even today, at bastions of higher education, some leading voices profess that we can reinvent business for good. Defenders of the notion and ESG abound in academia and beyond.[37]

And many of these institutions are funded by the fossil fuel industry—including, as climate scientist Michael Mann and activist Ilana Cohen wrote in the *Los Angeles Times*, "Stanford's Global Climate & Energy Project, sponsored by ExxonMobile and the world's largest oil-field services company, Schlumberger; and MIT's Energy Initiative, whose sponsors include Exxon, Chevron, Shell, Eni and ConocoPhillips. Cambridge University meanwhile hosts a Schlumberger research center."[38]

Benjamin Franta, formerly of Stanford University and today the founding head of the Climate Litigation Lab at Oxford University's Sustainable Law Programme, described the connection between the fossil fuel industry and academia: "We now know that at many universities, climate and energy research programs have become financially dependent on oil and gas funding, and that poses a huge problem in terms of independence."[39] Clearly, given their funding sources, many colleges and universities are forced to foster a philosophical argument that the status quo will enable the climate fix.[40]

It is not hard to see how academics arguing for emissions targets as a path to meaningful action on climate could be viewed as functionally parallel to oil company executives.

Some academics push back on conventional wisdom, arguing a different storyline—that business must engage at the political level if it wants to be taken seriously on climate and sustainability.[41] But these dissenters remain on the fringe. And even though some certification programs—like B Corp—include political activity in their rankings, political engagement has historically been a small percentage of the ranking. To be provocative: given the state of climate change, *political activity should constitute almost the entire value of the ranking.*

Because of the pervasiveness of conventional thinking, and because business wants nothing more, a sustainable MBA degree ensures graduates get buried in back rooms doing carbon accounting, stuck in a box made of win-win solutions and operational greening as an answer to the greatest threat ever to face civilization. They can't agitate, influence company policy, get political, or even talk to the CEO. Despite their titles, they can't affect climate change or real sustainability. Worse, pointing out the ineffectiveness of this broken strategy—because the criticism so blatantly counters the established status quo—can peg a staffer as unstable or scarily radical. A friend and colleague in a large corporation with aggressive green aspirations struggled mightily, over years, to get the company to finally commit to market-based carbon solutions, the absolute lowest policy bar. (And this was just to agree that such solutions were acceptable, not to actually *do* them.) The reality is that the labor of most corporate sustainability managers is worse than scut work: at least scut work advances toward a goal or leaves you with a clean toilet.

And oddly, with no exceptions, sustainability departments are just arms of standard business management. They do things with return on investment that cut energy use and make the organization more efficient. Those projects effectively have nothing to do with sustainability. The departments that could do the meaningful work, or should be doing it, are called *government affairs*. My suggestion: change the name of the government affairs department to Sustainability, and force it to engage on climate. Change the name of the currently named sustainability department to better represent what it does: operations management or facilities, for example. At worst, create a dotted line between what are now called sustainability departments and government affairs divisions.[42]

Sadly, most of us practitioners still haven't worked our way out of that box. Even a business that understands this—take Salesforce, for example, which is a leader in the sort of effective action I describe—still overwhelmingly emphasizes addressing its own footprint in its public materials and almost footnotes the critical power-wielding and lobbying it does so well, despite its membership in the anticlimate US Chamber of Commerce. The big whiff on the part of corporate America—missing the policy forest for the operational trees—may have begun with the blessing and boosterism of the fossil fuel industry, but it was bought and implemented by insiders, the gurus and sustainability leaders, the universities and businesses and think tanks.[43]

A Future of Our Own Making

Serious journalism, like that pursued by the truth tellers listed previously, is one way we can push our way out of this situation. But
mainstreaming that level of integrity and inquiry is difficult in an
owned world. For example, the progressive news outlet MSNBC
runs ExxonMobil ads about growing algae as a climate solution.
Exxon is being sued for greenwashing in these ads. This is why academia is even more important. Even though universities themselves
are heavily influenced by fossil fuel dollars, they are arguably more
independent than the media and could initiate a sea change in our
understanding of sustainable business. Universities could direct research and teaching curricula toward approaches that actually grapple with the climate problem instead of pretending to do so. The
obscure but noble Alliance for Research on Corporate Sustainability
is teeming with apostates and insurgents who understand the points
raised in this analysis. This group and others could begin to tip research away from erudite niggling over small points of interest and
focus academia's tractor beam on real climate solutions. The same
organization is also rife with good thinkers who lack courage and
true-believing practitioners of business as usual.[44]

Again, the academic solutions that matter would not revolve
around resource efficiency, carbon accounting, or intricate calcula-
tions showing that doing good provides shareholder value. Instead,
the solutions would focus on power wielding, the building of social
movements, and policy revolution, the sort of groundbreaking social
and political research undertaken by Harvard's Theda Skocpol or
Erica Chenoweth, but through a business lens. The question isn't the
traditional query of business classes: "How can business profit from
being green?" but "How can business be part of, even instigate, beneficial social and political revolution?" Milton Friedman fans would
push back: the role of business isn't to do good; it's to make money.
But in a time when the changes beset on the planet by business

directly affect present and future profit, might that perspective need to change?

Ironically, we know business is capable of driving the direction of governance, policymaking, regulation, social norms, and even public thought, because the fossil fuel industry has been wildly successful in doing just that to ensure an enduring fossil fuel economy.

Business may someday wake up and finally execute on the promise of the sustainability movement. While hope is a bad strategy, there are nonetheless signs that this is happening, even though the resulting actions are too evolutionary to achieve rapid change. Larry Fink, CEO of BlackRock, the largest money manager in the world, has been changing the conversation in corporate boardrooms, most interestingly through a call to businesses in his portfolio to achieve carbon neutrality by 2050. He has been crucified by the right for being too woke. People are asking for his resignation. Despite really good words, BlackRock is hardly a leader, and it's almost hilarious that Fink is being attacked. ESG funds tend to correlate very closely with the S&P 500. It's not as if these are woke funds.[45]

Ken Pucker of Tufts noted:

> Given their commitment to fossil fuels, State Controllers of TX, SC and LA should be cheering BlackRock for supporting only 22% of E and S [environmental and social] shareholder proposals this year, down from 47% last year.
>
> The same BlackRock that is a world leader in creating ESG funds and is accused of "boycotting" the fossil fuel industry . . . has, according to their release, invested $170 billion in US public energy companies . . . many of which (like Exxon and Chevron) are held in ESG funds (like the US Carbon Readiness Transition ETF [exchange-traded fund]).[46]

BlackRock's note repeatedly calls out its fiduciary duty . . . and its commitment to delivering "the best long-term results for our clients." The combined assets of BlackRock, Vanguard, and State

Street account for about half of the value of the S&P 500's.[47] Pucker continues: "[A]s such, these managers are exposed to systemic risks such as climate change. It seems to me, therefore, that advancing the fastest possible transition away from fossil fuels is what would be in the client's long-term best interest."

That said, after all the backlash, Fink's most recent note was about *the retirement crisis.*[48] So, progress is halting and sometime disingenuous, maybe approaching nonexistent, but the words and the talk are also changing social norms. Meanwhile, the growing climate threat is starting to change the banking industry, first in Europe and now in pockets of the United States, moving it away from financially risky and morally bankrupt fossil fuel investments. (Chapter 9 dives into this subject in detail.)

Government might wake up too, as it appears to be doing in the United States, with the passage of the Inflation Reduction Act, the biggest climate bill in the history of the world. And perhaps government will eventually pass regulation that prices out externalities and pushes corporations and the wider society to do enough of the right thing that it really matters. Joe Biden's commitment and skill in getting the climate bill through was one of the great bravura political performances of our time, but he and future leaders need support—*from the business community.* And he got little business support when pushing the act. But he was the beneficiary of a climate movement—Bill McKibben calls it the zeitgeist—that didn't exist when previous legislation was proposed. The zeitgeist meant that Senator Joe Manchin couldn't just say "I'm not voting for that bill" without consequences, as he could in the past. There were actually a lot of consequences—and outrage from a range of groups, citizens, elites like Bill Gates, and others when Manchin pulled his support. That's an incredibly hopeful sign.

Last, social movements like Black Lives Matter are bringing to light the inadequacy of corporate action on justice—and the duplicity of progressive talk undermined by backroom politicking and antiprogressive political donations. These social movements will naturally bolster meaningful climate action, since climate is a justice issue too and since solutions like decoupling money from politics and increasing voter access help the climate movement as well. Business support for Black Lives Matter is a piece of the difficult, moral, and seemingly risky trench work of the climate movement. (More on this later in the book.)[49]

What we can't survive is the status quo, because it pledges allegiance to a false deity, one that presumes that corporations, unrestrained, will save us. "That god," Cormac McCarthy writes, "lives in silence who has scoured the following land with salt and ash."[50]

 # Stealing Home: James Hansen's Choice to Be Great

In my office, I have a picture of a man testifying to Congress. He is haggard, with the look of someone under great strain. Behind him, engraved on the wall, is a quote from the Book of Proverbs: "Where there is no vision, the people perish." The man in the picture is NASA climatologist James Hansen, best known for bringing the danger of global climate change to the attention of the modern world in the 1980s and widely considered the planet's leading climatologist. In 2009, he published *Storms of My Grandchildren: The Truth About the Coming Climate Catastrophe and Our Last Chance to Save Humanity*. Because he's my hero, I bought the book immediately.[51]

As you'd expect, it contains enough charts and graphs to choke a rhino. And there's plenty of science, lots of it illuminating, even to jaded climate geeks like me. For example, how do we predict what a world with higher CO_2 concentrations would look like? Do we use computers to create climate models? That's one method, certainly. But we can find even more accurate information about what a warmed world will look like if we go back in time and rummage through the geologic record. The information we find there is extremely accurate. It shows that when the Earth was only 1°C warmer on average than now, the seas were several feet higher. Just 1°C makes that much difference.

The science is fascinating, especially when presented in the context of a thirty-year effort to make our government understand the dire need for aggressive action. But in the end, Hansen's book is about something else. It's about how one should live a life; the book is as much about Hansen's answer to this philosophical question as it is about climate change.

Hansen is, on one hand, a remarkable man with an exceptional intellect, perhaps a once-in-a-millennium, perfectly timed comet of a person, like a Muhammad Ali or a Jonas Salk. On the other hand, he's an everyman plagued with the same traits of regret and disappointment with himself that the rest of us also share. In the 1970s, the world's greatest climate scientist once froze up while giving a presentation and had to simply sit down, humiliated.[52] Then, after giving a talk to the Bush-Cheney White House, he agonized about whether he should have ignored the cooling effects of aerosols because it gave Cheney an out, enabling him and others to make the specious argument that aerosols somehow balance out the trillions of tons of CO_2 emitted every year.

Whatever his demons, Hansen repeatedly forces himself to do what he believes to be the right thing. Over and over, he swears that after one last effort to connect sound science to the policy it should inform, he'll go back to the lab. Fortunately for us, he never does; his conviction overrules his reticence. As just one example, Hansen publicly defended Tim DeChristopher, the student who received jail time for bidding on oil leases, without any money, to prevent drilling.

In his own office, it turns out, Hansen has a picture on the wall, too. This shot is of Jackie Robinson and the legendary 1950s Dodgers. I expect that this image must inspire him as much as his picture inspires me. Robinson, a fulcrum in another battle to save a piece of civilization, is known for doing the impossible: not just for integrating baseball, but also for stealing home base, the consummate statement of daring, hope, confidence, and simply being alive.

The task Hansen sets out for the reader—and for himself—in his book is similarly audacious: to take to the streets and save the planet. It's a task of limitless difficulty because it must overcome not only human inertia but also the fat-cat special interests and our glacially slow government. Hansen correctly notes that solving climate change is about solving money in politics and that the future of democracy depends on addressing both.

As the book concludes, Hansen has just undergone surgery for prostate cancer. With his grandchildren, Sophie and Connor, he is planting milkweed for monarch butterflies to nest in. Moving gingerly, working in the ancient Pennsylvania earth, and accompanied by two breathing miracles of existence, Hansen must have felt the crushing beauty of the world, the crippling weight of mortality, and the acute brevity and preciousness of life.

Hansen could have been content with just being a scientist. He could have done his work and felt—with justification—that he had contributed greatly to the world. This approach would have freed him from the personal attacks, the stress you can see plainly in his face, and the burden of being a living Cassandra, determined to try to change a world that stubbornly refuses to listen. But Hansen elected not to do that.

He chose, instead, to be a great man.

5

The False Promise of Corporate Carbon Neutrality

In 2022, Patagonia founder Yvon Chouinard *donated his company to the climate cause*. His visionary move, which earned well-deserved praise, lights the way for other progressive corporations—if they choose to follow. I'm not so optimistic.

One reason is that there's only one Yvon Chouinard. This is a guy who has only ever pursued what he loves. He'd buy discount dog food and a bag of potatoes as cheap food for himself while he slept under a truck in Yosemite so he could climb all summer. He invented new kinds of climbing equipment because it didn't exist. He pioneered clean climbing because he cared about the environment. Throughout my life, I've admired Chouinard. When I was twenty-two, I skied from Lee Vining in California into Yosemite in the spring. In the valley, starving, but also tight on cash, I bought a box of Mother's Cookies at the store and took them back to the rock I was sleeping under, eating them all in half an hour. (Pink-and-white frosted circus animal cookies; I still remember that meal.) On my way out, I had to cross a stream on a wet log. I slipped, fell off, and badly sprained my ankle as the weight of my pack exponentially increased the impact on my ligaments.

Unsure what to do (I had no friends nearby, no money, a car at the trailhead) I thought, "WWCD?" What would Chouinard do? I tightened my leather Telemark boots and limped up the trail toward Olmsted Point and Tenaya Lake. I dug a snow cave that night and downed a Percocet with the last of my whiskey, dreaming of Chouinard's adventures and toughness. I managed to get the rest of the way out over several days, but it was a long haul.

Not too many years later, I was eating lunch at Rocky Mountain Institute when my boss, Amory Lovins, mentioned he was going to visit Patagonia and Yvon Chouinard. "Really?" I said. "He's my hero."

"Want to come?" Amory asked.

So I became Amory's porter.

We arrived at Chouinard's house in the afternoon, and he greeted us outside. Describing what I did (sustainable business), Chouinard said, "There's no such thing." Awkward pause.

"Yeah, I get it . . ." I mumbled, looking down.

His house was made of recycled sidewalk and was completely solar powered. For dinner, he served us clam chowder from a huge pot. I ate three bowlfuls and then looked around to see what else might be on the menu. (I was in my early twenties and eating a lot.) But that was it. So I had a couple more bowlfuls. Amory and Yvon talked about inventions and highly efficient cookstoves that burned small amounts of wood. And I was paralyzed. Life lesson: it's not easy meeting your heroes. Especially ones who aren't so talkative. Even today, I'm not all that sure what I might have said to him.[1]

That night, we slept in the bunk room. Amory took the bottom bunk and handed me earplugs to block out his snoring. They didn't work.

. . .

Chouinard's radical move in donating his company to the environment is valuable on its face but more so in how it highlights the gap between real action and tokenism or cluelessness. Net-zero or carbon-neutral pledges are some of the most prominent examples of seemingly serious corporate climate actions that don't really matter. Here's why.

Last year, I did some sustainability consulting for a newer outdoor company. The group opened the conversation by saying they already had a strategy in mind. Their plan was to pursue a certification called Climate Neutral and, as part of that, to buy offsets so that they could claim net-zero emissions status.[2]

Offsets are reductions of CO_2 emissions in one place to make up for an activity releasing emissions elsewhere. A company that wants to keep polluting might pay a developing country to reduce its emissions instead. The company might, say, pay a landowner or country not to cut down trees. Burn coal in Schenectady, protect forests in Malaysia.

I spent the next hour explaining why I thought this was a terrible idea. As of 2024, Climate Neutral has certified more than 340 companies, many of them in the outdoor industry. And Climate Neutral is just one of many such certifiers. So from a brand-differentiation standpoint, this was reaching up to touch bottom. And from an environmental perspective, buying offsets is highly questionable. Why? Take tree planting. It has proven devilishly hard to demonstrate that the trees you protect will stay alive over the long term, that they weren't already legally protected but sold as offsets anyway, or that their preservation didn't ensure that nearby trees would be cut instead. The media, including Bloomberg, *Fast Company*, and John Oliver, is positively exploding with offset takedowns these days. Oliver spent a whopping twenty-four minutes brilliantly destroying the concept recently. Given the growing press storm, there's obvious brand risk to such a strategy as well.[3]

So instead, I suggested to the outdoor company leaders, why not use the money you would spend on offsets for something actually impactful, even if it doesn't allow you to make great claims? Retrofitting all the windows in your office to save energy, for example, or switching company vehicles to electric, as a model for your industry and the world. Or funding a lobbyist to go to DC on behalf of the climate and your own company. And then take the remaining time and energy and publish an op-ed in the *Wall Street Journal* about the need to pass climate legislation in the Senate. You'd be the only CEO in your industry doing that!

I was hopeful, but in the end, the company decided to pursue the Climate Neutral certification. The team meant well, but doing anything else felt unfamiliar and risky. And because the public and media give a pass to such not-too-effective action, there is no downside to doing less, and there is even a PR upside.

Never mind the no-confidence vote in my obviously limited powers of persuasion—this strategy is still a terrible idea. Setting carbon-neutral goals ("I promise to quit smoking by 2030!") and then buying offsets to get there has become such the norm in the sustainable-business world that if you're not doing it, you seem corrupt.

In fact, it's just the opposite. Net-zero or carbon-neutral as a concept is so hard to pin down, let alone achieve any version of, that it's by definition flimflammery.

If you google recent headlines to prove the point, your screen looks like the road to Baghdad during the first Iraq War: "World's Biggest Companies Accused of Exaggerating Their Climate Actions"; "The Truth Behind Corporate Climate Pledges"; "Companies' Climate Goals in Jeopardy from Flawed Energy Credits."[4]

The nonprofit community has tried to help improve corporate target-setting through science-based targets, which attempt to estimate a company's "fair share" of global emissions reduction.[5] But these targets miss the point, never mind that they replace unrealistic targets with *even more* unrealistic targets. The real problem is that "fair share" doesn't mean anything in a purely voluntary initiative. Today, a motivated business's fair share is arguably eliminating *all the emissions in the world*—because almost nobody else cares or acts effectively.

How did we get to a place where companies make bold climate pledges and then fall behind and end up trying to cram for the test by buying up dodgy offsets? One reason is that it's damn hard to cut emissions, which is really what we ought to be doing in the first place.

My own experience speaks to that. Mark and the missing garage door at Little Nell Hotel is just one story. But even the most obvious energy efficiency projects face stiff, unpredictable opposition, even if they have a seemingly slam-dunk payback. In my first book, *Getting Green Done*, I told a long story of trying to implement the most basic of all possible sustainability measures at the same hotel Mark operates but fifteen years before the garage door victory: a lighting retrofit with a 50 percent return on investment in the underground garage. (No smart businessperson turns down a 50 percent return, I thought, because you could *borrow* money from your fricking credit card at 19 percent interest to do the project and still make a ton.)

I encountered myriad barriers I had never anticipated (or that the starry-eyed gurus had never warned me about). These included opportunity cost, which I described earlier but which comes in many forms (the most frequent objection: if we've got twenty grand to spend, let's buy another bottle of Domaine Georges & Christophe Roumier Musigny Grand Cru, which costs about the same as the retrofit investment and which the Nell can make $10,000 on in one sale).[6] Other barriers include aesthetics (only Motel 6 has energy-efficient bulbs), business risk (what if someone sees these fluorescents and thinks we're not worthy of five stars?), and belief (I don't believe the lights will save energy).

But even after I had gotten through all those barriers and had the project approved, the engineers and contractors who would design and install the project blocked me. "You can't do that retrofit," they said. "There was a similar garage in Oakland with those new lights, and someone came in with a baseball bat, knocked out the lights, and attacked a woman."

"Let me ask you something," I said to the engineer. "Couldn't you take a bat to the *existing* lights?"

"Well, yeah."

"OK, so that's not a real problem. Let's do it!"

"No, I wouldn't do it."

"Why?"

"Well, if you put in those linear fluorescents, you can't power-wash the ceiling."

Let me pause here as the omniscient narrator and ask a question. How many times have you been to an underground hotel garage? What do the ceilings look like? They are typically hideous, often featuring steel beams covered with cobwebbed spray-foam insulation and fire retardant. Never in the history of the world, I can say with confidence, has the ceiling of a commercial garage ever been power-washed.

So it begs the question: What the hell was going on here? Why had it been almost infinitely hard—effectively impossible—to do a simple lighting retrofit?

The knee-jerk answer from the green left is this: These people are uneducated. They don't care about climate. They are troglodytes. Closed-minded. Maybe even stupid. That sounds harsh, but despite my better inclinations, I thought this way initially. In reality, they're just good people doing their job the best way they can. There's a reason the status quo holds: it works. Using the same technology that has always worked may not have environmental benefits, but you won't get called back in with complaints about performance, light quality, or other unknowns. You're providing the best service to your customer by using the thing you know works.

Busting past those last barriers was doable, but not copacetic. I played the trump card: "Just do this. We're the owner. We are doing this." But this story clarifies the problem with doing, well, virtually anything. (When I later told this story to my friend's father, Bill Drury, a captain in the Navy Supply Corps, whining that greening my business was hard, he said, "Anything in business is hard.")

In many cases, businesses set carbon goals that are impossible to meet because of conditions of their own creation. You can't meet aggressive carbon goals with light bulbs and motor retrofits alone—you need to change the carbon intensity of the electricity that powers those things. But long-standing business opposition to any regulation at all, and climate legislation in particular, means that key measures to decarbonize the electricity grid—a huge portion of the corporate footprint—never see daylight. And yet as we'll see in the next chapter, if you decarbonize the grid, you likely blow away your targets and then some, in a way that is good for society, not just your operations.

For a specific example of how industry creates the conditions by which pledges fail, take my favorite whipping boy, the beverage industry, which has made ambitious commitments to cut emissions by increasing the amount of recycled plastic in bottles. According to Bloomberg, "Coke, Dr Pepper, and Pepsi pledged to source a quarter of their plastic packaging from recycled materials by 2025, with Coke and Pepsi vowing to hit 50% by 2030. (Today, Coke is at 13.6%, Keurig Dr Pepper Inc. is at 11%, and PepsiCo Inc. is at 6%.)"[7]

But because recycling rates in the United States are so low under current conditions, there's no chance these companies can meet their goals, simply because of supply. These are conditions created by the bottlers themselves. Bloomberg again:

> Instead of taking ownership for the huge amount of waste that accompanied their shift to single-use containers, they worked to create the perception that this was the public's responsibility. Coke, for instance, launched an ad campaign in the early 1970s showing an attractive young woman bending down to pick up litter. "Bend a little," urged one such billboard in big bold letters. "Keep America green and clean."
>
> The industry paired this message with fierce opposition to legislative attempts to fix the growing mess. In 1970, voters in Washington State almost passed a law to ban nonreturnable bottles but fell just votes short after pushback from beverage makers. When Oregon enacted the nation's first-ever bottle bill a year

later, adding a five-cent deposit on bottles, the state's attorney general marveled at the political dustup: "I have never seen as much pressure exerted by so many vested interests against a single bill," he said.[8]

So it's hard to cut carbon. (This is the understatement of the century, perhaps the greatest understatement in the history of humanity . . .) But there's also another problem: carbon neutrality has captured the public's imagination because the climate issue is complex, and citizens and media just don't understand it well enough to know better. So even though setting goals and buying offsets is like suntanning in the 1950s—a supposedly healthy thing that is actually killing us—conventional wisdom rules.[9]

A corollary to this is that offsets *seem* to make sense. How could planting trees—or other measures, like buying resource-efficient stoves for people in Africa—not be good? But just one example of the growing body of discrediting research proves otherwise. Analysis by the emissions-modeling group Climate Interactive shows that even if we successfully deployed *all the possible natural carbon offsets in the world* without cutting emissions, we won't stabilize the climate.[10]

Tree-planting offsets are not the solution they appear to be, and they can threaten to undermine the entire effort to solve climate change. MIT's John Sterman lays out the terrifying logic:

> Large-scale investments in tree planting, paid for by revenue from carbon offsets, may harm the quest to cut global . . . emissions: corporations and individuals naturally seek to purchase the least expensive offsets available to them. But [high-quality] offsets will be more expensive than those that aren't. Without the ability to ensure an offset program is [meaningful], the offset market is likely to be flooded with cheap offsets that actually don't cut emissions, can't be verified, aren't immediate and aren't durable. Cheap but ineffective offsets make it appear that

the cost of cutting emissions is lower than it actually is, weakening the incentive companies and individuals have to actually cut their fossil fuel emissions.[11]

Indeed, in January 2023, a nine-month media investigation concluded that "more than 90% of rainforest carbon offsets by [the] biggest certifier are worthless." Most of these deforestation avoidance offsets—used by big companies like Shell, Disney, and Gucci—are, according to the report, "phantom credits" and may even "worsen global heating."[12]

Because of real-world challenges like these, most research on offsets shows that "the large majority are not real or are over-credited or both," as Barbara Haya, director of the Berkeley Carbon Trading Project, said in 2023. She added that every major offset program "has not just failed, but deeply failed."[13]

And that's why offsets are so cheap. The average price for what had become the most popular kind of offsets—the nature-based ones—is now a mere $2 a ton.

By comparison, the cost of directly reducing one ton of CO_2 in the regulated EU carbon market as of this writing was $72 a ton. If the world could solve the climate problem for $2 a ton, we would have done so long ago.[14]

But There's More! Now There's Legal Liability

Regardless of the obvious problems, until very recently, making grandiose claims about CO_2 emissions reductions was all the rage. But there are serious problems popping up for businesses making those claims, including the threat of lawsuits.

In November 2021, global consulting firm McKinsey & Company argued that the UN Climate Change Conference in Glasgow "made net zero a core principle for business." Net Zero Tracker reports that over one thousand companies from the *Forbes* 2000 list have made such pledges.[15]

But more and more, such corporate boasts are starting to look bogus. And they may even be a crime. The CEO of United Airlines slammed offsets in May 2023, saying "the majority of them are fraud."[16]

No wonder that by 2023, prices of the most popular carbon offsets have plummeted more than 90 percent since the Glasgow conference.[17]

In October 2022, the makers of Evian were sued over its "carbon-neutral" label.

In February 2023, a leading publisher for media and marketing companies wrote, "Firms relying on offsetting to hit net-zero targets risk greenwashing—and the law might be coming for them."[18]

In May, a class action suit targeted Delta Air Lines in federal court over its claim to be "the world's first carbon-neutral airline," a claim that, the plaintiffs say, is "false and misleading" and is based on offsets that were largely junk.[19]

In June, the Swiss commission regulating ads ruled that Switzerland-based FIFA (Fédération internationale de football association) misled fans by calling the Qatar World Cup "carbon-neutral" and told it to stop making such claims.[20]

The Real versus the Not Real

So how do we get out of this pattern? Let's start by asking what businesses really want in relation to sustainability. First, they need brand differentiation, which gets them employee attraction and retention, good press, and customer loyalty. But it can also be good for the environment. If a legitimately good company gets recognition for its climate work, then it will outperform others, force them to change, educate consumers, change social norms, and even put bad actors out of business. So media, branding, and press, if not based on greenwashing, actually matter environmentally. But to have good press, you have to be different, and that means not following the herd.

Second, in theory, businesses do want to solve the climate problem, because warming is proving to be so disruptive to global economies (do an online search for "flood Pakistan Mississippi" as just one example) that it must be addressed.

Which brings us back to the only viable business solution that truly cares and wants to stand out: the public wielding of its power to support policies that drive large-scale change. The Inflation Reduction Act was the most important piece of climate legislation in history. It not only fires billions of dollars at solutions but also reestablishes US leadership, pressuring other nations to act. The bill passed because of pressure from a social movement—citizens, NGOs, climate leaders in the House and Senate, and a few business leaders. It was the first time that elected officials felt real political and media pain for not acting on climate.

Conspicuously absent were some of the most powerful entities in the country: big business. In fact, until the very end, as previously noted, only Walmart, Salesforce, and Constellation Energy had spoken out in favor of the bill. (Microsoft ultimately joined these companies.) Some businesses now protest that they work "behind the scenes." That may be true, but it's not nearly as valuable as public advocacy, because part of what's required to solve climate is a change in social norms—the norm that it's taboo for businesses to speak about climate policy.[21]

This strategy—wielding corporate power for systemic change—grows in various dimensions the more one thinks about it. Some strategies have already been mentioned here, but there are many more, and the second half of this book is dedicated to real-life examples. Business can weaponize customers in the fight, as, you guessed it, Patagonia has long done. As discussed earlier, companies can pressure or exit trade groups that exhibit abusive relationships like those the US Chamber of Commerce has with its members when it takes climate-regressive positions counter to members' goals. Businesses can spend their lobbying dollars on climate instead of trade. And then, rather than buying offsets, they can use the money to do hard things that actually cut emissions, model solutions, and develop community expertise. For example, a business could convert an office building from natural gas to electric heat, donate to nonprofits, or build worker housing near mass transit. It's wide-open running for wannabe climate leaders; they just have to . . . *run.*[22]

A shrewd observation made in 1967 by Israeli politician Abba Eban (and sometimes erroneously ascribed to Winston Churchill) says that "men and nations behave wisely when they have exhausted all other resources." Carbon neutrality, carbon targets, and offsets neatly summarize "all other resources." Perhaps it's now time to do the right thing. What might that look like?

Possibility and Regret
The White Rim

The White Rim is a strip of manila sandstone on the edge of the Green River canyon. We've been following it for three days now, floating this sixty-mile flat-water stretch above Cataract Canyon in Utah, one small raft and a kayak. We did twenty miles yesterday, fifteen or so today. Sometimes delicately thin, sometimes robust and thick, the White Rim is faintly iridescent in the moonlight, oddly distinct in the day, always a gentle reminder of the past.

My old friend Randy Udall can't stop talking about it. Because the rim is rare, anomalous, within reach and tangible but immutable, it is, in his mind, the ultimate metaphor. He leers at it throughout the day, returns to it in conversation, speculates on its geology from beneath the rim of his purple sun hat in his seat at the oars.

He is pushing fifty, with encroaching gray in his beard and creases in his craggy neck from decades in the sun, entire winters in the Sierra, thirty years of fall fishing trips to the Wind River Range ("the Winds") in Wyoming. He and his wife have three teenagers now, a house, respectability. We've broken away from our jobs for this ten-day float in early summer weather, before the water gets really big, the weather gets hot, and the people come out.

Looking upstream, Randy can sift the sediments of his life, rifling through a grab bag of what Thomas Wolfe called "the billion deaths of possibility," to find, perhaps, catharsis in chaos. There are old lovers in that glowing rim of sandstone, uncorrectable mistakes, remembered strength, regrets, great heroics, forks in the road, youth. In a word, ghosts.

A woman passes us alone in her canoe, silent, too far away to talk. She wears a frumpy, broad sun hat and an ancient life jacket. We think she must be some kind of Annie Dillard character, philosophizing about her life, brave and adventurous, confident and a little wistful.

When she is close enough to talk, we engage her. She is a guidebook writer from Massachusetts, and she floats flat-water like this when she can; she's been doing it for twenty-five years. Randy explains what we thought about her and describes my role in the picture. "He's twenty years younger than me. We go on these trips together, and I reminisce about my past and about his future. He's my foil."

Annie, as we've dubbed her, is pleasant, friendly, and not shy. She eventually floats away. We see her again at the Anasazi ruins, then no more.

Evenings, Randy and I leave our camp among the cottonwoods and hike downstream until the sandstone turns pale gold and we are high on the canyon wall. We find infinite Zen gardens of rock, flowering cactus, white lilies, Indian paintbrush, and pools of water, all arranged in unique patterns in deposits of sand. Randy says, "Go on solo for three days, and you'll see God in these rock gardens. You'll be looking at them and crying. Trust me."

On the edge of a three-hundred-foot cliff that drops, overhanging, to the river, we look down onto a party of canoeists camped on a white sand beach, the tip of an island overrun with tamarisks. It is hard not to think of Huck Finn, harder to repress the loneliness that comes from watching a group of friends as an outsider. What could happen if we rowed our raft over with a peace offering of boxed cheesecake in a skillet? Who might we meet? What would their reaction be? How long would our friendships last?

The next day, we float the remaining flat-water to the Green's confluence with the Colorado River. Ahead are the rapids of Cataract Canyon, which wreaked havoc on John Wesley Powell and other pioneers.

We have forgotten our river map and so know nothing of what lies ahead, except that the worst of the big drops is called Satan's Gut. Randy turns to me, oars stowed and feet kicked up on a cooler of beer and ice, and asks, "If you could be with anyone now, who would it be?"

6

Holy Cross and the Energy Transition

You Don't Get to Clean Energy Unless You Get to Democracy First

I am a lineman for the county
and I drive the main roads
Searchin' in the sun for another overload.

—Jimmy Webb, "Wichita Lineman"

Imagine shaking hands with a big lobster. That's what it felt like to greet Tom, the president of Holy Cross Energy's board in the early 2000s. His hand was dry and cracked, recurved, meaty; arthritic, strong, and, like a lobster's, dangerous.

Tom was a cattle rancher, and he'd been on the board of our regional electric utility for a long time—decades, actually. And so had most of the rest of the board members, who were entrenched leaders governing what was a quite obscure, quite boring, but also vital service to local communities. And one that had deep roots in American history. Tom was a crusty guy. No bullshit. Doing the job of getting the power to the people as reliably as and at the lowest cost possible. Nothing fancy, just electricity supply. Climate change? Not apparently on the radar. In fact, taboo. Bringing it up would have been like ordering a craft beer at the Black Nugget in Carbondale, Colorado, thirty years ago, while asking "Any of you jerks know how to play pool?" Fightin' words.

Holy Cross was named after a famous feature on a local mountain—a cross-shaped couloir that, when filled with snow, is visible for miles, extending all the way up to fourteen thousand feet near the summit of Holy Cross peak. People have skied, it, climbed it, and photographed it for decades. So the utility wasn't named after the religious icon—an actual holy cross—but it might as well have been, given how conservative its board was.

Holy Cross provides electricity to Aspen Skiing Company, Vail, and about fifty thousand other customers in Western Colorado. It's a rural electric co-op, a kind of business created in the 1930s under Franklin D. Roosevelt. (Holy Cross Electric Association was formed in 1939.) Until co-ops came around, 90 percent of rural homes had no electricity. If you wanted to read at night or milk a cow at dawn, you did it by kerosene lantern, with all the associated risk and air pollution. You cooked dinner on a wood stove and used a washboard and hot water to do the laundry. No electricity meant that rural communities were locked into agriculture and locked out of a more diverse economy that might include manufacturing, offices, or other forms of business. Large utilities mostly ignored rural areas, and for good reason. It was hard to run power lines across hundreds of miles. Who would pay?

In 1935, Roosevelt solved that problem by creating the Rural Electrification Administration by executive order. The organization provided loans to farmer- and rancher-founded cooperatives. The program was a huge success. By 1953, nine in ten farms had electricity.

And rancher Tom was a natural part of that legacy. Rural electric co-ops were initially some of the most democratic organizations in the United States. The co-op model means that customers are also owners. The utilities were—and still are—run by elected boards of citizens. This structure seems amazing today, considering the complexity of electricity grids, power plants, and the wild engineering required to balance a grid composed of multiple power sources.

Over the years, however, the very forces that made co-ops democratic turned them into closed organizations. The ranchers and farmers still ran the show, but many more interest groups now lived in the West. The weirdness and obscurity of the boards meant that nobody knew about them. Nobody really voted. The papers didn't talk about the utilities or their elections. And so incumbents were reelected year after year in uncontested elections. The result was that the utility continued to do what it had done well and effectively for years: provide affordable power at a cheap price.

It turns out that over the past half century, the best way to do that was by digging up this flammable rock that humans found underground—coal—and setting it on fire. Scientists tell us that stopping coal-fired electricity is the first thing we need to do if we want to have a prayer of stopping global warming at manageable levels. Coal is also filthy dirty, releasing sulfur, mercury, soot, and other pollutants, including tons of CO_2, into the atmosphere.

Why Coal?

But for all the maligning of coal in the modern world, it's also worth contemplating this flammable rock as an amazing substance and a powerful agent of social change.

I have a chunk on my desk about the size of a volleyball. It's dense and black. And because it's a less sulfurous, sub-bituminous variety, it's slightly shiny and therefore less chalky—rub it on your face (make sure nobody's looking), and you won't look mascaraed like a coal miner. That chunk took millions of years to form: it is the concentrated remains of ancient plants.

If I were to throw a chunk of coal into my wood stove on a winter's day, and I have done that, it would simmer slowly for hours, glowing a candy orange as it burned, and emitting a thick, sweet, oily scent from my chimney. The smell isn't entirely offensive, even though coal smoke was the cause of legendarily deadly smog in England in the 1800s and 1900s and in Beijing today. When I hold coal-tar shampoo under the noses of fifth-graders, as I often do when teaching about electricity, half grimace and turn away, and half say they like the smell. Heating a home with a coal furnace uses what writer Thom Hartmann calls "the last hours of ancient sunlight," because of course, the supply of coal is finite, and the light that grew the plants that made the eventual coal is, in fact, ancient, not inconceivably from the same rays that warmed the dinosaurs.

Coal has been called "the rock that burns." And that may be the most amazing aspect. What could be more fortuitous, more seemingly God-given, than a rock you dig out of the ground and that burns and can constitute an entire society's energy supply? Most of the electricity in the United States has been produced using coal, though that number is blessedly in decline.

How do you burn coal to make electricity? It's the most analog thing you can imagine. You burn the rock under an industrial cauldron of water. The heat creates steam. The steam, under pressure like the jet from a teapot, spins a dynamo that makes electricity. The fact that coal was just some rock we found that happened to burn means it was more or less free, and because there was a lot of it, it enabled the entire Industrial Revolution. Whether you think that was a good thing or a bad thing, coal did lift human beings out of poverty. It improved our quality of life immeasurably with amenities like refrigeration and light. It powered steel mills that "made the cannon balls that helped the Union win the war," to quote Bruce Springsteen, and from the same song, enabled us to do "what Hitler couldn't do," which was win World War II. Remember that throughout history, until the recent present, half of all humans died before they reached the end of puberty. Coal was part of the reason people lived longer.[1]

And the people who dug and burned coal were not bad. At least initially, even management simply didn't know that coal had a carbon problem, that the CO_2 released by its combustion was changing the climate. They were just doing the hard and dangerous work of running the world.

We can best talk about and understand coal as a resource that was hugely valuable to the world but which today, we now know, emits unacceptable amounts of CO_2.

In short, to the people who enabled our coal economy, and to coal itself: thank you. And now it is time to move on.[2]

The problem is, Tom and the rest of the utility board didn't seem to want to move on.

A Carbon Footprint Conundrum

When I started in my job in sustainability at Aspen Skiing Company, we began calculating carbon footprint like most businesses trying to be green. We did this for several years while implementing programs to cut emissions. We did the sort of work described earlier at the Nell, but all over the company. We replaced old single-pane windows with double-pane models with special heat-retentive coatings and later argon gas insulation. We retrofitted old commercial washers in our housing units with new, front-load models and built new restaurants with the newest green techniques. We rebuilt ski patrol headquarters with fancy airtight and watertight blown-in foam insulation. And we did lots more, spending huge amounts of capital dollars in the process. After several years of implementing these programs, I recalculated our footprint, expecting to see real progress—after all, this was the vision I'd been hired to implement.

But something totally unexpected happened when I got the numbers back. To my surprise, our footprint had not gone down but had gone up! This went against everything I had learned and preached. What the hell was going on?

I had to dig around for a while. Were we using more natural gas to heat buildings? Was the winter colder than the previous year, so we had to use more snowmelt? Was there more snow or less? Did we install some big new energy users, like refrigeration or air-conditioning? Nothing checked out. But then I looked into the carbon-intensity factor we were using to calculate our footprint. Carbon intensity is how much CO_2 is emitted per kilowatt-hour (a dishwasher load's worth of electricity). As it turns out, the carbon intensity had gone up at Holy Cross, because marginally more coal had been used the previous year.[3]

Later, I found a story in the newspaper: "Xcel Energy has begun constructing its first new coal-fired electric generating unit in nearly 30 years. The Comanche Station near Pueblo, Colorado, is the site for a new 750MW supercritical pulverized coal-generating unit."[4]

Xcel Energy happens to be the main wholesale electricity supplier to Holy Cross Energy, our utility. And at the same time that Xcel was buying into Comanche 3 (the newest coal-powered generating station, in Pueblo), so was Holy Cross, which purchased an 8 percent stake in the coal-fired power plant.

"Oh my God," I thought, in one of the most powerful epiphanies of my career: "This work isn't about us—it's not about what we can do on the ground—because we can do all the state-of-the-art stuff, but if our utility decides to go big on coal, it deletes everything we've done. *So we have to change the utility, not just the light bulbs,* if we want our carbon footprint to go down."

Where to Start

How to move from epiphany to action wasn't exactly obvious. We didn't even know what the utility *was*. I had to begin a giant, grad-school-level research project. What is a rural co-op? How would you change your power supplier if you wanted? Could you even do that? I dug in.

As it turns out, co-ops have elections. And nobody knows about them. And why should they? Honestly, thinking about your utility isn't something most Americans want to do. They want the power (actually, they want the services provided by that power) and they want to be left alone. And so it was easy for Holy Cross—and the long-time board—to stay under the radar. The elections happened quietly once a year in various districts, uncontested, featuring a select group of ranchers or real estate agents, or friends of ranchers and agents, who ran the show. If there even was an announcement, it went out in a boring utility newsletter that people instantly moved to the circular file—after all, what could be more boring, and more of a waste of time, than reading the damn documents from your utility?

Knowing nothing about anything, I decided we should take on a particular board member from the far western and more conservative portion of the service territory, a man whose support and admiration for coal was unwavering and who happened to be up for election. His position was based on the utility's primary mission to provide reliable and affordable energy, and at the time, coal did that. Unfortunately, in my opinion, his stance was also informed by his resistance to acknowledging the climate impacts of coal. But first, we'd need a candidate.

I called all my energy friends and contacts: "Want to, uh, run for the utility board?" I struck out widely.

"I want to do it, but I'm not in the right district."

"I can't bear to do that, Auden . . ."

"You want me to do what now?"

I had rapidly proceeded through my entire energy Rolodex and couldn't find one person to run. The main problem was that the district in which the coal guy lived had a small population and was further west of my center of political power—I didn't know anyone out there.

So I finally resigned myself to the fact that I literally needed anyone at all to run for the seat. I just needed a breather, someone who would fog a mirror, as a warm body to replace this guy, because displacing his pro-coal voice was job one.

A friend suggested an entirely random person: Lynn Dwyer, who ran a greenhouse in New Castle, one of the small towns in the western district of Holy Cross. It turned out Lynn was more than just a warm body.[5]

"Hi, uh, Lynn . . . I'm Auden Schendler. I'm wondering if you're familiar with our utility, Holy Cross Energy, and the upcoming elections . . . and, where are you on the clean-energy revolution?"

To my joy and surprise, after a few conversations, Lynn said, "Sure, I'll run."

What Lynn and I didn't know was that her decision was monumental. After some basic research, I determined that there had never been a woman elected to the board. I called my old friend (and he was old, like, really old, looking a bit like a clean-shaven Gandalf) Ed Grange, who had been at Holy Cross since 1950.

"Ed," I said. "You guys have never had a woman on the board."

"That's not true, Auden," Ed responded in his creaky voice that sounded like a Walt Disney version of a kindly grandpa. "We had a woman on the board in 1937."

I checked—Ed was, of course, correct. There had been two women appointed to the first board of Holy Cross Energy in 1937. But they were the last to sit on the board—and no women had subsequently been elected.

So Lynn's womanhood gave us an advantage. For an electorate that had never been offered the chance to vote for anyone but older men, a woman stands out. And in this case, it seemed like co-op members would be simply more willing to vote for a woman than a man since they had never seen such a thing on the ballot, and why not try out one woman every seventy-five years? What could go wrong?

In some ways, this first campaign was like shooting fish in a barrel. We were up against a candidate who had *never had to campaign*! It was an election nobody knew about and where only a tiny select percentage of Holy Cross members—like 2 percent—voted.

The election had never been covered in the papers; the public had never had a choice of candidates. Nobody had ever run an email campaign. Nobody had ever used social media. Never ran ads in the paper. We did all these things—alerting the press (calling reporters directly and saying, "You have to cover this. It's the most important environmental election happening this year!") and driving up voter turnout. And, most importantly, we mobilized clean-energy-focused voters who had never even known about the election before but who cared and were therefore new votes.

We employed a strategy of lining up letters to the editor in local papers but holding them until very close to the election and then releasing one or two a day for two weeks in an onslaught. The letter-posting strategy caught the opposition by surprise, and by the time we had uncorked the letter flood, it was too late for them to mobilize their own news media campaign. And in small towns, everyone reads the newspaper.

Since elections occurred region-wide, we could amass progressive district votes when we couldn't reach conservative district votes. Since any given candidate on a ballot will get *some* votes, all we really needed to do was find the right number of incremental ballots—and it turned out to be very few. So if all the hippies—and by that I mean anyone who supported clean energy over coal—just got their friends to vote, we'd win.

And we did. One down, six to go.

Battle Royale

Now that Lynn had won, we needed to help her out. She was just one vote among many, and just one woman in an all-male establishment.

In the next election, the following year, we got Adam Palmer from the nearby town of Eagle to run. He was a lifelong environmentalist who had worked for Vail Resorts and various community entities on clean energy, energy efficiency, and climate change. Better yet, Adam was hilarious and all-in. He was a world-class athlete legendary for breaking trail all day at an unbelievable pace while backcountry skiing, wearing old equipment (like a bike helmet, instead of one for skiing), and dropping impossibly dry humor the whole time. (More on Adam at the end of this chapter.)

We could use the same approach as we did with Lynn Dwyer, same strategy, easy peasy, right?

Wrong. The first step in getting on the ballot is gathering signatures from membership. You need twenty-five. Adam did it—he brought in thirty-five or so, more than enough to certify. He submitted the petition.

Shortly thereafter, Holy Cross responded. Fifteen of the signatures had been invalidated—they didn't match the account holders. Adam was off the ballot. And there was no time left to gather more signatures. Adam was devastated—in fact, one of my enduring images of him is with his head in his hands over eggs at Breakfast in America, our local restaurant in a strip mall. We were trying to figure out what had happened.

As it turned out, we had run smack into intentional and unintentional antidemocratic practices that helped protect the status quo.

When Adam called Holy Cross to find out why so many signatures were invalidated—after all, the people who signed the petition lived at the address supplied by Holy Cross—he found out that the names hadn't matched the specific account owner. Meaning that if your name is on the account but your wife or husband signed the petition, it gets invalidated.

"OK, understood," said Adam. "So how does a fella know whose name is on the bill?"

"Oh, that information is on cards in the basement of our headquarters in Glenwood Springs. You can make an appointment and come look at them while we supervise you."

What was this, the Soviet Union? Remember, by the time Adam ran, Holy Cross was not happy at all about people coming in and screwing with *their* organization. So it wouldn't have exactly been a comfortable situation if Adam had decided to check out the base-ment. But since he hadn't even known about the mismatch problem, he never had the chance. And that was it for the next year. We had lost before even getting on the ballot.

But we continued to fight. The next year, Adam ran again, this time with double the number of signatures needed to qualify, each of which had been confirmed as the account owner. He made the ballot, and we used the same approach we had with Lynn: community net-working, social media, email, other electronic campaigns, daylighting the election in the media, letter-to-the-editor campaigns timed to re-lease as mail-in ballots arrived, and mobilizing large groups of people at organizations like Aspen Skiing Company and local environmental groups. Many citizens chipped in with their own networks of voters.

Early on in these campaigns, the very mention of green or anything else environmental in your flyers meant you'd win. In one election, an older candidate we hadn't recruited decided to run. He touted his army service and electrical engineering background in his flyer but didn't mention anything about environment. And he lost.

But our effort was never easy and always controversial. One tenet I've always held about climate work is that it's not sexy; it's not fancy. It's much less like a TED talk than it is like digging a trench. If it's difficult, awkward, and uncomfortable and takes a lot of energy, to the point that if at the end of the day you're craving a cheese-burger, it's probably effective. If you're wearing a thin headset mic and standing on a stage, you're probably not moving the needle too much. We need more of the foot soldiers who will canvass for utility elections and fewer people trying to be thought leaders and vision-aries, as many people on LinkedIn inexplicably describe themselves. (You can't call yourself a thought leader. That's for others to do.)

The unsavoriness of the campaign meant that it was hard to recruit others. When I called other regional businesses served by Holy Cross that had expressed interest in environmentalism and clean energy—Vail Resorts and Alpine Bank, the leading regional bank and an incredible supporter of community—both declined to participate in our campaign. To be fair, there was even some consternation at Aspen Skiing Company—public activism, especially in small towns, is incredibly uncomfortable.

One morning, I was invited to have breakfast with Tom and Roz, his wife, at the Village Smithy in Carbondale. The very idea made the hair on my neck stand up and spiked my blood pressure.

Trench work.

I went to this meeting with a full case of the dreads. And despite the succulent mushroom and spinach omelet in front of me, my appetite was wavering, with the tension as thick as my side of country ham. Roz confronted me immediately as a wealthy elite. "You Aspen people"—I live in Basalt—"can afford this expensive wind power. But the rest of these communities can't." In Roz's defense, wind *was* more expensive when we were having this conversation. My counterpoint was that wind would not always be more expensive and that with climate impacts growing, coal would become costly on its face but would also have a cost to our community health and survival. True, there was an element of faith and calculation to my comments, especially back then, but it all played out. Wind and solar are now coming in cheaper than new coal and natural gas power by a long way. That's partly because the technology has arrived, partly because the fuel is free, and partly because markets have finally scaled. And of course, the climate impacts have become obvious.

Nonetheless, it was clear the Turnbulls thought of me as a spokesperson for the wealthy, effete, and elite, and that hurt because, frankly, I identified more with Tom and Roz than with the Aspen crowd. I grew up wearing hand-me-downs; dorky checkered bellbottom Toughskins and JCPenney jeans; I never learned about stuff like how clothes are supposed to match or track with the seasons. I still don't know. I spent summers visiting my grandparents in North Dakota, hanging out at Rotary and the country club with World War II vets and farmers, Goldwater Republicans all. My grandfather's recurrent advice to me: "Work hard." If in pain: "Take aspirin." So I didn't take kindly to being batched with the Aspen elite.

Press coverage at the time illustrated the tension in the community, as this excerpt from a piece by Scott Condon of the *Glenwood Springs Post Independent* shows:

> Elections for a utility company's board of directors are usually about as exciting as watching a windmill twirl, but this month's Holy Cross Energy contest has been spiced up by the Aspen Skiing Co.'s intervention.
>
> The Skico [Aspen Skiing Company] is lobbying to oust incumbents, George H. Shaeffer and James. G. Snyder, according to Auden Schendler, executive director of community and environmental responsibility. The Skico endorsed challengers David S. Campbell, who is running against Shaeffer, and Lynn E. Dwyer, who is running against Snyder, because of their support for increasing renewable energy.
>
> "We spoke to them. They seem to be the more progressive candidates on this issue," said Schendler. Holy Cross . . . has a reputation for being one of the more progressive energy providers in the state—a point that Schendler acknowledged. But the Skico is lobbying for the challengers because it feels Holy Cross can be even more progressive.
>
> The Skico's endorsements puzzled Shaeffer, who has served two 3-year terms on the board. Shaeffer, who has been the owner and operator of a construction company in the Eagle Valley for about 30 years . . . believes Holy Cross has a good record on its renewable mix and providing incentives to its customers to conserve and seek alternative energy sources. Information on Holy Cross' website said 55 percent of the company's power supply is generated by coal-fired plants; 24 percent comes from natural gas; 15 percent is a mix of plants that use coal and natural gas; and 6 percent is from renewable sources . . . .
>
> Specifically, Schendler was critical of the board majority's decision to invest in a new coal-fired plant near Pueblo. The Skico is taking a low-key approach to the campaign. It contemplated

placing advertisements with its endorsements, but decided against it for reasons Schendler wouldn't specify. Schendler wrote a letter to the editor endorsing Campbell and Dwyer, but he signed it as an individual and not as the representative of the Skico. The company also is circulating an e-mail urging support for the challengers . . . . Shaeffer said he supports many, not necessarily all, of the environmental initiatives that Holy Cross Energy has taken during his six years on the board. He said he understands the "fever" over renewable energy, but "there are so many more issues." One critical issue is helping employees find affordable housing . . . . He is also concerned about providing reliable energy and affordable prices over the long-run. The continued integration of green power must be undertaken in a way that keeps rates affordable.[6]

The tension in that article is palpable. The utility, considered progressive at the time, was only *6 percent renewables*! And you can see the waffling, coded talk by the incumbents: "There are so many more issues."

Beyond elections, one of the many battles was against the sorts of antidemocratic practices we identified at the co-op. We had many conversations with then CEO Del Worley, a smart, open-minded guy who didn't look the part. Del had a drooping horseshoe mustache and wore an enormous belt buckle. He always wore jeans. And his pastime was weightlifting, particularly, as I recall, squats. At Holy Cross events, the song most played was Glen Campbell's classic "Wichita Lineman."

But Del worked closely with us (and our colleague Randy Udall) on the climate question. He took an executive course on climate at MIT at Randy's urging. And he implemented many of Holy Cross's early clean-energy programs, including one of the first green power purchase programs in the country. He was a true pioneer.

Nonetheless, the pressure from Aspen Skiing Company eventually frustrated Del and forced him to ask us what we were asking of Holy Cross. Acting in the company's name, I provided Del with a letter explaining our understanding of the climate threat and how we proposed that the utility could lead on the solution. One of the pieces we needed to fix was co-op democracy. Here's a snippet from that part of the letter, included here because the problems we identified are almost universal in rural electric co-ops across America. You don't get to clean energy unless you get to democracy first.

> We recognize that ASC's [Aspen Skiing Company's] involvement in Holy Cross Energy elections has troubled some HCE staff and board members. But the cooperative structure is meant to be democratic, that's the whole driving principle.
>
> We believe full member participation and education is an important piece of solving our energy problems. It's good to have contested elections. It's good to have a debate about our energy future. It would be good to have a much higher percentage of HCE member/owner votes in the board elections. As we've become involved with Holy Cross elections, we've identified what we believe are structural problems that hinder member/owner participation in Coop decisions. A series of simple and straightforward "sunshine provisions" could improve member awareness, education, and customer participation in Holy Cross elections. They are as follows:
>
> 1. Announce elections in the Holy Cross Newsletter. This year, there was no announcement of elections in the Holy Cross Newsletter in time for candidates to consider running. This may be part of the reason why so many elections have gone uncontested.
>
> 2. Simplify the process of qualifying for the ballot. There are substantial obstacles to candidacy for the Holy Cross board. A major obstacle is the lack of transparency as to who in the household is a member of Holy Cross. There are a variety of ways to fix this: one is to allow any member of a household to sign a petition.

3. Daylight membership (ideally by listing members online) so that the information is both open to the public and to candidates for campaign purposes, and so that petition signers know if their signature is valid or not.

4. Post board meeting minutes (current and historical) and board member votes online. Currently this information is difficult to come by. Why not post it online?

5. Change the date of dividend disbursement. Disbursing checks to HCE members during the week of the elections tends to support incumbents. This is not HCE's intent, and it can be easily changed.

6. List board candidates alphabetically or randomly on ballots. The current practice of listing incumbents first favors incumbents. Again, not HCE's intent, and easily fixed.

7. Set a goal of 20% election participation by 2020 and work to achieve that goal through advertising, newsletter, email, website, and other means. This would be roughly triple the current participation, and in line with the goals of a very successful direct mail campaign, though well below what is considered minimal participation in a democracy.

8. Create board term limits. Term limits would encourage greater participation in governance by coop member. Perhaps board members should be limited to serving four 3-year terms.

In conclusion, it's worth pointing out that ASC is fundamentally focused on climate change as the pressing issue of our time. We don't want Holy Cross to misconstrue this focus as personal criticism of the staff or board at Holy Cross. On the contrary, we have enjoyed working with HCE over the years and respect

and admire the staff and board. And we look forward to working with you on the next stage of this journey.[7]

Del responded, "Good letter." And our conversations continued.
The next year, though, we had to take on the big guy: Tom. An *Aspen
Times* article describes *that* fight, and it's included here because the
language used in slow-walking the climate fix will be familiar to any
community activist. Combating that sort of response *is* the battle.

A longtime member of Holy Cross Energy's board of directors
says the Roaring Fork Valley's biggest power supplier has to
take a "balanced" approach to business despite growing pressure from the environmental movement.

Tom Turnbull, a Carbondale rancher, is being targeted for
ouster by environmental activists after nearly 30 years on the
utility's board of directors. The Aspen Skiing Co. and individuals in the green community have endorsed his opponent, Carbondale resident and Glenwood Springs businessman Marshall
Foote, in the current election. They believe Foote will embrace
renewable energy to a greater degree.

Turnbull, the current board president, said he is proud of
the steps the power distributor has taken to reduce carbon
emissions. He supports the utility's direction to add increasing
amounts of renewable energy to its mix and to promote energy
efficiency among customers . . . .

While he supports those steps, Turnbull also said Holy Cross
must take a balanced approach to business to make sure electricity remains reliable and affordable for its members. That
means investing in power supplied by coal plants. Energy generated by coal-powered plants costs between 4 and 5 cents per
kilowatt hour to produce. Electricity from wind and solar farms
costs triple that amount, Turnbull said.

He sees renewable energy as a big part of Holy Cross' future,
but the timing is what has him at odds with critics.

"I just hope we do it at a pace and a cost that's more manageable," Turnbull said. "I would be bothered if we had to do it in the next year or two, because it would be really expensive."

He strongly defended Holy Cross Energy's decision to invest in the Comanche 3 coal-fired plant in Pueblo. That plant is considered one of the most efficient and cleanest, as far as non-carbon pollutants. It will open by the end of the year . . . .

The investment in the plant is exactly the type of balance Turnbull believes Holy Cross needs to make along with investments in renewables.

"It's a baseload that we own," Turnbull said of the Comanche 3 power. "We get it at the cost of production."

In addition, Turnbull isn't convinced that Holy Cross will be able to meet the forecasted growth in demand from customers by relying solely on renewable energy sources. Locking up dependable power from a coal plant was critical, he said . . . .[8]

Now, however, it appears that savings might not be as great as when the Holy Cross board made its decision. Congress and the Obama administration are examining possible ways of taxing carbon emissions, so power from plants like Comanche 3 might get more expensive.

In a recent newsletter, Turnbull wrote to Holy Cross members that he hopes carbon tax policy will receive thorough, deliberate debate and that the government won't act in haste. His report also riled critics who perceived he downplayed the significance of global warming.

"There is no doubt that we are witnessing a warming trend but, historically, civilization has benefited and thrived in warmer periods as opposed to ice ages," Turnbull wrote.

"It's not clear that Tom feels climate change is a problem or even human-caused," said Auden Schendler, Aspen Skiing Co.'s executive director of community and environmental responsibility . . . .

Turnbull declined to comment on the Skico's endorsement of his foe.[9]

How did the election go? We lost. And had to wait four more years before we could again challenge Tom Turnbull for his seat. But in that later election, we prevailed.

It's hard to explain how difficult all this work was. In 2011, Megan Gilman, an engineer from Eagle, Colorado, won a seat in the northern district. Young, effervescent, sharp, and friendly, Megan joined the board as the second woman ever elected. She shortly encountered another board member, a man, who on an elevator during a tour of some energy facility said, "Is this making any sense to you?" Megan told me that story, laughing, over coffee.

These campaigns are wrenching experiences, the stuff of 2 a.m. wake-ups and epic instances of the supermarket problem (as mentioned earlier, the assaults you experience when you take an unpopular public stand). These are the kinds of things nobody would wish on their enemies, let alone their friends. The campaigns make enemies and hurt your reputation because it's hard to be nice and kind all the time when you're at war. But if we're going to solve the climate problem, we're going to have to learn to love, even relish, these uncomfortable battles.

As of the writing of this book, the board supermajority supports climate action. It includes only two women now, but at one point there were three. The new CEO is a climate scientist, and the utility has achieved over 70 percent renewable energy, with a goal of 100 percent by 2030. When this book is published, the co-op will have achieved 90 percent: a truly mind-blowing accomplishment that inspires profound hope. Holy Cross achieved this in part by divesting from Comanche 3, something I suggested previously and was sneered at. "That's forty million in loan guarantees you have to get out of," critics told me. "Never happen."

Holy Cross's clean-energy conversion—they will achieve 90 percent renewable power supply by the end of 2024, and 100 percent by 2030—will more than cut Aspen Skiing Company's footprint in half.[10] And it will eventually zero out the climate impact of electricity for every business and household in the region—at rates that are also some of the lowest in the country. In this time of climate despair, there's almost something sublime to this accomplishment, maybe even holy.

. . .

One of the unanticipated benefits of our utility work is that it served to elevate community members—often women—and climate progressives into positions of power.

In 2020, Colorado governor Jared Polis appointed a new member to the Public Utilities Commission, a regulatory body with wide-ranging authority over electric and natural gas utilities and a key player in state energy and climate policy. The new appointee was a smart, tough, and capable engineer who had served on the board of a rural electric co-op on Colorado's Western Slope.

Her name was Megan Gilman.

With a Wink and a Grin, Adam Palmer Had Missions in Life Far Beyond Himself

My heart went out to lonely sounds in the misty springtime night of wild sweet America in her powers, the wetness on the wire fence bugled me to belief, I stood on sandpiles with an open soul, I not only accept loss forever, I am made of loss—I am made of Cody, too.
—Jack Kerouac, *Visions of Cody*

The climate movement is anchored in the people who make it happen and the fighters in the street. We can better understand how to drive change by knowing the people who do. Adam Palmer was a seminal player in the climate movement in Western Colorado, as well as a character in the previous story about Holy Cross Energy. He tragically died in an avalanche in the winter of 2021. On the following pages is a memorial I wrote about Adam, because he is an example of what it takes to be a true climate warrior.

. . .

Adam Palmer is sitting next to you on a chairlift. You are lost in thought. But you feel eyes. You turn, and there's that smirk, the penetrating stare, waiting for you to respond to the wisecrack that was so dry you already missed it.

Later, after his death, my wife Ellen said, "I just can't stop thinking of his smiling face."

It wasn't quite a smile, though. It was the sly grin.

Along with two companions, Adam died in the winter of 2021 in an avalanche near Silverton in Colorado's San Juan Mountains.

Adam was the Norse god Loki of Eagle County, the Coyote of the climate movement and of our community. He was a trickster, an Odysseus, a delighted warrior, highly dangerous to the status quo, whether that status quo was the serious thread of your conversation or the global order. If he had been born in China or Russia, I can tell you where he would have been living: in jail. Instead, in America, he was a town councilman, a utility board member, a family man, and a leader on climate solutions for the country.

His chosen work was serious indeed, incredibly discouraging labor because it is so hard. And yet Adam performed it with energy and joy because he saw in it a hopeful future for the world. It wasn't his community Adam cared about so much as everyone in the world.

He achieved what the physician and antipoverty activist Paul Farmer described as an almost unmanageable task: the ability to love a stranger's child as your own. To love the world community as your family.

Yes, he struggled and succeeded mightily for his wife, Kalie, and his daughters, Montana and Savannah, but he did it just as much for you. His friend Jason Blevins summed up the Palmer worldview: "He would haul a cabinet-style speaker down to the surf wave in Eagle he fought so hard to build . . . blasting his punk tunes, he would set up lights on towers and we would surf all night long, drinking beer and shredding . . . (well, *he* was shredding . . . most everyone else, except for the pre-teens and Adam, were crashing)."[11]

For such a jokester, Adam was insistently mission-driven.

"The two most important days in your life," Adam said, attributing the words to Mark Twain, "are the day you are born, and the day you find out why."[12] But you'd be forgiven if you weren't quite sure which was Adam's "why": the mission or the joke. Making them almost equal was the core of his resilience and his empathy. Tacked onto an email on the social cost of carbon and clean-energy percentages, he'd add a picture of himself in a new trucker hat emblazoned with "Energy Smart" or his "badass Freddy Mercury" mustache he was admiring while poring over some code document.

A memory I often recalled to him was not a happy one, but it defined who he was. As described earlier, he is sitting with his head bent in his hands, in despair over a plate of huevos, fifteen or so years ago over breakfast with Randy Udall and me. He had just been disqualified from running for the board of Holy Cross Energy. It was a nadir for us: it felt like we would never win this fight, would never turn the ship of this coal-based utility, would never make progress on climate change and clean energy. Randy and I were there to give him succor and counsel. Over a decade later, Adam had become an essential element in what led to Holy Cross's complete transformation and commitment to 100 percent renewables.

But it's hard for me to know if I was his mentor or if he was mine. I never knew someone to so persistently care about the success of others, to so joyously celebrate and foster their progress, even as he himself excelled.

When I wrote a book, my Eagle County party was at his house, he insisted. When I had a new idea, he brought me over to speak. And then in between, it was Adam who kept our friendship going: "Amigo, [this was how all his emails began] we had an email thread going around soil carbon sequestration and they were suggesting a Zoom meeting which I said blows and meetings on the slope are much more productive. It looks like Friday, February 26th works for us, can you join us hiking the bowl?"

This active connection is why so many loved him so much, but it is also the rare trait of a good and great friend.

Adam was massively talented, but his talent was beyond himself, a talent for the world. He was a music prodigy (I think he *was* a prodigy as a kid). My friend John Gitchell first learned about his skills when Adam played keyboard at John's grandmother's nursing home some twenty-five years ago. He biked across America but spent summer weekends building single-track mountain bike trails in his neighborhood. He was known as a dreamer and a doer.

He was a physical animal, but unlike some of the bros to be found in the Colorado backcountry who are just out for the stoke, Adam laced his badassery with a potent drug: kindness and an outward focus.

Jason Blevins again: "He would always break trail when skinning uphill on skis . . . . He was oblivious to gear . . . wore his bike helmet skiing, a jacket from the 90s. He was indefatigable . . . literally could not be worn down . . . . He fought hard for his community . . . . Every time you saw him you were stoked . . . . Every. Time."

His talents were also imbued with humility and self-awareness: "We just got the baby bike trailer thingy hooked up," he told me, "and took Montana out for a ride. It was awesome until I rode by a big store window and saw our reflection. I suddenly realized I had become the dad-with-the-munchkin-in-the-trailer-with-reflectors-who-cruises-on-the-bikepath guy."

Adam liked to quote his dad. "As my dad, who spent some quality time on the front of a patrol boat in the Mekong Delta says, always be ready for an ambush."

We got ambushed by Adam's death. As we age, especially if we are involved in a difficult, maybe impossible battle greater than ourselves—which, well, we all are—it is hard to escape the creeping and desolate feeling that the world takes the best and leaves the rest of us to muddle along, lonelier, slightly crippled. I have to remember Adam's relentless faith in us, his urging and encouragement and certainty in our eventual success.

Some years ago, Adam was playing with his band at Bonfire Brewing, wearing a big floppy Mad Hatter top hat, singing and moving from keyboard to guitar, his five o'clock stubble glistening with sweat, accepting beers and joyously reveling for hours and hours, the king of the room, Robin Hood of his merry band, the groom at the wedding, the center of the world. This was a man who, even in the heart of Dionysian debauchery, was using that escape and release to repower for the important fights to come. He had reached a state of transcendence unattainable by many of us. A hero on a pedestal, a model for the world.

And yet, if you looked his way, he'd grin and wink.

Maybe I will leave him there.

7

Asymmetric Warfare, Kimberly-Clark, and ExxonMobil

One day in the early part of my career at Aspen Skiing Company, I was sitting at my desk trading stocks as I am wont to do. My old boss David Bellack and I used to call it the "Aspen Skiing Company Trading Desk," and we advised Amy and Chris, our unsuspecting office mates, until the 2008 crash wiped everyone out or discouraged them out of the market and away from our counsel. The trading desk closed for good.

The phone rang. It was a group called Forest Ethics (I'd never heard of it), and it was working with Greenpeace on a boycott of Kimberly-Clark. "Would you ban Kleenex?" the person on the line wanted to know.

"Well, tell us why you ask," I said.

In short, Kimberly-Clark, one of the largest paper-based consumer products corporations in the world, was still making Kleenex without any postconsumer waste. (Postconsumer waste means the paper scraps like those you'd find in your office shredder or home recycle pile—they have been used and then would be recycled into a new product.) So, to be clear, you blow your nose in the stuff, but it's got only virgin tree fiber in it. Blowing your nose in the Tongass National

Forest. Beyond that, the company was logging endangered forest and wasn't openly communicating with the environmental community.

That's why Forest Ethics was calling. Greenpeace had organized a boycott of Kleenex, and the group had over seven hundred participants. Would Aspen like to join?

"Uh, sure," I said.

As it turns out, Aspen Skiing Company was small potatoes. We spent about $30,000 annually on tissue, much of it in restaurants, hotels, ticket offices, and the ski lines, where almost everyone has a runny nose. To swap it out for a Georgia-Pacific product would be relatively easy, though we'd have to modify the dispensers for a differently shaped box. But sure, let's do it. In fact, how society manages forests is a huge piece of the climate problem. If we could influence one of the world's largest corporations and how it sources fiber, that would be a legitimate climate win. And so we joined the boycott.

I told much of this story in my previous book and won't repeat it here other than in summary and to tell you the second half, which hadn't played out in 2009. The end of this story is a quintessential example of the complexity of corporate climate action, which I'll return to in chapter 9's discussion of banking and carbon emissions.

We joined the boycott and were immediately crucified by the local press and community. It was greenwashing, they said. Tokenism. Hypocritical. Who were we to talk? Our company was a luxury ski resort, where people flew in from Europe carrying small dogs on their laps and wearing leather pants. Then we moved them up and down a mountain for no reasons, using, for years, coal. Who were we to accuse others of anything? I had to grovel in apology to Pat O'Donnell, our gruff sixty-nine-year-old, shaved-headed, gym-jacked CEO who was wondering WTF I was trying to destroy with my unnecessary and completely gratuitous PR face-plant. Pat didn't need this literally weeks before his retirement.

And yet, something wild happened about ten days after the debacle began. My phone rang. This time it wasn't a hippie environmental group, my usual fare, but Ken Strassner, vice president of global environment, safety, regulatory, and scientific affairs at Kimberly-Clark. He was calling on behalf of the then CEO, Tom Falk. Simply put, Falk and the company as a whole weren't happy that a big, internationally famous brand like Aspen Skiing Company was banning Kleenex. Falk wanted to have a conversation with our new CEO, Mike Kaplan, and send a team to talk to us.

We agreed, and the conversations between Mike and Tom began, both on the phone and via mail. We also accepted the offer to meet with a team of Kimberly-Clark representatives who would fly down to Aspen, under the condition that they not present a dog and pony show about how great Kimberly-Clark was. Our point was, we don't care how good you are; we are asking for three specific changes: postconsumer waste, engagement with environmental groups, and changes to forestry practices to reduce or eliminate logging in endangered forests.

A team did fly down, and they did, to our chagrin, give us the dog and pony show. However, the meeting wasn't without value. At one point, after we reiterated our request that Kimberly-Clark engage the environmental community, Strassner pointed out that Greenpeace had *occupied their main office*. Would *you* talk to people who did that?

To me, his outrage at Greenpeace's actions illustrated the difference between old-school and new-school business management around environmental issues. Because, yeah, we would engage. In fact, the first thing our CEO would do if we were subject to a mass protest would be to wade into the crowd and talk to people.

Regardless, Kimberly-Clark was thinking about how to deal with the boycott. Our conversations continued, and in 2009, two years after our initial exchange, a news article appeared. Kimberly-Clark had done an about face on its forestry practices.

> Paper products giant Kimberly-Clark Corp joined forces with Greenpeace on Wednesday, pledging to conserve forests by getting wood fiber from environmentally responsible sources.
>
> In an announcement with the environmental group, which waged a nearly 5-year campaign against the company for clearcutting in Canada's boreal forest, Kimberly-Clark said it would

stop buying wood fiber from the vast woodland which stretches across the country unless it is certified by the Forest Stewardship Council.

"We are a 100-plus-year-old company. We want to be around here for another 100-plus years or more, and the only way we can be is by using sustainable forest practices," Kimberly-Clark's Suhas Apte, vice president of global sustainability, said in a telephone interview.[1]

"Holy cow!" I thought. "We've won!" And I immediately drafted a letter of congratulations to Tom Falk from Mike Kaplan, saying we would end our boycott, thanking him for his responsiveness.

And then, in a moment of doubt, I called Allen Hershkowitz at the Natural Resources Defense Council to get his take on Kimberly-Clark's move.

"It's not enough, Auden," he said. Kimberly-Clark made a limited move, but there was far more to be done. My blood pressure and cortisol spiked immediately. What had we done? We let them off too easily!

I charged into Mike's office and said, "I think we blew this. We need to push them more."

This was when Mike realigned my thinking. "Hey look," he said. "If a corporation engages with and then responds to the demands of an environmental group or movement, and then every time they do something positive, it's not enough, they are going to stop engaging. This is real progress, and they should be recognized for it, and we should end the boycott."

Techno Lock-In

Except there was a problem. There's something in the policy community known as *technological lock-in*. The concept is often applied to the idea of natural-gas-fired electricity as a "bridge fuel" to renewables, since natural gas is perceived as lower carbon than coal when combusted. Nevertheless, it still emits CO_2. It's not really a bridge, because studies show it's as bad as, or worse than, coal when you account for methane leakage.[2] And worse, once you build an expensive, complicated (and useful) natural gas plant, you're not going to just mothball it when you have enough renewables—it's going to get used. That's technological lock-in. And we were experiencing this situation with the Georgia-Pacific Angel Soft tissues we had replaced Kleenex with. Angel Soft was in a cube holder, and the Kleenex container was rectangular. We had changed the dispensers, and to change them back was a pain in the ass. At the same time, purchasing had gotten used to ordering the new product, so even though we *wanted* to switch back, we couldn't!

Meanwhile, I started to wonder about the product we had switched to. Was it actually better, environmentally speaking? I dug in and found out to my horror that Georgia-Pacific was owned by . . . *Koch Industries*. Yes, the same company owned by Charles and David Koch, who together have done more to undermine climate action and science than arguably anybody else in the world.[3]

Once again, I got a horrible feeling in the pit of my stomach. What if we had switched away from one bad actor to an even worse one? I called Allen at National Resources Defense Council in a panic. "Chill out," he said. "Georgia-Pacific actually has quite good environmental practices." He then added, "And yes, while they're part of the Koch family, their on-the-ground actions are good relative to the industry."

Another heart attack dodged.

Meanwhile, Kimberly-Clark continued to show it cared about forestry. Indeed, in 2010, it invented the first toilet paper roll without a tube, meaning it eliminated the waste of the cardboard tube. On one hand, the product was kind of goofy. On the other, it showed that Kimberly-Clark wasn't screwing around: it was taking the issue seriously, innovating, and continuing to think about improvement. And just as important, the company was participating in societal norm-changing, forcing people to think about these issues. This is an important but underrated role of smaller environmental actions.

As an example of the norm-changing value of the tubeless toilet paper roll, here's Emily Flitter covering the tubeless rolls in the *New York Times*:

> Kimberly-Clark is the first and only maker of toilet paper without cardboard tubes. Scientists at its Wisconsin facilities designed and patented a way to make the paper roll up around a stiff, hollow center that would hold its shape during packaging and transport. They also designed various accouterments, like a special dispenser for industrial-volume tubeless paper, the kind you might see in a public bathroom but which is not available for retail purchase.
>
>   . . . [After the product was discontinued] Scott [the parent company of Kimberly-Clark] Tube-Free's website has been flooded with more than 2,000 protests from devotees of the product begging Scott to reconsider its decision, with all-caps titles like "DON'T DISCONTINUE." . . .
>
>   Another fan said: "Scott tube free toilet paper is the highlight of most of my days!!!! I NEVER want to see an empty brown tube in my bathroom again. I love you more than my family sometimes!!!!"[4]

Asymmetric Warfare

When Aspen Skiing Company engaged with Kimberly-Clark, we were a tiny company. In fact, we were at a nadir in our profitability: I remember our CEO pounding the table at executive meetings and saying, "Stop . . . spending . . . money!"

So, on the bigness ledger, we weren't noteworthy. But we had other power: our fame, our media appeal, the influential guests who visit, and the fact that we're Aspen, one of the most famous ski resorts in the world and therefore a place where brands want representation. The resort town has always had retail shops that everyone knows aren't profitable but that are there just to be in Aspen. They come and go, but they feature names like Prada, Banana Republic, and Gap.

When we engaged with Kimberly-Clark, the multinational company had $20 billion in revenue and was bigger than half the countries in the world. But because of who we were, we got the ear of the CEO and we played a role—however small—in moving that company in the right direction. The military has a term for this kind of action. It's *asymmetric warfare*, where a lesser force is able to defeat a much more powerful one. Like Vietnam. Or Afghanistan.

Finding Your Power

Perhaps the most common question I get from citizens and counterparts at other companies on the climate issue is, How can I be effective? What ought I do? And the answer isn't the common bromides like "Vote!" or "Write your senator!" or other rote responses. These things are all great and important. But they should be price of entry in a democracy. And it hasn't been enough, in part because the movement, the oomph, doesn't exist to ensure that people do those seemingly obvious things. The answer is to get a case of beer—I highly recommend Fat Tire—invite a few friends, and sit around for an evening thinking about where your power lies. Each person, business, government, or NGO has their own unique power. But we never dive deep enough to understand our power, and so most Americans default to actions that neither realize an individual's agency nor drive real change: recycling plastic being the absolute most annoying example of a total waste of time.[5]

When you're into your second beer or cup of coffee and really digging in, you'll start to find power you didn't know you had. If you're a teacher, you have the respect of the community and an opportunity to educate a generation of students. If you're a kid, you may think you're weak, but you actually have astounding power: think of Greta Thunberg or the children who marched in the civil rights movement and were a fulcrum on which that movement turned. (The so-called Children's Crusade forced President John F. Kennedy's hand. He effectively said to Martin Luther King Jr., "Get the children out of the street; we're going to act."[6]) If you're a corporation—well, if deployed, your power is potentially vast. And there's a low bar. Almost any action to wield this power would far exceed anything currently being done on climate by most *Fortune* 500 businesses. Our Kimberly-Clark story and our Holy Cross Energy battle are just two ways to think about the problem. Another approach we found— perhaps the most exciting of all—began just like the Kimberly-Clark story, at the Aspen Skiing Company stock trading desk. As usual, I was interrupted by a phone call out of the blue.

Operation "Destroy the Company"

For years, one of the biggest possible levers in the climate fight hadn't been used at all or had only been used in obscure cases: the legal system. And yet it was lawsuits attacking the harm caused by tobacco that significantly damaged the industry, killed off Joe Camel and the Marlboro Man by banning ads and the targeting of youth and generating funds for antismoking campaigns across the country. Smoking has been in consistent decline in the United States partly as a result.

The climate movement started aggressively using the courts around 2017, when various constituencies uncorked a host of suits by governments, including New York City, San Francisco, and the state of Rhode Island, claiming that the fossil fuel industry has long known about the devastating impact of their products on the climate but has ignored it. Those suits were followed by legal action by crab fishermen and then the government of Boulder, Colorado, as reported on the county website: "In April 2018, the Colorado communities of

Boulder County, San Miguel County, and the City of Boulder—with legal support from EarthRights International, Hannon Law Firm, and Niskanen Center—filed a lawsuit against Suncor and Exxon-Mobil, two oil companies with significant responsibility for climate change. The communities have demanded that these companies pay their fair share of the costs associated with climate change impacts so that the costs do not fall disproportionately on taxpayers."[7]

At the time, Aspen Skiing Company had been invited to join the lawsuit. As I understood it, or as it was being publicly framed, the plaintiffs seemed to be suing ExxonMobil for the damage associated with the fossil fuels it produced. It struck me as optically difficult for a ski resort that had consumed those fuels (and still does) to file a suit blaming Exxon. I was interviewed in the press about it, and I said something on the order of "We're not going to join this suit, but we'd absolutely be interested in a lawsuit against ExxonMobil and other fossil fuel companies for burying the science on climate change, and therefore preventing an energy transition and causing harm to our industry."

That statement got the attention of some in the environmental community, and in short order I was in conversation with one of the OG climate lawyers in the country—one of several attorneys who had played a role in *Massachusetts v. EPA*, the Supreme Court suit that established CO_2 as a pollutant under the Clean Air Act and on which all subsequent climate law has been based.[8]

That lawyer was looking for a client with particular standing in particular states to become the first private party to sue ExxonMobil for damages. This idea really grabbed me: it lived up to our mantra of using big levers to drive large-scale change on climate and justice, and I was also feeling some desperation around the closing window to keep warming at 1.5°C.

The plan: Aspen Skiing Company would sue ExxonMobil for causing harm to the ski industry by knowingly obfuscating established climate science for decades. It was the best idea I'd come across in my career, an absolute crackerjack play, by a business, to move the needle on climate.

What was so good about it was that our chances of winning the lawsuit itself—a total Hail Mary—were not nearly as valuable as the collateral effects, and this played right into Aspen's strengths. The *fact* of the lawsuit, and the resultant press coverage, would be embarrassing as hell for ExxonMobil and would further erode its social license, which had been a major goal of the divestment movement. Coverage of the lawsuit would also daylight Exxon's malfeasance in the press—essentially, that it knew about a threat to human civilization and intentionally buried the information. It would be consistent with our company's effort to be an agent for change, not just a place where people slide downhill on snow.

Between the Idea and the Reality . . . Falls the Shadow

We took the idea all the way to Aspen Skiing Company ownership offices. I arrived the night before and met our lawyer for a steak dinner and two Manhattans. The next day, we walked over to the headquarters and into a room where several staffers were clearly there to do some ninja-level due diligence.

Here's the upshot of the conversation: there's a reason people or businesses don't sue big, eight-hundred-pound gorillas like ExxonMobil. Firms like Exxon, part of the most profitable industry in the history of commerce, have limitless legal resources. At the advent of a lawsuit, a big oil company can bury a plaintiff in discovery, legal requests for information. That alone could bring a business to a standstill and incur huge costs. One concern that emerged was that the lawsuit wasn't winnable. My point was that simply filing the suit would be a victory, because it would be PR coup that would begin to chip away at ExxonMobil's social license.

We aired out our thesis, the lawyers and our ownership listened, and we went back home. In the chaos of the moment, it might have been easy to miss what was actually going on: our idea got an audience. A serious one. In fact, it was months later—months of thought and analysis—before we got a lengthy document explaining why it seemed like a bad idea to sue ExxonMobil.

Ultimately, between the risk, the weirdness of the suit, the distraction it would create for the business, we decided not to sue. While I was disappointed that the idea was too radical for Aspen Skiing Company, it's worth noting that it has been too radical for *anybody*. Not a single corporation, no matter how progressive—not Patagonia, not Ben and Jerry's—has been able to take this leap. But I still tried to find a taker for the idea.

I made a run at a company known for its environmental activism in the beer industry. "Any interest in suing ExxonMobil?" I asked their senior legal counsel. I got no response, a familiar silence. Just another reminder that solving climate change is not going to be easy. But then, if it were easy, we'd have done it already.

Still, I'm not giving up. In this book, I'm doing the next best thing: I've open-sourced the proposal as an appendix so that perhaps someone else can grab the ball and run. You'd need to have standing in a state in which ExxonMobil operates if that was the company you chose to sue (Colorado and New Jersey are a start), some serious cojones, a plausible case for harm, and a good lawyer to vet the idea.

As noted earlier in this book, we don't have a whole lot of levers when it comes to the climate fight. But one humongous one, with a history of success, is the law. And corporations have been absent in this fight, with most suits being filed by citizens, trade groups, or governments. One challenge in using lawsuits in this way is that they are run by lawyers, and lawyers think about cases in terms of whether they'll win or lose. But as I've explained we don't need to win to achieve our objectives and move the needle. So we really need PR agents who happen to have studied law or lawyers with a good nose for PR. In any case, if you were waiting for your aha moment—the realization of your life's mission around climate—you just found it, sister: use the legal system as a climate lever, however you can.

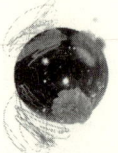 # Considering the Wider World

My anxiety-prone seven-year-old son Elias was so nervous about his first baseball game that he felt sick. "Those are called butterflies," I said. To help him out, I took him into the backyard and pitched some balls, all the while reciting a litany of "great athletes who got nervous" stories. I told him that the Islanders goalie Billy Smith used to throw up before every game. I told him how Wade Boggs, one of the great hitters of all time, used to be horrifically anxious.

After a little research, I found that most of my stories were false. In fact, the goalie who threw up before games was Glenn Hall. Boggs didn't get nervous, particularly; he just had a series of rituals on game day—like eating chicken or taking batting practice at an exact time. But never mind that; what mattered was the spirit of what I was saying, the parenting.

I told Elias not to worry, since probably nobody else would really pay much attention to his performance. The people would be focused on themselves, and they were all going to screw up to some extent. Anyway, in baseball, much of the time you're just standing around. And remember what Gandalf said to Bilbo, I said. "You are a very fine person, Mr. Baggins, and I am very fond of you; but you are only quite a little fellow in a wide world after all!"

Indeed, small-town Colorado coach-pitch baseball is a melting pot of characters, personalities, and ambitions, boys and girls alike. One player, with permanently and defiantly untied shoes, looked over at me in right field one day and said: "My throat hurts."

"You should drink some water," I said.

"My legs hurt. I can't do this."

"If your legs hurt so much, you shouldn't have come out for practice," I said, perhaps being too harsh. But I was thinking of the tragedy of Lucy in the outfield, the ultimate in unreliable teammates, "backing up" Charlie Brown.

We have kids who are slightly older than Elias with the coordination of Michael Jordan, one kid who can rope-throw from shortstop to first, directly on target ten out of ten times. Others are slower, or shorter, or younger, and still others can't follow directions and wander around the outfield like lost souls. But they're all in the mix, batting and fielding and training.

The coach, Bob, has a major league bellow, which modulates down to a low growl. He's a strategist: "If you run through first base hard, I guarantee you'd get on base half the time!" And "If we can just field, we'll win!" One day, he roars at the kids coming off the field: "Run! There's no walking in Basalt baseball!"

As a helper coach, it's all new to me. I grew up with nontraditional sports like hiking and climbing. I look out at the kids hustling in behind Bob, and I take the tough-guy talk for granted, until I see Bob grinning widely, looking at me, his back to the team.

"Baseball is a thinking game!" Bob says. I like that. There is more here than victory at all costs. What I fear most is what the writer Peter Maass calls "the wild beast"—the dark aspects of human nature that get unleashed at certain times. Maass found it in Bosnia, but I worry about finding it during games. For me, the wild beast is the irrational desire to win, even when winning isn't the only point. It's omnipresent, but most alarmingly, I find it not just in others (where it's annoying) but also in myself (where it's scary).

My friend, who has three boys of his own, all athletes, heard about my fear and told me that 90 percent of the coaches get it. He says most understand it's about teaching kids the game. Later he adds, baseball is about teaching kids about life.

I thought about the gamut of children on Elias's teams, the vast range of abilities—players with swings like George Brett and speed like Rickey Henderson, kids who couldn't catch a pop fly if you offered them Twinkies, and players so distracted, disaffected, or just slower to develop that they sometimes frustrate coaches as well as their peers.

But as our coach-pitcher, Larry, said when one boy whiffed thirty times in batting practice and notes of derision burbled from the bench, "Hey, he's your teammate. You need to support him."

A civilization is measured, the saying goes, by how it treats its weakest members. The Little League field is, in fact, a wider world. And this game offers up, like Larry's soft pitches, some small lessons in how to get along in it.

8

Dirtbags, Powder Hounds, and the NRA

The Protect Our Winters Strategy

A man arrives at the gates of heaven and asks to be let in.

St. Peter says, "Of course. Just show us your scars."

The man answers, "I have no scars."

St. Peter responds, "What a pity.
Was there nothing worth fighting for?"[1]

When maybe the greatest big-mountain snowboarder in the history of the sport, Jeremy Jones, called me one morning in my office, the voice I heard on the other line was, as far as I could tell, "the Dude" from *The Big Lebowski*. Jeremy has a laconic Southern California drawl; he's a *snowboarder*, which is akin to being a skateboarder, a punk rocker, or a pirate. With no offense intended, he often looks like he just crawled out of a snow cave, with wild hair and a five o'clock shadow, because he's often just off some expedition or hor-rific travel schedule, and all that put together made me skeptical that this guy had the kind of game to be taken seriously; his appearance belied his greatness.[2]

I did know that long before any other athletes in the industry cared about climate, he did, making a video about the issue during the 2006 Olympics. I remember hearing about it, then watching it, and thinking, "Well, God bless this guy, whoever he is. At least someone from snow sports is finally talking about climate."

But it actually *was* a big deal. Jeremy had cred. He became famous for riding some of the most aggro lines in the world on remote mountains, from Alaska to the Himalayas. He was an extreme athlete of the highest order.

Aspen Skiing Company was the most prominent environmental advocate in the ski industry, and Jeremy was calling to ask if I'd sit on the board of a relatively new nonprofit he had created, Protect Our Winters, or POW. Jeremy created POW after he visited a childhood ski resort (he grew up in Massachusetts) and found the snow almost entirely gone. "Shit, man," he thought. "Climate change is a real problem. I better give some money to the snow sports industry foundation working on this threat to the whole sport." And he looked around, and . . . there was no such group.

So he founded one.

"Oh boy," I thought, "another board." But at the same time, this organization was doing exactly what our industry needed, and why wouldn't I, also in the industry, try to help? So I said yes.

On Dirtbags

What I was missing about Jeremy is that you don't survive years in the high mountains, snowboarding incredibly dangerous lines, without being smart, wily, and strategic. Jeremy was all that. True, he was also a *dirtbag*, an outdoors lover who cares little about material things so that they can focus on the real stuff, like climbing, skiing, hiking, and expeditions into the snow. The most famous dirtbag is Patagonia founder Yvon Chouinard, who famously never used a ground pad and who still rolls out his sleeping bag on Tom Brokaw's couch when he visits him in New York City. Of course, Chouinard became one of the leading businessmen and environmentalists of his generation, but he was part of a tradition. Before him, there was John Muir, the founder of the Sierra Club, who was known to head out into the wilderness with his signature metal cup and *a crust of bread tied to his belt* for sustenance. The first energy bar.

I myself am a dirtbag and proud of that credential. I have spent the summer in Alaska working cannery slime lines and National Forest Service remote work camps, all while squatting in an abandoned shack with a moldered *Playboy* centerfold plastered to the wall and later sleeping behind the stove in a boardinghouse mostly occupied by Filipinos working at the cannery. After college, I lived in a closet in Telluride for a summer. (The place had a functional washer and dryer hookup, but no washer or dryer, and I accidentally turned on the washer hookup once and doused my sleeping bag.) I eventually moved into a trailer in El Jebel with four roommates, one of whom drank all our milk whenever we went shopping and another (the milk drinker's girlfriend) who regularly asked me why I hated her. (I did not.) This is dirtbag stuff.

To this day, most years I spend a few weeks sleeping under the stars, and despite my work at a ski resort that owns hotels and restaurants, I find being waited on in anything but a cursory way highly uncomfortable.

Important note: dirtbags are not political actors. For example, civil rights leader John Lewis, as great a man as he was, was not a dirtbag. Dirtbags would rather spend all summer eating discount cat food so they could climb a mountain than march in the streets. They prefer backcountry skiing to voting. They are almost by definition disinclined to be political engaged.

And yet, occasionally they catch fire. Muir, a mountaineer from California, became one of the great environmentalists of his era. Almost the same story applies to the great David Brower, a later head of the Sierra Club, who was, in his time, a leading American mountaineer. I thought, Jeremy is also a dirtbag mountaineer living in California; maybe there's something here.

A few months after joining the board, I walked into my first meeting at a trade show in Denver. The room seemed empty. Sitting around a table was Jeremy; his executive director Chris Steinkamp; Matt McClain, who then worked for the Surfrider Foundation; and Christina Thomure, the environmental coordinator at a small ski resort called Stevens Pass.

"Where's the board?" I asked.

"This *is* the board," Chris said.

"What foundations are supporting you?" I asked.

"None."

"What major private donors do you have?"

"None."

"OK, cool."

All this is just to say the organization was nascent, ambitious, and just beginning to find its way, and I was lucky to be part of an environmental startup.

Over the years, POW's vision and purpose evolved into an incredibly powerful idea in the form of a question. What if you could take a huge sector of the population—outdoorspeople—who are naturally *dis*inclined to be involved with politics or movements (after all, we're talking dirtbags here) and mobilize them in the climate fight, as part of the movement, and as a voting block?

Think about it: the National Rifle Association, at its peak, reportedly had five million members (or less), about two million of which were active.[3] There was money in the organization, too, but more important, studies of the organization's success show that the constituency was rabid and mobilized on legislation whenever it was needed. *They showed up.* And because of that, they owned their issue in Washington.

The outdoor industry is arguably much larger than the gun community. (And just as wildly driven.) Consider that outdoor retail company REI alone has 23 million members. Depending on how you measure it, the outdoor community in the United States is anywhere from 40 to 168 million people. And these folks aren't just blobs; they are intense fanatics, as much as, or more so than, gun owners. Skiers are so rabid that in places like the Pacific Northwest (Mount Hood, say, where the weather is legendarily bad and you can ski boilerplate, crud, powder, and slush all in one day), they are known to ski in trash bags with armhole cutouts on rainy days. Climbers are also notoriously obsessive, often spending whole summers working on *one particular move* on one particular climb. Runners, hikers, and surfers also tend to skew wealthy, influential, and, most importantly, environmentalist. There isn't a skier who doesn't, through affiliation with the outdoors, have some sense of identity as an environmentalist. Indeed, you can't have been on a ski mountain or anywhere else in the beauty of nature and not have some level of environmentalism burgeoning in you. Because the thing you love is the thing that is also threatened by pollution, by climate change, and by extraction. So, what if you could mobilize this group politically?[4]

Importantly, these mobilized dirtbags would be *incremental* votes, new voices and activists from a cohort not typically inclined to speak up or to participate actively in democracy. Moreover, states with robust outdoor communities tend to map one-to-one with purple states, blue states with swing senators, or even flippable red states. Montana is a great example, as is Colorado, Arizona, Maine, Michigan, and Nevada.

What the environmental movement has long missed is just such a play on identity politics. NRA members are gun people. They are members of gun clubs. They socialize around guns, and they wear gun T-shirts. In the same way that I sometimes go to sleep thinking about particular rock climbs, they think about types of rifles and handguns, shooting technique, scopes, holsters, bullets. Guns are part of their identity, and so when they are called to engage on the gun issue, when they are called to show up for their very selves, they really show up.

This is equally true for the outdoor community. An old rock-climbing partner of mine tells people, "I'm a *climber*. I don't climb, *I'm a climber*." What he is saying is that climbing is his identity. It affects everything from how he reacts to snow when he leaves a restaurant to how he might deal with a flat tire or respond to an offer of free food (take it—see "dirtbag").

It's fun being part of a tribe: it gives our lives meaning, purpose, vision, and community.

POW exhibits these identity qualities on steroids. At one meeting we had in Salt Lake City, POW board member and legendary climber Conrad Anker (who found Mallory's body on Everest and put up numerous high, difficult rock and ice routes and first ascents around the world) approached me at the check-in desk. "Auden," he said, "do you mind if I crash in your room? If not, no worries, I can sleep in my car." *Which was in the hotel garage . . .*

"Conrad," I said. "You're welcome to stay with me. But we are grown-ups here, and POW has a budget for your room, which isn't that expensive, and so let's just get you a room." (I needed to get some sleep, which is a delicate and desperate enterprise for me. I knew Conrad could sleep under a rock and be fine, but it was me I was worried about. But what's not to love about Conrad's core instinct, which is to not spend money if you don't have to? That predisposition used to be called conservatism.)

POW grew over the years, partnering with the Natural Resources Defense Council to visit Washington, DC, with groups of Olympic medalists, lobbying state commissions for clean-energy legislation, and over time, it put theory into practice.

The Tester Test Case

A test case was Jon Tester's 2018 Senate race in Montana. POW, Patagonia, and other groups activated outdoor industry voters in places like Missoula, Bozeman, and West Glacier using influential outdoorspeople and state residents like Conrad and fly-fisher Hilary Hutcheson. An important sociological effect we were tapping is known as *elite cues*. In short, if Michael Jordan tells you to eat Wheaties, you're not going to say, "Well, how much iron is in there? Is it too sugary?" No, you're going to eat the damn Wheaties. If Hilary, your fishing hero, tells you to vote for Tester, you'll vote for Tester.

Tester won by eighteen thousand votes, a tiny margin. While it's hard to be sure how many votes this effort was able to deliver, the strategy seems right. In the 2020 presidential election, POW applied that thinking in key swing states that have outdoor economies: Michigan, Maine, Colorado, and Nevada, targeting climbing gyms, colleges, ski hills, outdoor shops, and social media. POW even placed ads in the Georgia senate race in 2021—after all, that state, too, has a huge community of boaters, bikers, hikers, and climbers. Heck, the Appalachian Trail starts there!

POW thrived by being opportunistic and creative but never losing sight of its role: mobilizing the outdoor industry as a force on climate. One of POW's better ventures was a partnership with New Belgium Brewery and Ben & Jerry's. The brewery is a longtime leader in legitimate sustainable-business practices and, more importantly, the makers of the great Fat Tire beer. Ben & Jerry's, whose sustainability programs have been led for years by an epically smart and dedicated former Bernie Sanders staffer named Chris Miller, is one of the most innovative activist companies on climate and justice.

Ice Cream–Flavored Beer

The vision was . . . well, initially it was . . . Salted Caramel Brownie Brown Ale . . . with POW on the label and sold as a fundraiser.

The limited-edition ice cream (Salted Caramel Brownie Brown Ale *ice cream*!) and beer was a massive hit and raised $100,000 for

POW, which at the time was a huge portion of the annual budget. But the other vision for the collaboration was the idea that one might mobilize people as climate activists *at the bar* more easily than elsewhere.

So the beer bottles had back-label information on climate and POW and a link to a website. On the website were directions for how to call your senator and what to say. (These are two huge barriers to citizen engagement: people don't know who to call or what to say. But it's pretty simple: find your senator, call, and say, "I vote, and I care about climate. Can you do more?")

The vision was that people would be sitting at the bar late at night, peeling off the beer label as we are wont to do, and, being slightly relieved of inhibition, would be more inclined to dial up their senator. Did this work? We don't know. But it was fun as hell, and like many of POW's projects, it seems like the right way to think about activism.

While this kind of stunt might see random or scattershot, the truth about the climate movement is that we don't know for sure what's going to tip the scales, catch fire, or drive the movement. That's why leaders like Bill McKibben are always trying new stuff—divestment, banking reform, uncorking the power of the senior citizen vote. The climate battle is a little like a bad bar fight that you're losing: You have to try stuff. Throw chairs. Flip tables. Improvise.

The Inflation Reduction Act Play

For years, POW had been arguing—along with Aspen Skiing Company—that while small, individual, or operational actions are good for business and help change social norms, the only way to solve a systemic problem like climate is through a movement, and then through the resulting legislation enabled by that movement. But after years of failed policy in the United States going all the way back to the Waxman-Markey Cap and Trade Bill that nearly passed but ultimately failed in 2010, no federal climate legislation had passed. And by 2022, such legislation seemed even more unlikely, with a split Senate and no clear path forward.

The circumstances changed, however, when the Inflation Reduction Act, a carve-out from the Build Back Better Act, got traction. Seeing a narrow shot at a win, POW sprang into action.

As climate nerds will remember, the bill's passage first hinged on getting past Joe Manchin of West Virginia, the nominal Democrat who serves a coal state and a conservative constituency but who was the key swing vote. As it turns out, West Virginia is home to a ski resort named Snowshoe. And Snowshoe is owned by Alterra, a conglomerate.

Since its inception, Aspen Skiing Company has been urging industry peers like Alterra to wield power on policy in addition to traditional ski industry (and broader business) approaches of focusing on carbon footprint and emissions targets. Alterra understood the value of weighing in on the Inflation Reduction Act and allowed POW to reach out to the CEO of Snowshoe. Would she be willing to contact Manchin, since she knew him personally? The answer was yes, and POW came in to help, drafting a two-page letter outlining why the Inflation Reduction Act was an important business play for West Virginia. (Many other business leaders, including Bill Gates, similarly weighed in.) The letter was hand-delivered to Manchin, and miraculously and thanks to many forces, not just POW's, he voted yes. That was step one.

Then, however, Arizona senator Kyrsten Sinema became the swing vote. POW has a coalition of outdoor athletes interested in climate action, and two of them, POW knew, were admired by Sinema and followed by her on social media. So POW had those athletes directly tweet Sinema, asking for her vote on the bill.

Did POW single-handedly pass the Inflation Reduction Act? Of course not. But the nonprofit was part of the movement that meant that climate legislation could no longer be ignored.

Give a Flake

Aspen Skiing Company had tried for years to address this glaring gap in the climate movement: that there were no consequences for elected officials who ignored climate change. One approach was to use advertising. Think about it: What does the typical ski ad look like? It's a skier on a blue-sky powder day. But who cares? That's what every ski resort does. It's like advertising your beer with a picture of a can of beer. It doesn't offer you anything unique, doesn't differentiate the brand at all. What if instead, you did something totally different, something that aligned with a cause? We decided to launch the Give a Flake campaign, the third marketing campaign we'd done around climate change, this one focused on direct advocacy.

As part of the campaign, we released hundreds of thousands of tear-out, postage-paid postcards in national magazines like *Outside*. Those cards targeted specific Republican senators who were potential swing votes: Lisa Murkowski of Alaska, Rob Portman of Ohio, and Susan Collins of Maine. Take a look at one of the cards.

We did something else. Considering where we might have the most power to address climate in our hotels, we thought about our

I GIVE A FL✳KE

Dear Senator Murkowski:

I'm writing you as a fellow skier, lover of winter, and concerned citizen. I can't think of another place in the world more on the front lines of climate change than Alaska, yet you remain indifferent to the issue. How can that be when "ski" is right there in your name? Your state's annual average temperature has warmed 2.4 degrees since 1988 and an astonishing 5.4 degrees in the winter. Alaska has some of the best skiing and riding in the world. But the whole economy—and entire villages built on melting permafrost—is threatened. Despite the obvious impact on our world, you choose not to take the lead on climate. That's gotta change. Of all people, you're the right person in the right place to Give a Flake.

Sincerely,

_____

To learn more and take action, visit GiveAFlake.com

guests: they are often wealthy, influential, and environmentally minded. What if we gave them a chance to be climate activists?

So we created a lobby kiosk to help guests send a prepaid postcard to Joe Manchin. The kiosk had pens and suggested language: "I'm a skier, and I vote. You need to do more on climate!"

You might imagine this kind of thing would be seen as a stunt and dismissed. But the day the campaign launched, the phone rang in the office of our then CEO, Mike Kaplan. It was Murkowski's office.

"What are you guys doing? We're trying to help you with ski industry legislation, and you're attacking us on climate?"

That, of course (and I was used to this by now) triggered a call to me from Mike.

"Uh, Auden, I got Lisa Murkowski wanting to talk to me about this ad campaign we're doing . . ."

I prepped Mike for the call, and he had the conversation with their office. "Look," he said, "you just simply need to do more on climate. You need to step up."

The story didn't end there. Murkowski wrote to *Outside* magazine, where many of the ads had been published, to protest. That led *Outside* to fact-check her claims and to a back-and-forth between Murkowski and me in the magazine.[5]

Did we move the senator? Nope. But this was one of the first times an elected official felt big-time national pain for not doing enough on climate. And it was the beginning of a trend that culminated in the Inflation Reduction Act, which was also the first time in American history that elected officials saw large-scale consequences—political pain and public outrage—over their inaction on climate. For years, elected officials could do anything they wanted: outright deny the science, claim to care but slow-walk action, and fund fossil fuel companies as if they were climate solutions without ever being called out. That era has ended.

. . .

POW was blessed by the vision of its founder, by having a genuinely good idea, and by filling a niche that offered open-field running without competition. It also had a slew of strong board members and generous donors. But early on, Aspen Skiing Company played an important role building the organization, and did so through a strategy that more corporations that profess to care about climate should adopt: they *seconded* me. (*To second* means to lend an employee to a different job for a short period.)

While I did my board development, strategy, and fundraising work for POW, I worked on the Aspen Skiing Company payroll and had its blessing. For this reason, the company could contribute to the climate movement in a meaningful way, with a major investment of time and money, but also with a multiplier effect: instead of changing light bulbs, we were helping build a movement.

Aspen Skiing used this strategy repeatedly. In 2018, I was appointed by then governor John Hickenlooper to serve on the Colorado Air Quality Control Commission. This is the state commission that develops climate and pollution law. It required a monthly drive to Denver, a four-hour journey, and multiple days of meetings, sometimes a week at a time. I did the drive in an electric Audi e-tron issued by Aspen Skiing Company, with the company's blessing, and on the company's dime. Instead of lobbying elected officials, begging for better policy, Aspen Skiing Company was *actually making the law.*

During my tenure with Colorado's Air Quality Control Division, it passed the most rigorous restrictions on methane emissions in the United States (methane is a super greenhouse gas). It also passed a ban on hydrofluorocarbons (the second-generation refrigerants that replaced chlorofluorocarbons, notorious for destroying the ozone layer and that are also super greenhouse gases, even more potent than methane). And Colorado became the first state in the central United States to adopt California's low-emissions standard and then its zero-emissions vehicle standard. I was lucky to be there, and easily the least qualified guy on the board, surrounded by PhDs, pulmonologists, engineers, and even a former special forces guy who worked to find rogue chemical weapons in breakaway Soviet republics. (He and I had some interesting conversations over beers . . .)

Businesses and individuals need to think differently about how they can influence the climate fight. We need to get out of the box. If you just look around, opportunities—in the form of dirtbags, beer bottles, state commissions, and ad campaigns—abound.

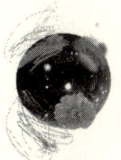 ## Debris Huts and Other Skills

A *debris hut* is a crude shelter constructed out of desperation with materials at hand. It is designed to serve as an emergency shelter while you get something else online, find your way to a road, or figure out what you're doing screwing around in the woods without a tent. Built opportunistically from sticks, leaves, grasses, and dirt, it might be considered a stepping stone to a better life, the trailer home of the backcountry. Nobody wants to end up in a debris hut, but sometimes you find yourself, like me, looking up at the stars and wondering how it came to this.

I first learned about debris huts growing up in New Jersey. There, five minutes from Manhattan, I could only fantasize about the backcountry, which I saw as a place of salvation. So I did what any real New Jerseyite wannabe outdoorsman does: I read the Tom Brown Jr. wilderness survival series. Brown, a Jersey boy who cut his teeth in the Pine Barrens, produced quite a body of work, ranging from his autobiographical *The Tracker* to tomes on edible plants and animal prints. Brown even expanded his expertise into urban survival, where he taught such techniques as climbing into the Salvation Army clothes drop boxes as a way to overnight in suburbia.

A clothes drop box would have been preferable to the debris hut I found myself in one fall in my twenties. I had set out for some fishing in the Wind River Range with my friend Randy and his daughter, Tarn. The Winds in autumn was such an enchanting prospect that I brought the most whimsical book I could find, Proust's *Remembrance of Things Past*. A clean break, if there ever was one, from Tom Brown. Though my pack was heavy with a week's worth of food, I thought the sacrifice of carrying the brick of a novel would pay off in self-improvement. Not physically: it would hurt my knees. But my idea was that, locked in the mountains with my taciturn friend Randy, hours of twilight, mediocre autumn fishing (the August hatches would be over), and nothing else to read, I might possibly get myself educated.

Conditions, it turned out, were good for reading. It snowed the entire week. No fish rose. A sense of melancholy in the fall weather and in the gold light on the fading willows made reading optimal. Randy was himself, tending to go off on his own for long fishing ventures or peak climbs. Tarn managed to read, write in her diary, and generally keep herself occupied. I was happy during the days, but evening reading (and sleeping) was difficult in the three-person tent. Too many limbs from six-foot-four Randy, and I worried about rolling over and crushing Tarn or putting her into years of therapy with my snoring and drooling. When snow made travel increasingly difficult, we set up base camp near the Little Wind River for a couple of days to wait for clearer weather. It was time, I realized, for a debris hut.

The theory is simple: pile enough dirt, leaves, and other detritus onto a lean-to skeleton of sticks a foot or so off the ground, and you've created a more or less weatherproof mini-wigwam. Make a pine-bough floor and fill the thing with leaves and grasses as insulation, build a small fire at the head, and you're styling. Unfortunately, faced with wet leaves and grasses, and inherently lazy, I only managed a shelter that, propped against an overhanging rock, barely kept off the snow. A mouse moved in and nibbled on pieces of leftover Pop-Tart. I had reached, I felt, a new low, a sort of return to the New Jersey I had escaped, but worse, because it occurred in the most beautiful place in the world. The weather was terrible, the fishing poor, mobility limited, and I couldn't even build a debris hut to spec.

Even with my newly created personal space, reading Proust was too much. After fifty pages in his boyhood home, I couldn't get out the front door. The book was more boring than a subtitled film, more monotonous than *La Traviata*. I would rather have wasted my time trying to catch nonexistent fish in the dark—at least that would have been a form of meditation.

So, affected by the weather and the time of year, and maybe a little by Proust's reflective tone, we told melancholy stories when we ventured forth to the fire. Randy told me about his friend who found out, at fifty, that he had Huntington's disease, a time bomb that erupts and incapacitates with a cruelness that suggests cosmic punishment. Unlike Job, this man could not converse with God. He wrote a letter to friends, then jumped from a bridge in Seattle.

I told a story about my father. He grew up during the Depression, so poor that once, returning home, he found his mother and all her furniture on the sidewalk: the family had been evicted. Talk about urban survival skills. His father had long since left; to stay warm they stuffed their jackets with crumpled newspaper in the same way that survivalists might stuff their pants with grasses for insulation. They became mobile debris huts, as many people did then.

My father described sitting, ear to the speaker of a tube radio in a dark corner late at night, listening to a symphony. Deep into the last movement, as my father drifted off to sleep, an aria exploded: it was "Ode to Joy"; the symphony was Beethoven's Ninth. My father said he was spellbound. Not yet a teenager, he had never heard anything so beautiful in his life. Beethoven's biographer Maynard Solomon called that symphony "an expression of humankind's search for the divine." Critic Martin Goldsmith called the fourth movement "a universal expression of unity and exaltation."

In that story there was, I thought, hope for something risen out of the ashes. If, on short notice, we can descend into hell from a place that might be heaven, perhaps we can climb back out on something as ethereal as a song. The weather "moight a kilt us," to paraphrase Faulkner, "but it hadn't whupped us yit." And with that thought, I crawled back into the hut, careful not to crush my mouse tenant, humming off-key tunes into the quiet of the new snow.

9

Taking On Carbon Banks

Many years ago, I was on a chairlift with a friend when he looked down onto the ski slope and commented, with some surprise: "That guy only has only one ski! And he's ripping!" I pointed out that while that was true, the material point was that the skier only had one leg. As it turned out, the skier was a pioneer in adaptive skiing, which later grew explosively and, along with newer technology, made the sport accessible to far more people.

As with my friend's perception of the skier, in the environmental and climate movement, often the thing people focus on isn't the most important issue: cutting carbon footprint at businesses versus driving political change is a good example. Sometimes, fixing the problem that's in your face and seems most obvious doesn't yield the highest leverage. Take Aspen, for example, where wealth is often the target of climate activism. Indeed, Oxfam has reported that the richest 1 percent of the population emits as much planet-warming emissions as the poorer two-thirds of society. We think of those impacts in terms of private jets and yachts, but most of the emissions come from something less obvious: cash. Wealthy people all have sizable bank accounts, personal or business. And it's the cash they have in the bank that matters most when it comes to climate.

Financed Carbon

Here's a weird thing about cash: if you hold it in the bank, it doesn't just sit there. The bank uses it for stuff. All kinds of stuff, including mortgages, investments, and loans used to make money. As it turns out, most banks also have fossil fuel as part of their investment portfolio. And that means that your cash will be funding, at least in part, some level of fossil fuel development, extraction, or refinement.

The Backstory on Banks

When it comes to efforts to tackle climate change, there's not a lot of love flowing to bankers. In March 2022, the SEC proposed a new rule requiring banks to disclose the carbon footprint of their loans—so-called financed emissions. A bank that lends money to a coal mine developer, for example, would be required to report on the resulting emissions. Environmental groups such as Rainforest Action Network and 350.org have expanded campaigns targeting Chase, Citibank, Wells Fargo, and Bank of America, among others, for financing tar sands and other fossil fuels. And "The Carbon Bankroll: The Climate Impact and Untapped Power of Corporate Cash," a 2022 report produced by several nonprofits, showed that climate-concerned businesses are effectively misstating their carbon footprints and failing to account for cash holdings that banks repurpose, at least in part, to fund fossil fuel development.[1]

To put an exclamation point on it, here's what Bill McKibben wrote about "The Carbon Bankroll" report when it came out:

> According to these calculations, Google's carbon emissions, in effect, would have risen a hundred and eleven per cent overnight. Meta's emissions would have increased by a hundred and twelve per cent, and Apple's by sixty-four per cent. For Microsoft in

2021, the report claims, "the emissions generated by the company's $130 billion in cash and investments were comparable to the cumulative emissions generated by the manufacturing, transporting, and use of every Microsoft product in the world." Amazon, too, has worked to cut emissions; it plans to run its delivery fleet on electric trucks, for instance. But in 2020, the report claims, its "$81 billion in cash and financial investments still generated more carbon emissions than emissions generated by the energy Amazon purchased to power all their facilities across the world—its fulfillment centers, data centers, physical stores."[2]

Climate advocates have a point: it's hard to call yourself a green company if your cash assets are underwriting global warming.

So what's a responsible business to do?

One conventional approach would be for corporate leaders to double down on cleaning up their own house. They could purchase more offsets, ramp up energy efficiency and renewables to cut emissions, and even switch to, say, Amalgamated Bank, a leading, if relatively small, low-carbon bank. That act would further decarbonize operations, and coupled with campaign pressure and media daylight, it might also force banks to create meaningful policies banning new coal extraction, halting new gas exploration, and eliminating other high-carbon investment like tar sands development.

The problem with these tactics is that they lack the power to drive enough global emissions cuts to stabilize the planet's temperature below 2°C in the time we have left. There are other problems we've encountered before. The offsets are often bogus; efficiency can only go so far; and capital will still flow to fossil fuel extraction from other sources, from uncooperative banks, or from the lengthy winddown. Meanwhile, there just aren't that many low-carbon or no-carbon banks to switch to. Because they tend to be small, few have the expertise and staff required for complex international deals. It's not that this path isn't valuable in some way, but it's business as usual, and it's just not enough.

A more promising approach could result from a thorough understanding of the whole climate-banking landscape, including new SEC rules, climate campaign demands, and "The Carbon Bankroll" report. If they recognize that finance as currently practiced ensures climate chaos, businesses might conclude that they can't escape climate change unless they fix the whole enchilada: creating an economy that operates on clean energy, with legal guardrails in place to restrain the worst aspects of capitalism. Such a change fundamentally requires a finance system that isn't complicit with the status quo.

What Is a Green Bank?

What might a higher-leverage, bigger-picture business strategy look like as applied to banking? Ivan Frishberg, senior vice president and chief sustainability officer at Amalgamated Bank, described some practical steps businesses can take to support a reform movement.

First, businesses could simply change their corporate carbon measurement to account for financed emissions. This would lead to further public and media awareness of the problem and to conversations between banks and businesses. To its credit, Salesforce has been wide open to the dialogue, even providing a blurb on "The Carbon Bankroll" report. This is the sort of engagement that could lead to meaningful next steps.

One such step was suggested by a former sustainability director at a major American bank who asked to remain anonymous: "A company with the influence of Google could likely set rules for the use of their cash deposits—if you want our deposits, you can't use them for X, Y or Z." Such a practice would also start to steer financial institutions toward a "good bank, bad bank" strategy, which would split riskier, less desirable carbon-based assets from cleaner ones. An example of this model is Citi Holdings, created after the financial crisis to bundle and eventually sell distressed assets. Under such a model, market forces might then take hold. "Good bank" operations would likely attract and retain talent disproportionately (it's less attractive to say "Hey, Mom and Dad, I'm off to work for an evil bank!") and could even price products differently—since there would be less risk in the good bank than in the bad.

It's not a radical idea. Ford has already created two units, splitting its electric vehicle business from its internal combustion production, though both will remain under the Ford umbrella.

And second, Frishberg noted that businesses could also *partially* leave a bank—moving cash to a low-carbon financier while continuing to work with larger banks on projects that require international deal making and finance expertise not available elsewhere. This approach would also generate media attention while allowing for continued engagement, which a complete divestment would not.

Daylighting big finance's role in the climate crisis can be incredibly valuable. But only if business leaders learn the right lessons from it and reject incrementalism for action appropriate to the scale of the problem.

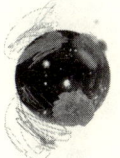

Love, Loneliness, and How to Treat Each Other

My favorite of the Cassini spacecraft's photographs is of Saturn's rings, with Earth a small star in the background, barely visible. Sometimes I think my daughter Willa can relate, navigating the oxygen-deprived deep space of eighth grade.

"At least she's not buried under rubble after an earthquake," my wife Ellen reasoned, thinking of staggering tragedies in the news. "True," I replied, "as long as you're not speaking metaphorically."

Of all the parenting challenges I've faced—my son carrying a gnome obsession into his second decade, my time-deprived wife harboring standing piles of papers in our study—helping my daughter navigate the apocalypse that is the middle-school social landscape has been the most punishing.

The indignities are both diabolical and omnipresent. They include friends cliquing up with a mean girl, whose social traction seems to rest on her being slightly prettier than the others. Once attached to the new mothership, the "friend" no longer looks Willa in the eye.

Willa is baffled on one hand, but also consciously unwilling to play the game on the other.

It's sad to me that her closest soulmate would be the sheriff in *No Country for Old Men*. Like Willa, I observe, he knows that to engage, "a man would have to put his soul at hazard. He'd have to say: 'OK, I'll be part of this world.'"

She tries, though, to a point. At recess, Willa asked if she could join a game of boxball. "No," the gaggle said, laughing. "Don't feel bad. It's not about you. It's us."

Unfortunately, it's easy for me as a middle-aged man to choose whom I associate with and to embrace my nerdishness. For a teenage girl, I know it's a universe in which my advice is a foreign tongue.

"Those girls, if they act that way, they were never your friends," Ellen tells her. "It's not like they abandoned you."

The tragedy is that this is Willa we're talking about: a real human, worthy of great, not petty, associations. Like her namesake Willa Cather's most famous character, Antonia, she is a rich mine of life.

She likes the fact that she wears glasses because it lets her appreciate the beauty of the world in focus.

She has so much empathy, she will still unconsciously mime parts of a story you are telling, just as she did when she was little.

This is a teen who completely understood that, when a vicious, pounding hailstorm caught us in our kayak on the river, it was a great, unique, and amazing experience. "This is awesome!"

We go to art house movies together, and afterward, while I'm quietly mulling things, she's incorrigibly conversational.

In short, this is a real person, with an adult sensibility, forced into complete adolescent madness.

She asks about finding new friends. "I don't know what to say," she says. "I don't know how to be."

On one hand, this is an easy problem. I tell her she has to go up to people and talk to them. "You ask them about themselves. You're kind to people. There are no losers." I want Willa to learn how to be a good person, regardless of the social cost.

My namesake, the poet W. H. Auden, famous beyond any standard in his time, was known for finding the least important person in the room to talk to, not the acolytes or rich people. It's a simple question or just the oldest one in human thought—how should we live?

Willa wonders what it takes to forge these middle-school friendships: What makes me interesting to people? Who am I if I stop martial arts or if I'm not a soccer player? Am I just a person? Am I, like the drifting Earth, just that spot of light Cassini saw from so far off, one of billions, undifferentiated, fragile, ephemeral?

I tell Willa that in college she will have the intense friendships she deserves. They will explode onto the scene just as fast, with the same violent romance as that of poets Arthur Rimbaud and Paul Verlaine. "Come, dear great soul," Verlaine wrote to Rimbaud. "We await you; we desire you!"

For now, instead of meeting a wild cadre of friends, Willa and I will go to dinner and a movie. I will treasure it, even if it occurs in the context of her own social collapse.

Before it cut power to its cameras and plunged itself into oblivion, Cassini took one final shot: its impact zone, roughly ten degrees north of Saturn's equator, visible as a hazy and rippled cloud pattern. The picture was no more or less foreboding than the yawning gaps of time before the eighth-grade bell rings each morning.

With its last glimpses, it was hard not to personify Cassini, cast about on the stars, like Lot's wife, looking back.

And as it fell, juxtaposed against Earth so small and distant, one had to wonder which corner of space might be the lonelier of the two.

10

Talking about Climate Change at the Rotary Club

The toughest, but in some ways the best, venue for giving talks about climate change is a Rotary breakfast.

First, there is an endless supply of bacon.

Second, there are all these chants and songs and incantations and pledges and "Happy Bucks," where you put some money into a hat and say something like "This is for my son-in-law, who graduated from college," and it's a bit cultish, with rituals that seem out of the 1940s, not the new millennium. (At one meeting I attended, we sang "Take Me Out to the Ball Game," and I melted into my chair.) Don't get me wrong: Rotary International is the stuff that binds civil society—its mission, similar to other groups like the Lions Club, is to build community. Its "four-way test" is as good a guide for how to live as any: Is it the *truth*? Is it *fair* to all concerned? Will it build *goodwill* and *better friendships*? Will it be *beneficial* to all concerned?

The members are weird and old-school but also philanthropic and wonderful, and my Grandpa Joe was a member of all these groups and more in Jamestown, North Dakota. He lived to be ninety-seven, in part because of these social connections. But I can't imagine that

Rotary gets a lot of new members, because the vibe is conservative and patriotic in a blind-faith way that doesn't hold for many younger Americans. It is (and I hate to say this, because I resemble it) goofy in an embarrassed kid's "oh Dad!" kind of way. Which is actually a wonderful and human trait but one that might put off younger generations. And then, the final challenge to visitors: the meetings take place butt early in the morning, which is not my time to shine. And so to get invited to speak at Rotary has always been something I feel obliged to do but dread. There is, however, one ameliorating factor: bacon.

But when I speak, I talk about climate differently than I do elsewhere, because it's an older and more conservative audience than I usually encounter.

Talking Climate to People Who Might Not Want to Hear It

So, we're going to talk about climate change, but it's not going to be what you're used to. We're going to start with coal. Coal has been used for heat since the time of the cave dwellers. Imagine digging around in the ground and finding a black rock. Imagine being bored and sticking it in the fire. And imagine your surprise when it glows and pumps out heat for hours. The rock that burns. A miracle.

Coal started getting used in earnest at the beginning of the Industrial Revolution, around 1850, to run engines and, later, to generate electricity. Later still, another thing found in the ground proved useful: oil.

Coal, oil, and other fossil fuels like natural gas aren't *bad*. Nor were the people who pulled those substances out of the ground for our use. Quite the opposite: fossil fuels were a blessing to humanity (as described in chapter 6).

The problem is, by about 1950, scientists started to realize that all that carbon being burned was going to change the climate. And this wasn't radical thinking or radical science—much of it took place at Exxon itself in the seventies. CO_2 and other greenhouse gases are why we're alive at all on planet Earth—we'd be freezing without that atmosphere to trap heat. It makes basic sense that adding more heat-trapping gases would make it warmer, and indeed, that's what's happened. We've warmed the planet by about 1.3°C since the Industrial Revolution, and we'll be well on our way to 1.5°C in the next ten to fifteen years. (Tragically, in September 2023, global average temperature spiked to 1.8°C above preindustrial times.)[1]

While the hard workers who pulled these resources out of the ground were good people helping society, the people in leadership at the oil, coal, and gas companies weren't so good. Although they initially recognized the climate problem and realized they could be part of addressing it, they soon pivoted to sowing confusion about the science, lying, hiding information, and either obfuscating the truth or flat-out funding science denial. This obfuscation by industry is all known, documented information, in records from ExxonMobil and elsewhere.[2]

So the problem isn't coal and oil, and it isn't coal miners or well drillers. It's the fact that fossil fuels release CO_2 and that we can't keep burning things for energy. It's just true. And then a second fact is that if we keep releasing CO_2 at current levels, the result is going to be catastrophic for society. Many of the models used to predict the future climate are proving to be more conservative than what's actually happening on the ground, and these underestimates are a real problem.[3]

Now, there is the issue of hypocrisy. After all, despite knowing that fossil fuels spew carbon, I still use them to drive my car, heat my house, and power my lights. And all of us were asking for cheap energy, and fossil fuels were cheap. But as discussed in the introduction, what's missing from that accusation of hypocrisy is agency. You see, none of us—not you, not me, not even most of the businesses outside the fossil fuel industry—were in the room when governments were making decisions about how we'd power our economy. None of us said, "I want hot showers and cold soda and light and warmth and comfort. Any chance you could provide me those services in a way that will eventually destroy civilization? (Oh, and while you're at it, let's fill up the oceans with plastic.)" That didn't happen, because decisions were made behind closed doors as a result of the crippling effect of money in politics. Remember, fossil fuels have been one of the most profitable businesses in the history of commerce.[4]

Any reasonable citizenry, given the facts on the fossil fuel connection to climate change, would begin pivoting away from these fuels. The problem, to remind you of Naomi Oreskes's comment, is that we were confused because people were trying to confuse us.

So we need not feel like hypocrites—that would have required intent and full information. Instead, as mostly victims of a carbon economy imposed on citizens, we are like fish in water, swimming in fossil fuels. And because we're all in it together, the climate problem isn't partisan, it's a manufactured climate culture war. It's just a wicked problem we have to figure out. And there are ways to do that.

We should also consider—even if you don't agree—that the people who are trying to confuse are also trying to divide us, and the reason is always money. On fossil fuels, the motive is obvious—monetizing proven reserves—as described earlier. But the intentional polarization is part of what Robert Reich, former US secretary of labor, calls a pattern of "manufacturing fears of 'the other' to distract from where all the wealth and power have gone . . . all the way to the top"—a tactic that has created an unprecedented divide.[5] Instilling fear and confusion is the best way to keep people distracted from the astounding inequity of the economic divide in the United States (or Russia). So in the same sense that we are complicit with a fossil fuel economy if we take blame for it, we are also complicit in maintaining an inequitable status quo if we participate in this manufactured polarization. That we are fighting about something so obviously in need of repair as climate change shows that the oligarchs have won.

Reich also notes that this movement has been "bankrolled by an American oligarchy—Rupert Murdoch, Charles Koch, Rebekah

Mercer, Peter Thiel, and other billionaires . . . . Sowing racism, homophobia, and transphobia creates life-or-death dangers for many people in our society. For both Putin and the American right, it serves to divert attention from the economic plunder by the ultra-rich . . . . They want people to fear one another rather than unite behind higher wages, better working conditions, and a fairer economy—and against authoritarianism."[6]

It's on this point—and against this common enemy—that the climate movements, the social justice movements, and even the labor movement intersect, and that's the subject of the next chapter.

Free Markets Are Not Free: Unwinding the Ouroboros

Americans like to think we operate in a free-market system, where the price of something represents its value. Digging into capitalism just a bit shows that isn't true. For example, as discussed earlier in this book, you can't just dump your trash on the sidewalk. You have to pay to have it disposed of. From that standpoint, the market effectively puts a price on the impact of your household waste. But at the same time, people and businesses can emit as much carbon pollution as they want—and it's just like the trash, a physical volume of stuff. Indeed, as Randy Udall used to observe, if you drive any standard American SUV, your emissions are the equivalent of chucking a twenty-pound bag of charcoal briquettes out the window every twenty-five miles or so.[7] But we don't see it. And yes, the whole suite of emissions from fossil fuels causes all kinds of measurable harm to society, including the health impacts of traditional pollutants like mercury, sulfur dioxide, and nitrogen oxides that come from coal and the immense impacts of warming on virtually everything, from agriculture to supply chains to human health, coastal real estate, and so on. These impacts are known and measurable. That analysis has been done by Nobel Prize–winning economist William Nordhaus at

Yale and others. (Nordhaus is a conservative, and so he's a useful citation for Rotary talks.)

Exactly how we fix the problem of free markets that aren't free is up to us to decide—but the upshot is that the solution is an improvement on capitalism, not a gutting of it. There are many ways to do it, with differing support along the political spectrum. You could tax pollution, for example. But if you just, say, increased the price of gasoline, electricity, and natural gas to send a market signal that it's bad stuff, you'd disproportionately impact poor people. So maybe the tax should be based on income. The point isn't to solve the problem here. It's to say that there are all kinds of policy solutions on the shelf, some of which are amenable to all political persuasions.

One of the problems today is that people settle on a solution—nuclear, carbon capture, carbon fee, and dividend—instead of settling on *the need to act on climate*. It's the latter commitment that we need, but Americans being Americans, we want to win, we want to have a team to root for, and so we pick a lane—nuclear power, say—and fight from that platform. And of course, the fossil fuel industry will put its finger on the scale as well, arguing that its products are a viable solution too, as they have done with natural gas and propane. But there are so many climate solutions, and we as citizens will have a hard time ensuring that the one we prefer is selected by a capricious and unpredictable legislature. So it's best to prioritize policy action of any sort, however imperfect it may seem, as long as the gist of it is to create incentives to reduce the combustion of fossil fuels as the first priority.[8] The Inflation Reduction Act, passed by the US legislature in 2022, is a good example. It has incredible incentives for clean energy and technology. And it also has bad policy like incentives for ethanol. But on balance, we need the bill.

This focus on reducing fossil fuels is important because they account for some 75 to 90 percent of the total greenhouse gas problem. To move away from them, we need to generate electricity with renewable, geothermal, and some existing nuclear technology and store that energy in various ways. We then need to use the clean electricity to heat and cool buildings and to power transportation. And we must do this at huge scale, and quickly. At the same time, it's going to take a while to wean society off fossil fuels, and that's understood. We can't turn off the spigot tomorrow, as the right often complain. Fair enough. But we do have to move relatively quickly, because there's another thing scientists and economists, including Nordhaus, generally agree on: it will cost more to do nothing about climate change than to solve the problem. And that the longer we wait, the more costly it will be.[9]

Remember, wind and solar power are free and clean. Coal is expensive and dirty, and natural gas is expensive and still emits CO_2. It's common sense to move on.

Oh, and nuclear. It should be on the table. Let it compete on the market. But remember that, at least in the United States, banks don't want to finance it; insurance companies don't want to insure it; neighbors don't want to host it; and nuclear plants have rarely been built without astronomical cost overruns. And we still don't know what to do with the waste.

What about the waste—and mining—associated with the batteries that will be essential for large-grid energy storage and the electrification of transportation? Aren't children mining cobalt in horrible conditions in the Democratic Republic of Congo, and won't batteries present a massive waste problem? In a renewable economy, yes, you'll mine stuff. But then you use the material for twenty-plus years in wind turbines, batteries, and solar panels. That's in contrast to the fossil fuel economy we live in now, where you mine oil, coal, and gas (often under terrible conditions and, for coal, often by children) and then *you use it up*, and then you mine it again. Indeed, one analysis showed that a renewable energy economy would require the extraction of 1/535 of the material that our current fossil fuel economy requires. That's a hell of a lot less waste.[10]

Bill McKibben laid out this case clearly in an interview with Ezra Klein of the *New York Times*:

> Mark Jacobson at Stanford, who I think has been proven so far to be the most reliable calculator of these things, estimates that the total mining burden on a planet that ran on renewable energy would drop by about 80 percent. That's the direct reflection of the fact that when you mine for coal or drill for oil, you have to keep doing it over and over and over again because you consume it.
>
> So none of it's beautiful or pretty. No one's ever going to make, no matter what they do, a mine that's clean and attractive. And we should be careful about where we site them and how we site them, and we should be especially careful about the human rights abuses that too often have accompanied mining of all kinds.
>
> But we also should understand that we are in an emergency, and that when you're in an emergency, you act on the ways that you have to act. Nine million people a year die from breathing the combustion byproducts of fossil fuel. That alone would give you lots and lots and lots of reason to take steps in another direction.
>
> Add to that the fact that climate change is the first truly existential risk that we've faced as a globe. If we don't get it right, the death toll is measured in numbers we can't even imagine. The UN estimates that unchecked climate change on the kind of path we're on at the moment would produce a billion climate refugees or more by the middle or end of this century.
>
> Try to imagine that world. Try to imagine the instability, chaos, destruction of that kind of planet. And when you do, the incentives for moving quickly in the direction of sun and wind seem profound.[11]

There's a final kicker that really has to make sense to professed conservatives, and that's the fact that saving energy is cheaper than producing it, a maxim around which my old boss physicist Amory

Lovins has framed his career. If a refrigerator saves you $100 a year over another model that provides the same service, wouldn't you buy the more efficient one? If a hybrid truck gets you all the power and glory of an internal combustion engine truck but uses half the gas (like the Ford Maverick hybrid does at forty-two miles per gallon), well, it's up to you. You can buy a gas guzzler and pay more every time you fill up, or you can buy the hybrid or the electric, and spend your money on beer or movies or dinners out or you can save it. Isn't having extra money in your pocket without having to compromise lifestyle the dream for both liberals and conservatives alike? Maybe that's something we can all agree on? And national policy can be built around these ideas too, with improved and expanded energy efficiency standards—that protect consumers' wallets—and more widespread and visible labels for appliances, which enable customers to make the right choice, at no additional cost. It's not a nanny state that would do this; it's a "don't keep citizens in the dark" state.

My rock-ribbed conservative Grandpa Joe from North Dakota would agree. And so should we.

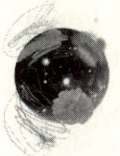

A Lifetime of Service on the North Dakota Plains

A slide show: Old pictures narrated in a yell by his daughter. Joe Sorkness is turning ninety-seven and is deaf. He still lives in Jamestown, North Dakota, where he spends time piled into a chair and squinting at the *Wall Street Journal* through Coke-bottle glasses that make his eyes look as big as eggs.

"Here we are in Norway," she says, "where we met a young boy who could raise one eyebrow, traveling with his mother. Do you remember? We kept running into him at hotels. He and his wife visited me in August. They live in England."

Joe says it was a long time ago. This slide show is a walk through his hometown covered in thick gauze. It is broadcast on a wall in need of paint: the studs show like bones on a March elk. Joe's shoulders are hunched and cockeyed; one leg is much longer than the other from a broken leg, then a broken hip. When he lifts a knee to get into bed, you can see the outline of his femur.

What comes clear to Joe are the people he never really knew: his father, his brother, his son.

He asks, "Have you seen Sidney?"

His daughter tells him, "Your brother Sidney died in a car wreck forty years ago."

"I was out of town when Sidney died," he tells her, "so I couldn't go to his funeral." This statement is a breach of reality to cushion deadening fact: in some slides, you can see Joe by the grave.

Joe volunteered for World War I, only to be rejected because his father was on the draft board and knew his birthday: January 1901. "I missed my chance to be a hero," Joe says. His father saw no need to have his son slaughtered at seventeen. Joe volunteered for World War II. But he was the only doctor in Jamestown, and so, condemned to a place so broad and flat that the horizon curves, he missed the battles his friends knew: Leyte Gulf, Pointe du Hoc, Hürtgen Forest.

But there were compensations. When Joe was in the hospital with a broken hip, a man came to his bedside. "You saved my son's life forty years ago," the man told Joe. "He's a doctor now." A woman, recalling her surgery, called his voice and footsteps outside her room "the most reassuring sound in the world."

And the hospital supply foreman says he told his assistant to stall on doctors' orders while he was away. Except for Joe: "Give him whatever he asks for; have it shipped as fast as you can." Because Joe didn't mess around.

Joe's son, Paul, also a doctor, died of a stroke at sixty-five. "How did he die?" Joe asks. "And where is he now?"

What is it like to volunteer for and miss the two most deadly wars of the century, then outlive your son and older brother? Do you begin to feel immortal? Because in America, at ninety-seven, you almost are. His daughter asks, "What do you make of it all, Joe?"

"What?"

"The last hundred years."

"I don't know yet."

"OK, the last ninety-seven."

"It was fairly interesting."

Interesting like a ruptured appendix or pneumonia in the 1920s, before penicillin or even sulfa drugs. Perhaps the vestiges of such helplessness are what made him gruff, attentive mostly to real illness, scoffing at all else.

"Take some aspirin!" he'd growl if your ailment didn't pass muster.

"What did you do during the Depression, when no one could pay?" his daughter asks.

"People paid however they could, sometimes with a bag of grain, or a chicken." Two Navajo rugs on the living room floor recall a hysterectomy sixty years ago.

"And the rest, who had nothing?"

"They always paid." House calls made in the Depression were paid off after the Cold War. Monthly installments of $10 came in—twenty years after Joe retired.

His father was the first of three generations to graduate from the University of Minnesota Medical School. Joe drove his father's cart through Fargo, North Dakota, during the 1918 flu pandemic and remembers him pointing and saying, "Two will die there tonight. And one will die there." In a small town on the prairie, the people dying are friends and relatives.

Joe's father wore himself out during that plague and died at fifty-three. Joe's mother died shortly after his birth. Assuming he would die young, too, Joe never worried about the cigars he smoked for seventy years, or about his diet of meat with few vegetables and a crushing work ethic. He turned out to be durable, and North Dakota air is clean.

Time for him must make a rushing sound, like other strong things he knew: a train or a twister. A four-year-old great-granddaughter recently commented on the difference between Pacific and Central Time. "Two hours is a long time," she said. Joe might disagree.

One slide is of "the boys," Joe's duck-hunting buddies, all in their seventies and eighties in the photo. Two are still alive. Many fought in wars; the others had good excuses. They took summer trips to a cabin in the pothole country. Hunched and worn-in, all Republicans, and all kind and hardworking if set in their ways and their thinking, they ate jellied beef loaf on rye with A.1. Sauce: a relic of Norwegian taste, probably Viking.

Joe remembers: Warm summer winds smelled of sweetgrass after rain. The rain that fell on Sidney, the wind that blew Paul's kite. They mowed the lawn and sometimes took target practice at cans.

One of them, a doctor friend of Joe's, ran while pushing the mower, as if the fast-growing grass threatened to make him a prairie version of Sisyphus. Or maybe he ran from habit: old-style anesthetics like ether and nitrous oxide wore off quickly. You learned to work fast.

Joe does a crossword puzzle while his birthday presents are unwrapped for him. He squints at an obscure gift: a can of cashews—"I don't know what that is"—and peers tentatively out the window into the night sky. It was never remarkable to him as a boy, even though the sunsets were pink. As a man, he worked too hard to look for the long curtain of the aurora borealis. Now, the stars are circled with ghosts.

11

The Climate-Equity Connection

How Climate Action and Justice Are the Same Issue

When Quincy "Q" Shannon visited Snowmass, Colorado, he asked us how he'd know if he'd be safe here. I wasn't sure what to say.

Q is a leader in the Denver community, a reverend, an avid skier, a father, and an administrator at a Denver middle school. He's African American, and he runs an outfit called Ski Noir, which helps Black youth learn how to ski. We had connected with him after George Floyd's murder, when we realized, again, how white the ski industry was.[1]

To start with, our ads feature white people skiing in white powder. Our employees and guests are mostly white. Years ago, I made the catastrophic mistake of helping a climate nonprofit do an ad campaign with the slogan "Keep Winter White." (That was a long time ago. But still, someone saw a relic of it and sent me a note: "Whoever did that should be fired.")

If you're Black and in a ski town, you run into a wall of whiteness. The message, Black employees, guests, colleagues, and friends told us, was that the Black community wasn't welcome here, or at least, there was little effort being made to include it.

I was the climate and sustainability guy, but I got tasked with leading the effort to change all that. In truth, I had little expertise or background that would qualify me, other than being part of a society—and extended family—that is as mixed race as many American families are becoming. I wasn't thrilled with the task, in part because I rejected the notion that all progressive causes were connected: "He's the climate guy. So he can do the justice work too." At the same time, the effort seemed necessary and obvious. I grew up in New Jersey and went to school in a very diverse New York City. When I moved to the mountains, all my friends were white. The racial homogeneity was disconcerting at the most basic level, never mind its implications.

We invited Q to visit to help us with these questions. Tall, friendly, outgoing, and in your face, Q was the perfect facilitator. And his question was baffling to me. I didn't know how to answer it, because I didn't know the answer.

Q explained that showing up Black in a mountain town wasn't easy. In some cases, even getting gas put one at risk of harassment, dirty looks, even threats. Would Aspen or Snowmass be any different? And why, actually, were we trying to do anything about this at all?

Syracuse and the Marxist Boycott

I was thinking about all this but was still possessing a climate Buddha nature when I flew out to Syracuse University to give a talk on business and climate change. Before I went on stage, my host professor pulled me aside.

"Hey, uh, just so you know. I don't think there will be any grad students here. Probably none."

"Why?" I asked.

"Well, most of them are Marxists."

"Say what?" I asked.

"The students think capitalism is bankrupt. They don't want to hear from a corporation on climate. Business has nothing credible to offer them," he said. The students felt that absent a clear and nontoken effort to solve the two crushing problems of our time— climate and equity—business wasn't relevant anymore. This was the first connection: climate change and equity failures originated in the same broken system.

On one hand, I was like, "You go girl!" I loved the students' conviction. In my experience too, corporate America isn't particularly trustworthy, and the more I work in this field, the more convinced I am that business might be incapable of solving society's problems. For just a sense of why the students were pissed, here's a sample of a letter from a corporation after Aspen Skiing Company's CEO asked this company for help supporting the Inflation Reduction Act, the most critical piece of climate legislation in history. While I've kept the identity of the company private, it is a *Fortune* 500 business with an elaborate sustainability website with lots of talk about climate change.

> We appreciate and agree on the urgent need for action. As Congress works through a myriad of challenging issues including climate change, [X company] remains eager to review the language of a bill when one emerges and then gauge our position and interest. Legislation addressing climate is almost always complex, complicated, and convoluted, so we prefer to review specific language before taking a particular public position.
>
> In addition, sweeping climate legislation often touches the lives of all Americans who are currently beset with a sharp rise in the cost of living generally and consumer goods specifically. [X company] is very sensitive to current anxieties and concerns among citizens and wants to be very strategic in our approach and messaging so that we can advance climate discussions in the future and not be set back in our efforts by current

> politics in the present. In the meantime, we will continue urging
> policymakers and stakeholders to bring their authentic ideas for
> honest discussions.

Let me paraphrase: "No. We're not doing anything. You understand, right?"

No, we don't. But the company's preceding response could be
simply copied and pasted from virtually any major corporation in
America.

In any case, even though I loved the student response, I was also
taken aback. As a career corporate environmentalist with twenty-five
years of experience building and writing about sustainable business,
I care about the same issues the students do. As the previous chapters
amply demonstrate, I believe the role of business in the green universe is not only to keep one's house in order by reducing impacts but
also to wield the substantial power that brands hold. I had personally blown the whistle on greenwashing and tokenism many times,
including, as readers will recall, on myself.

I also care because I'm a progressive. In my view, government,
laws, and tax policies are not a burden but instead impose consensus
limits on freedom so that we can thrive as a society. Free markets
are good, and therefore pollution should cost money. Free speech
is bedrock, but you can't use it to incite people to do harm. But
I'm not a wonky idealist—I simply think climate and equity issues
can't be ignored. Americans today seem to agree—a majority across
the political spectrum support a conventional progressive agenda,
including abortion rights, climate action, gay marriage, and beyond.[2]

An Air Conditioner on Low

Still. As we've seen time and again in these chapters, companies'
action on climate and its corresponding issue—equity—has always
been what my poet friend Mark Scott might describe as being like

"an air conditioner on low," which is to say nominal, ineffective, and hardly denting the problem. By definition, businesses' actions will fail to catalyze the broader change that an increasing number of people, especially young people (also known as future customers), care about.

Take Microsoft's announcement to go carbon negative by 2030. The statement made no mention of a commensurate push for climate legislation, arguably the only real path to a systemic solution. (Nor did Microsoft mention the company's conference in Saudi Arabia, taking place the same week as the carbon-negative announcement, which discussed how to more efficiently extract fossil fuels.) A *Newsweek* column by two climate experts asked, "Why—in the face of Big Oil's continued, if repackaged climate obstructionism—does Big Tech fail to show up on climate policy? Why, on the brink of such a high-stakes struggle over climate policy [the piece was written as the Inflation Reduction Act was being debated], is Big Tech still devoting only a measly 4 percent of its lobbying activities to climate?"[3]

And that was the second connection I found between climate and equity. On the equity front, I noticed that the disingenuity was strikingly similar. The reluctance to act meaningfully was of a piece with business's natural inclination to battle anything that even remotely smells like regulation. The US Chamber of Commerce has waged this battle so well over decades. And the reason for companies' reluctance to change was that the system we have right now works pretty damn well for business.

For example, in 2021, leading Georgia companies participated in conversations with legislators about a new restrictive voting law in the state but didn't publicly oppose it until it passed. They tried to appear on the side of justice, but only after the fact. Sometimes, the press even seems to bless this strategy by not pointing it out. The duplicity, slow-walking, and untrustworthiness—this commitment to corporatist status quo—are often hidden behind superficial positions on justice, broader responsibility, and climate. A 2019 *New York Times* headline, "Shareholder Value Is No Longer

Everything, Top CEOs Say," appeared to signal that many *Fortune 500* CEOs are leaders of a new progressive business movement that values the environment and employees. But some of those CEOs run banks that have invested more in fossil fuels than any other entities on earth. And shortly after making those commitments, many of the same businesses responded to Covid-19 with furloughs and layoffs.[4]

No wonder the students are angry. They want to reform a system that has overt, entrenched flaws. Most people believe that modern-day capitalism does "more harm than good in the world," according to the twentieth annual Edelman Trust Barometer.[5] That fact alone ought to be quite a wake-up call for the architects of that world, as well as for businesses.

Climate Is a Stakeholder Whether Companies Like It or Not

Focusing on climate for a moment, it's clearly putting pressure on business as usual—on our entire economic system—from all sides. In my office, for example, our international sales guy Bob took me aside and said, "Hey, Auden. Thanks to Greta Thunberg, European visitors to our resort are saying they don't want to fly here. They're flight-shamed. What should I tell them?" This is real: the mere idea of climate change—not even its actual impact—and the quality of our response is affecting our workers' jobs and our ability to attract business.

That same day, the risk and complexity of our own activism emerged: our insurance lawyer warned us that we probably shouldn't lean on our carrier to reduce its support for fossil fuel projects, as we'd been considering. He told me that insurance companies are so hammered by the effects of natural disasters (like the wildfires that hit us in the last two years and even closed our airport) that rates are rising sharply. The companies are looking to drop clients, not appease them, and we couldn't afford to lose our insurance in a tight market.

(So just to be clear: we could have lost our insurance coverage by asking insurers to get out of climate-damaging investments *because* those insurers were being hammered by climate-related disasters.)

Climate is not a side project that's part of a corporate social responsibility effort; it's central to strategy and decision-making. It touches everything. It's the everything problem. And yet, so too are equity and justice, which affect every aspect of American life.

In this context—two everything problems—the connection between climate, equity, and business doesn't seem all that radical. Indeed, the Green New Deal was criticized by centrists for trying to make this very linkage. Instead of just tackling carbon and climate, it rolled up social equity, Medicare for All, and job guarantees into the mix. *But that's exactly the point.*

After I was stood up in Syracuse (to be fair, there were plenty of less jaded undergrads at my talk), my host professor handed me a paper by Matt Huber, an award-winning associate professor of geography and the environment at the university, and a Marxist. He has published in many left-leaning journals and is the author of *Climate Change as Class War: Building Socialism on a Warming Planet.* Huber's paper, "Ecological Politics for the Working Class," argues that "the key is to build a movement where masses of people connect the dots to see the solutions to all our crises of climate, health care, and housing require building mass social power to combat the industries profiting from these very crises." And this is precisely what the Green New Deal was trying to do, offering all Americans a job with family-sustaining wages, adequate family and medical leave, paid vacations, and retirement security—which sounds a lot like real stakeholder capitalism. (Yes, that bogeyman, Marxism, takes into account the concerns of *all* people practicing capitalism. But no blue-blooded stakeholder-capitalist would make that case.) If nothing else, the Green New Deal was a direct assault on the corporate status quo.[6]

A key takeaway for business leaders who are trying to stay on top of social responsibility issues and climate at the same time: fixing climate requires fixing equity. You are taking on a system that has failed because of the unrestricted dominance of the corporate sector, and reining that in solves those problems and more. Stakeholders know this and will increasingly call foul if a business doesn't demonstrate its understanding of this connection. An important note: this is not a call to overthrow capitalism or a critique of capitalism writ large, as writers like Naomi Klein have made. Instead, this book envisions a future whereby guardrails are placed on capitalism to enable success and free markets. After all, neoliberalism—free market fundamentalism, which rejects government regulation—has arguably led to our crises of housing, health care, education, *and* climate all together. For example, we could reduce money in politics and price pollution that leads to economic and personal harm. As Naomi Oreskes and Erik Conway point out in *The Big Myth*, even Friedrich Hayek, the darling of the free-market fundamentalists, didn't argue against all market regulation. An example of a beneficial free-market regulation that has been good for all is the Clean Air Act.[7]

Climate Is Equity Is Climate

It may seem like I'm talking about a sliver of the population here—a group of angry university students and a few others. But that would be misleading. The fundamental reason climate and equity are *politically* tied is that any attempt to tackle climate alone won't have the support of a big-enough movement. That sentiment was confirmed in a report on decarbonization in the United States by the National Academies of Sciences, Engineering, and Medicine, which emphasized that the costs and benefits of the transition must be shared equitably. Why? Sharing is necessary, as *Vox* reported, for "getting buy-in from a wide coalition for the major changes needed to eliminate greenhouse gas emissions. Otherwise, there could be strong resistance that would undermine progress."[8]

Professor Huber agrees with that argument. Historically, he notes, environmentalism has been the hobby of the elite, who feel guilty about their role in global warming and who also have the time and money to care on the margins. "Save the Whales!" gets mocked for good reason: to care about whales, most people have to be in pretty good economic shape and completely secure.[9] As a result, the climate movement, such as it is, has been small. And its message has been unappealing to Americans—drive less, eat the tofu, harangue your coworker for throwing out a can, bring reusable and uncleanable cloth bags to the supermarket. To become part of the climate movement, the huge swath of people facing debt, stagnant wages, and job insecurity need to see that joining up would help more of their needs be met. The fact that the Green New Deal had even *some* level of traction is just one sign that this approach is beginning to play out on the ground.

Listen Up, Business

Business ignores this at its peril. Corporations that zero out their carbon footprints through offsets are assuaging a very small slice of society and possibly enraging the rest by ignoring the things employees and customers need to live dignified lives. ("We don't need offsets," they might say to the CEO. "We need housing!") Maybe sustainability programs have been weak because, in truth, customers simply didn't care. But combine sustainability with equity, and suddenly your customers and workers have a compelling reason to pay attention. In Aspen, this was starkly evident. The community places huge priority on sustainability, but equity issues—availability of housing and level of pay—literally determine if we have enough staff to run our restaurants. And yet housing employees close to their work—or to mass transit—is a key climate solution.

Meanwhile, other stakeholders, including visitors to our ski resorts and hotels, are starting to understand that the causes of the climate crisis—a poorly regulated capitalist system that in many aspects fails to value life and factor in the cost of pollution—are some of the same causes of inequity. This connection came starkly to the fore in the Covid-19 pandemic, where death rates for people of color far exceeded that of any other group. These same people of color are those who disproportionately suffer from the impacts of pollution and climate change. The movement sparked by George Floyd's murder is in direct response to the same capitalist system, one that has baked into it the systemic oppression of Black citizens. In a sense, the social justice revolution now simmering in American streets *is* the climate revolution, because the goals are effectively the same. The candidates who would support those goals are the same, and the solutions to justice and climate issues are often the same too.

As an on-the-ground example, in 2021 Aspen Skiing Company built the Hub, a new four-story employee-housing building. The project was all electric, which is a key climate solution. (Buildings heated by natural gas emit CO_2 for the entire life cycle; an electric building becomes greener each year as the grid adds renewables. In our region, thanks in part to the company's work, the utility will be 100 percent clean power by 2030, meaning the building will be net-zero when the grid gets there.) The roof is covered in solar panels, the building itself is on a public bus line, and the parking lots have electric-vehicle chargers and bike-share stations. So the project is green as can be, but it's also equitable, in the sense that workers can live close to where they work and not have to commute for hours, spending precious mornings and evenings in their vehicles, losing income in gas money and missing time with their families. The project also cuts down on traffic and associated pollution from the commute while reducing wear and tear of the roads. As we'll see in chapter 12, though, most communities don't like these sorts of projects. They hurt "small-town character." They're too dense. They clog the neighborhood. When we were permitting the project, one member of the public said they found condoms on the berm near the highway, and if we put more employees there, the problem would get worse (!).[10]

True stakeholder capitalism, which most broadly is about equity, almost always helps solve the climate problem. For example, as

Huber points out (and the Hub demonstrates), public or employee housing can integrate green building techniques that save residents money. And expanded mass transit and incentives by businesses for employees to use it could cut carbon and reduce dependence on cars while enabling people without a vehicle to get around. Additional investment in electrical grid improvements (with funding from both the government and the automobile sector) and clean energy creates jobs lost from the decline of oil, gas, and coal. In fact, the very same people with the skills to work in the fossil fuel industry have the skills to help rebuild the utility grid. At the same time, bending the curve of emissions will eventually ameliorate the impacts from flood, fire, food insecurity, and disease that will disproportionately affect poorer members of society.

If society and government were to take on climate and equity in meaningful ways, the economy-wide implications would be political gold. Trying to imagine how those changes might affect business has long been the role of scenario planning. To make a measurable impact on our biggest problems, the United States would have to accept more-progressive taxation or a wealth tax and restructured priorities in government spending; move away from natural gas, oil, and coal subsidies; cut down our massive military expenditure; and reprioritize programs like rebuilding public education funding, reducing college costs and debt, and perhaps providing guaranteed minimum income, a form of which came in both Democratic and Republican stimulus bills during the pandemic. Given that there is public support for much of the preceding outcomes, these approaches are a perfect starting point for corporate planning.

Opportunity at the Nexus

In the end, the nexus of climate change and equity seems to be creating a societal movement, one supported by a majority of Americans and represented by a new base. That movement consists of young people, Americans of color, and college-educated progressive voters. To become more durable, this coalition could add blue-collar workers, as they are numerous and uniquely able to wield power over the industries with undue influence on policymaking. Enlisting the blue-collar segment won't be easy, as many such workers are migrating to the right, aligning with a coalition that has been less receptive to a climate-equity argument.

Still, we can imagine that with a new coalition buying (or not buying) their products, voting, and therefore making policy decisions, businesses will actually have to step up.

There have already been some successes. Against much criticism and at risk of alienating its customers, in 2021, Major League Baseball pulled the All-Star Game from Atlanta in response to Georgia's restrictive new voting laws. That action will help MLB's brand catch up to the truly impressive equity and justice work done by the National Basketball Association. Equally important, it will shore up relationships with a key constituency: its employees, the players, and its customers, who support the league's progressive action and, because they do, are also likely to support climate action. But simply ensuring the franchise, which is what MLB's action was about, is itself good for the climate, since most Americans support action.

In the tech industry, Salesforce added climate change as a key component of its public policy lobbying platform, meaning that climate changes has equal billing with more-mainstream corporate concerns. Salesforce was one of only a few *Fortune* 500 businesses to weigh in to support the Inflation Reduction Act, even though, sadly, the company still paid dues to the US Chamber of Commerce to oppose it.

Of course, there continue to be failures. After making loud statements in support of Black Lives Matter, Wall Street banks urged shareholders to vote against racial equity resolutions. That, on top of banks' empty statements in support of climate action, may further sink their credibility in the public eye. Time will tell.[11]

The changes that are happening shouldn't scare business. They're a golden opportunity to reinvent the economy in which a business engages in commerce and to rebrand around issues of vital interest to current and future customers. These changes also enable business to stabilize both society and climate—key elements for staying in business forever. The upside is huge. After all, this isn't the first time Americans recognized the systemic nature of their problems and then responded together to address them. The aftermath of the Great Depression and the rollout of Social Security and the New Deal was one example. A second was Lyndon B. Johnson's Great Society, which created Medicaid and Medicare. Yet another was the Declaration of Independence—and what it produced was a new nation and a better world. It would be smart for business to anticipate the future of that new land and assist in its formation.

. . .

My son Elias plays high school basketball in our rural town in Western Colorado; the town is named after the rock deposited here in abundance by an ancient volcano: Basalt. During halftime, non-player students, some parents, and other random folks will often get out on the court and shoot baskets just for fun. At a game in the high school gymnasium two years ago, this was going on, and one parent from a neighboring community, who happened to be Black, was taking some shots. A mom from another town *started making monkey sounds and movements directed at the man.* I wish I didn't have to say this happened, but it did. It happened so fast that I didn't even know it when our athletic director kicked the woman out of the school, escorting her to the door. When I understood what had transpired, my blood pressure spiked and I almost passed out with rage—but also with embarrassment that this could have happened in my town. But it *did* happen, and I thought about Quincy's question: "Will I be safe?"

. . .

When we left Q that night in Snowmass, he decided to wander around the lobby, talking to various people—there are few humans more socially adept than Q. He struck up a conversation with a guest who explained that he was there for the balloon fest (Snowmass is famous for a hot air balloon festival). "Wow!" Q said. "Tell me about it." And the man did, and closed with an invitation: "Would you like to come up with me tomorrow morning, early?"

Q said yes.

And so the next day, for the first time in his life, Q was twelve thousand feet up, levitated only by heated air, welcomed by one friendly member of the community, and embraced by the gentle morning thermals of Snowmass Village. Q posted a euphoric video on Instagram. Always ready to overinterpret any experience, I saw his balloon flight as a good omen, a wish for the future—a sight, in modern America, for sore eyes.

In the end, there are two reasons racial justice and climate are tied together. One is utilitarian. The other is moral. Yes, there are all kinds of good, effective, and practical reasons that racial justice and climate action are complementary. That we need each other, and are stronger together. But ultimately, there's the moral reason. A society that hasn't fully dealt with a moral insult in its face will not be equipped to deal with the intergenerational justice questions that climate change poses.

The truth is, we need to get right with ourselves before we can get right with the planet.

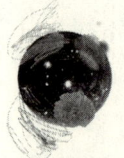 ## Letting Go

When Willa was seven, she came home from school one day and said she knew what sex was. Her friend Melissa had told her.

"OK, what is it?" my wife Ellen asked, as I poured the bourbon for the Manhattan I knew I'd need.

"It's when a man and a woman lie down together and kiss."

There was a long and thoughtful pause. I looked at Ellen, holding the bottle of bourbon tipped, still pouring it into the shaker. Perhaps a stiff cocktail tonight.

"No, that's not what sex is, Willa," Ellen said. And she muttered to me, "I'll be damned if Melissa is going to be the one to teach her about sex."

"I can't believe this is happening," I thought. The iconic experience of parenthood, coming five years early, on a nondescript fall evening with no time to prepare.

Parenthood can be summed up simply: you try to insulate and protect your children, at least for a while, and you fail right out of the gate. The true nature of the world, experience, maturity, the meanness of things—it all sneaks up. The world offers endless hardship along with its graces, and only luck can tip the scales.

Willa and Ellen retreated to her room, protected by its flowered comforter and small glass animals.

"Uh, hey, do you want me in here, I mean—"

"*NO!!*" Willa and Ellen both yelled. I started doing dishes. Then went back and hovered outside the door, missing the most important conversation of my daughter's life. (Though I did overhear Willa ask, "Do you have to go to the hospital to have sex?")

I felt I should be there, but was relieved I wasn't. To be honest, I had no idea what I would say, though I'm certain my first word would have been "Uh . . ."

I scrubbed at the cast-iron skillet, a legendary culinary instrument meant to work flawlessly, the original nonstick. Never for me. I chipped off vulcanized omelet with a paring knife.

I ought to have known all this was coming. Not even six months ago, I was brushing Willa's teeth. She asked me to stop.

"What do you think of this?" She pulled the strap of her pajamas over her shoulder, a red and white ensemble that said "Cutiesaurus" below a ridiculous cartoon dinosaur. She let a curl of hair hang over her eyes, canted her hips, and looked into the mirror with a sultry pout. Six years old then.

The poet Julia Kasdorf says the first gesture we learn is goodbye.

"You look beautiful," I said, panicking. "Open wide, I got to get the molars."

One summer afternoon, I biked to the supermarket with Willa and Elias, who was then five. Almost there, we stopped to pet horses and play on a stump by a ditch. The weather had been threatening all day. Now, ominous clouds billowed to the south. You could see the arcing lines of precipitation; there was thunder, lightning. It was spectacularly beautiful, and also terrifying.

"Hey, guys," I said, "we'd better head out now. It's probably going to rain."

They played. The storm was about four miles off; we had maybe fifteen minutes. But the weather had been odd that year, and the storm came onto us faster than I had anticipated.

"Yeah, OK, we gotta go here!" I said. The kids hopped on their bikes, and within thirty seconds, it was pouring. I was as wet as if someone had doused me with a bucket from the blind side.

"Come on, guys! Let's go!" I hollered.

I looked back, and they were pedaling their tiny bikes frantically, expressing some slight concern, getting soaked. And then came the hail.

"Dada!" little Elias was yelling, the ice hitting hard on his hands and face, on the verge of tears.

Willa looked terrified. "We have to stop!" she said. And I was thinking, stop where? And do what? Crawl under a tree? Or into a culvert? What could I do, short of lying on top of them?

"We can't stop! We have no choice! I can't help you!" I yelled, drowned out in simultaneous lightning and thunder. I didn't want to circle back, because I worried they'd stop and we'd get annihilated. So I stayed ahead, yelling and exhorting like some fanatical World War I lieutenant with a bugle and a soccer ball, leading my men off into catastrophe, an apt metaphor for parenthood.

Squinting back into the sideways-blowing, bitterly stinging hail, I watched my two children, their heads down, hands bright red, legs pumping furiously, making their way as best they could into a world they'd find to be part pig iron, part gold, and theirs alone.

12

"A Republic, Madam, If You Can Keep It"

What Does Citizenship Look Like?

All noble things are as difficult as they are rare.

—Spinoza

"I should get my .45 and shoot that guy in the leg," an obviously disturbed citizen said to me before one town council session. The implication, as I took it: "I have a gun, a pretty big one. And I could shoot you, too!" The guy didn't even live in town, but he showed up at most meetings, lobbied hard for or against various development projects, and appeared to be on the payroll of some applicants as a kind of thug or fixer. Since I was a town council member myself, he made me feel uneasy much of the time. If you shook this guy's hand, as I had to do often as an elected official, it was cold and clammy, like grabbing a fish. I asked my friend the police chief, "Should I be afraid of this guy? Should other council members?" He answered, "We're watching him closely." One day, around this time, I found a military field dressing for a sucking chest wound in my mailbox at town hall. What the hell was that about? (I put it in my first aid kit. I'm kind of an emergency medicine geek.)

Does this all sound great to you? Like, did you think, "Mmmmmm . . . I want me some of that"? If you did, then you're ready for the modern climate movement. If not, you'd better learn to love it.

I had to deal with this ridiculousness (and trust me, this was only a small piece of it) because I was foolish enough to run for town council in Basalt, Colorado. But the reason I ran—and the reason you should too—is that I was tired of not being a citizen. For years, the same old farts had governed the community—they'd run for council unopposed, then run for mayor, then get term-limited out, then wait four years and run again. They were all—without exception—well-intentioned people. And God bless them for stepping up. But they represented just one point of view, and as a result, our town missed out on modern town design opportunities. We have a gas station in what urban planners call the town's *100 percent corner*—the place everyone walks by every day. We have an employee housing crisis (to be fair, just like every other community in the United States). In the literal dead center of town, we have an abandoned, empty supermarket that has been sitting there for fifteen years and that should have been condemned a decade ago as urban blight.

I thought, "Man, this decision-making is bad and inside the box. Someone else should run for council to bring fresh ideas." I looked around, and nobody was stepping up. So reluctantly, I decided the someone who should run was me.

In my tenure, I got almost nothing done. I tried hard to open an alley behind the old supermarket to make it easier to walk around town. It had been open years ago, and without it, people had to walk a giant circuit to get from Main Street to another part of town. I failed. I tried to install little free libraries as a way to bolster community and thoughtfulness—I got one completed. I approved at least two terrible development projects that ended up wildly unaffordable. In my defense, we did upgrade building codes (a huge win on climate) and declare a climate emergency (which didn't really mean anything). There was at least some affordable housing beyond code requirements in those approved projects. We also helped fund and encouraged a net-zero, all-electric development for teacher housing adjacent to the high school. That development became a state model, and the developer hosted the governor on a tour of the site. I went on a ride-along with the police at night. That was cool, going to 7–Eleven at 2 a.m.

Oh yeah: I did create a Gnome Home Building Ordinance, establishing districting in the park by the river outside the library to enable little kids to build fairy houses out of bark, grass, and sticks. That effort was supported by the town manager, just before he left and sued the town for half a mil and got a lot of it in settlement. Winning!

The point is, citizenship is hard. It's boring. It's difficult. And it's Sisyphean. You can only hope to move the ball uphill for the next guy. As Reinhold Niebuhr said, "Nothing that is worth doing can be achieved in a lifetime."[1] And yet, almost for all those reasons, just because it's *not* a TED Talk that has a lot of flash but not much substance, just because it *is* hard work and requires conversation and physically showing up, that's the reason it matters. But it only matters if you bring, in addition to the willingness to suffer, the perspective of a citizen, not an individual.

Fundamentally, that means doing something almost unheard-of in modern America: basing decisions on what is good for society at large, not just on what benefits you and people like you.

In small towns and even city neighborhoods, people *think* they're being good citizens by "protecting community character," which is their operating thesis of governance. What's not to like about this approach? Keep things the way we always remembered them. It's how you get elected. It's how you govern. And people love it, even though it's hurting them.

It's worth digging into small-town housing and how to fix it, because it's a perfect case study in the differences between citizenship and selfishness. Housing is a key concern facing all communities, including cities, in the United States; it's a key climate solution, because where you put housing and how it's constructed are climate issues that determine traffic and commuting patterns and quality of life. Meanwhile, working on housing puts citizens in the same uncomfortable situations that any meaningful activism does. For this reason, it's a good metaphor—and training wheels—for what's needed in much broader political engagement.

Housing and Citizenship

John Steinbeck said that there's only one story in the world, and we tell it over and over. If you live in a resort town or, for that matter, really, anywhere now, that story is about the lack of affordable housing, which leaves no aspect of the community untouched. And it's about people's ironclad opposition to fixing that problem, whether they believe that's what they're doing or not.

Here's an example. About ten years ago, in my neighborhood, a homeowner proposed adding an accessory dwelling unit (ADU), also known as a mother-in-law unit. It's a small stand-alone apartment, often above a garage or adjacent to or connected to the main house.

Let's briefly consider what the mother-in-law unit would do for the applicant and the community. The owner was a ski patroller and a carpenter, and his wife was a teacher. They are, you might imagine, the sorts of people we want to live in our community. But it's hard to do that in an increasingly unaffordable mountain town. An ADU would provide his family with a little more income, enabling them to remain in town. Just as important, the ADU itself would provide affordable housing (by definition, because it's so small) to someone else locally. So, the project provides a range of good things. But it doesn't stop there. Adding housing within town boundaries instead of outside the town means that new residents are accessing existing infrastructure and services (water, sewer, electric, police, fire, trash) without requiring, as sprawl does, resource- and energy-intensive build-outs of new municipal plumbing, police services, fire coverage, and so forth. Mother-in-law units prevent the need for sprawl by providing housing within the town. They also eliminate one commuter and that person's associated wasted time, traffic congestion, and air pollution, or they at least situate the commuter closer to work. The new resident also contributes to the local economy and helps provide the throughput needed to help small businesses survive outside the summer and winter rushes, without commuting in from the outside, in traffic, to do that.

OK, so what did the neighbors think about the proposal?

Without exception, they all showed up at the planning and zoning meeting to oppose it. Why? Construction? It would be burdensome. Traffic? There would be another car near them, coming in and out. Density? They didn't want more people in their neighborhood. Old-school environmentalists consider any construction at all to be bad. Neighbors just don't want to be bothered. Development bad. Density bad.

Here's how they rationalize these anticommunity decisions that directly opposed their own neighbor's desires and community well-being and go against their own self-interest: "It doesn't fit with community character." This is a catch-all phrase that means "Not in my backyard" (NIMBY).

This worldview is widespread. Mountain communities are often run by environmentalists from forty years ago whose thinking has not kept abreast of the developments in their hometowns. They came up in an era when land conservation and open space protection *was* environmentalism. Climate was just emerging as a problem, and the solutions, it appears to the old school, threaten the things they care about: solar panels scar public land; wind turbines block ocean viewsheds.[2]

They champion stasis over change and open space over density, and they consider development evil. "The only thing these guys hate more than sprawl," an architect told me, "is density." Get the irony there? Density is a solution to sprawl . . .

To that point, doing well by the environment usually requires housing. And you'd be surprised about which seemingly unrelated issues tie back to housing.

As just one example, consider composting.

How Composting Requires Housing

Many restaurants compost food waste in and around Aspen. But not every restaurant does it. In one location, a guest asked a manager, "Why don't you compost here? Don't you care about the environment?" The manager responded, "You may not be aware of this, but my business had a severe labor shortage this year—region-wide, we are down sixty employees. Composting takes labor. If we were fully staffed, we'd be able to do it no problem. But right now, we don't even have enough cashiers."

Why the labor shortage? It turns out that employers can't house their workforces. In the winter of 2022–2023, Aspen Skiing Company, as one example, was short some one hundred beds alone, even after spending tens of millions of dollars on housing. Workers apply for jobs, realize there's no place to sleep, and move on.

Let's dig deeper. The person who asked about composting is likely part of that old-school environmental community that practices preservationism—the preservation of small-town character, of land, and of history. This person also focuses on the small and individual actions over the systemic. They almost certainly also opposed recent efforts to increase density—read affordable housing—in our town in the name of, you guessed it, protecting the environment.

Many years ago, the town of Telluride, Colorado, spent tens of millions of dollars to protect a large parcel of open space at the entrance to town. The move was consistent with what environmentalists had done for decades. But protecting open space, while lovely, also makes existing housing more expensive, for two reasons. First, the open space is beautiful, and unthreatened by development. If you've got a view—or a house in town—it gets more valuable. Second, the open space protection eats up the very limited space that exists for housing. In Telluride, I pointed this out in an op-ed that generated an infuriated response from some environmentalists there.[3]

A friend of mine who recently sold his house in Telluride for $2 million recently saw it listed for $5 million. (He told me the sight of the listing made him throw up a little in his mouth.) The open space is a material portion of that price increase.

Back in Aspen, sections of the town look like they did decades ago, with Victorian houses and big, lovely parks. There are, however, no people in those houses (which are often second, third, or fourth homes), and a long line of traffic runs through town every morning and evening as people who are forced to live down valley, where real estate is cheaper, end up commuting twenty, thirty, and even fifty miles to work.

There's nothing environmentally friendly about any of this. The long commute creates pollution. It blocks guests from the ski hill. It wears out the road and creates small particulate pollution from road dust and tire wear. It's the exact antithesis of all the ideas Aspen was founded on—about renewal and escaping from your usual life.

But voters argue they don't want to destroy the place they love by building more housing. "What's the carrying capacity?" they ask. "We can't just build housing forever!" One older, quite famous environmentalist told me about her opposition to a four-lane highway (one lane for a bus) into Aspen: "You should want to slow down and look around when you come into Aspen." Let them eat traffic. It'll give them a nice break, for reflection.

There's truth to the idea that you can't build out a community forever. But the goal isn't to let everyone in. It's for communities to be able to house their workforces, so that those people have reasonable commutes, so that the community isn't congested with traffic from the outside, and so that businesses can function for the good of the local economy. In doing that, we should respect urban growth boundaries and oppose unmitigated sprawl. But we must also welcome changes to our towns and understand that nothing living gets locked in time.

All resort towns—including Jackson Hole, Wyoming; the Colorado resorts of Telluride and Crested Butte; and North Conway, New Hampshire—experience the same challenges. "But we don't want more people in town!" a local radio host told me once. But if we're talking workforce housing, *those people are already in town.* Still, residents, who mostly base decisions on what will affect their property values, vote density down every time.

Race and Open Space

There is also a troubling aspect to American urban planning built around open space, nature, and low density: racism. And it has a long history.

A key piece of that history was the City Beautiful movement, which arose at the turn of the nineteenth century in the United States and aimed to add architectural grandeur and beautification as part of a social reform movement that would promote *moral and civic virtue.* (That should already set off alert readers: "beauty, morality, and civic virtue" are too often code for "only white people.")

As historian Kathleen Lamp writes:

> As City Beautiful moved across the country, immigrants remained a chief focus of the movement, at least in the Midwest and Northeast. The driving anxieties of City Beautiful regarding the urban poor and immigrants in the North easily grafted onto anxieties about race in the post-reconstruction South. While there is a long history of neoclassical architecture in the antebellum south, many Confederate statues in the South date from the City Beautiful era. While this is the period in which it became cheaper to mass produce statues, [historians] Andrea

Douglas and Jalane Schmidt clearly connect City Beautiful with the use of Confederate statues to control public space. They explain that, following the Civil War, memorials were erected and "interlaced with ideas about race," and "part of what was beautiful was who needed to be removed, supposedly, from public space in order to beautify them."

. . . City Beautiful-era Confederate monuments were used alongside other "terror campaigns" to segregate physical space and discourage civic participation, community, and commercial involvement by black people. The controversy of the last several years regarding Confederate statues has made evident how those statues were (and are) used to control public space—that is, specifically to further white supremacy by excluding black people from public, often civic, spaces.[4]

Urban planning often continues the practices established by the City Beautiful movement. Indeed, simply the lack of dense housing near mass transit ensures that no people outside the elite can live in these communities. But even in a place like Aspen, even in 2023, the symbols implicitly designed to keep certain people out remain. Outside Veterans Memorial Park on Main Street in downtown Aspen, there was a plaque containing a Robert E. Lee quote. The quote itself is beautiful. But the person who said it was a traitor who fought to preserve slavery in America.[5]

Bad urban planning isn't just bad for our towns; it's bad for our souls.

These stories serve as examples of the supermarket problem, just in another context. Dennis Handley, an army veteran originally from Boone, North Carolina, now lives in Aspen. He spent four years trying to get rid of that Lee plaque. The conversation was radioactive. Some veterans opposed it. County staff said they had more important things to deal with. But, as Dennis realized, it's just part of the job of citizenship. He plugged away. And in 2024, he won. The Lee quote went down, and in its place was Lincoln: "With malice toward none, with charity for all." Any meaningful position you might take on policy, in whatever venue, will be controversial. As a concerned community citizen working on climate, you'll soon learn that many of the policies that are critical to solving the problem are reviled.[6]

Gas-X for Methane

Here's another example around the issue of natural gas. If we don't stop building new houses heated with natural gas, we will ensure that the built environment emits CO_2 forever, because of combustion. So a key climate solution at the municipal level is to ban natural gas in new buildings. Contractors hate such a ban because the expertise to install electric heat pumps instead of gas boilers is nascent—many communities don't have the installers. And there are concerns about the cost of installation, operations, performance, and even access to new heat pump technology. That said, the only way to increase expertise and bring costs down is to get more people doing it, through policy. The same thinking applies at the state level, where public utility commissions are increasingly banning the extension of gas lines into new neighborhoods: if a new subdivision is proposed, instead of approving an extension to the gas infrastructure, states create laws banning those extensions. The subdivision must consequently be all electric. This statewide policy approach achieves the same goal of eliminating new natural-gas-heated buildings.

It's really difficult to take policy positions that will make you reviled in your community, confronted by people with gripes that seem legitimate until you factor in climate change. And it has always been hard to counter people's immediate concerns of cost and affordability with any other inputs. Even though the climate threat is real and urgent, to take a position on the basis of climate alone still makes you seem like a hippie.

In skiing, there's an expression "If it were easy, they'd call it snowboarding." (This is an unfair knock against snowboarding and snowboarders, who are often maligned for being unwashed malingerers, the snow equivalent of skate rats.[7]) But a corollary in public service would be "If it were easy, it wouldn't be citizenship." Being a leader and a citizen is tough. Citizenship involves justice, not just loving kindness; it is highly charged and controversial.

Affordable Housing as Climate Fix

How we as a society and individuals embrace our responsibility as citizens is a larger question and one for individuals to explore. But how we address housing is less complicated but important because urban planning is a key part of the climate fix. But it is also a key part of how we take care of each other.

Broadly speaking, we need to embrace density. Basic urban planning principles offer some solutions. Build infill housing in the urban core, or at least within the urban growth boundary, along transit routes. Make it dense, which means small units that go up vertically instead of out. Deed-restrict the housing by capping appreciation and total value or controlling rent. (This is essential because regardless of size, units on the free market in desirable locations will become unaffordable over time or even instantly.) Change zoning codes to allow for smaller houses, which are more affordable (Carbondale, Colorado, for example, eliminated *minimum* house size requirements), and enable mother-in-law units with occupation requirements as well as deed restrictions.

There are gnarlier answers, too. Proposed legislation in California would get rid of zoning restrictions around transit hubs in bigger cities, making it easier to build thousands of new units near bus stops and train stations. You can see how this change would scare residents concerned about community character. But it was their unwillingness to plan and accommodate others that led to the housing crunch in the first place. And yet neighborhoods rose up to oppose the proposed zoning because they wanted to protect community character.

They wanted to keep what they had. But their decision-making was based entirely on themselves. Not even remotely did it include others, society, or the common good.

How do we get past NIMBYism and arrive at smart solutions? We need to support the nascent YIMBYism movement—"Yes in my backyard!" We need a civics revolution, whereby younger citizens—the very ones who need housing, the very ones who are starting to show up in our national elections—or enlightened elders either run for office or amp up pressure on those already in power.[8]

That may seem like a big ask, but the question I get from individuals more than any other is, "What can I do?"

Well, fellow citizens, here's something you can do. The only problem is, it's hard. Are you tough enough to be a citizen?

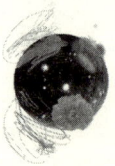 ## Gnomes and Community

> *Up the airy mountain,*
> *Down the rushy glen,*
> *We daren't go a-hunting,*
> *For fear of little men;*
> *Wee folk, good folk,*
> *Trooping all together;*
> *Green jacket, red cap,*
> *And white owl's feather!*
> —**William Allingham,** "The Fairies"

Collecting gnomes wasn't just a hobby for my son Elias before he became a middle-schooler; it was a way of life. In the morning, he would don his bathrobe and check on the gnome home he built under a juniper bush. He would leave notes and receive them in return. When one of his goldfish died, the gnomes sent a condolence card.

He responded with a drawing of a house shaped like a mushroom and a smiling face: "Your note did cheer me up, and I will be fully cheered-up soon. Thank you for all your kindness. You are very good friends of mine. You make my life awesome."

Gnomes are the diminutive, pointy-red-hatted custodians of the natural world: master farmers, animal doctors, vegetarians, they have names like Geronimus B and Thelonious. They are kind and quiet and decent. In these fractured times, they connect us back to what we care about and what makes us happy: a place-based life that integrates landscape with community.

By chance, a reporter for a national publication wrote about Elias's growing collection. Overnight, he became famous.

Shortly afterward, packages began to arrive, wrapped in twine as if from across the ages and addressed in shaky penmanship. They contained not the bombs or anthrax I had presumed but gnomes and notes. Many began: "I live alone. After my husband died . . ." They recalled days past, telling stories of cross-country journeys to live with children, of loss, of unspoken but implied loneliness—"I wish my children were little again"—signed with names from several generations past: Marva. Eunice. Arnie.

A professional gnome carver from Ohio sent Elias a custom figurine clearly intended as a talisman: "This good luck gnome eats little, drinks less but only water, is house broken, dances and sings occasionally, and wears indoor-outdoor finish . . . . Best of all he has the power to give his master the confidence to take on difficult tasks and be successful."

A ninety-plus-year-old woman from North Carolina still sends cards to "Her little gnome, Elias," on holidays. When I received emails asking for Elias's address from gnome lovers, I shared it without thinking, only to be scolded by Ellen, who warned me about the modern world's impure intentions. "But," I protested, "these are the best people on earth!"

One such correspondence led Ellen to a prearranged meeting in a Starbucks parking lot, where a woman named Patricia handed off two cement gnomes, lifted from the trunk of her green Citation.

The transaction felt illicit—trafficking in humanity in the early twenty-first century.

Improbable human connection is the domain of the gnome.

They seem to answer in the affirmative to Bruce Springsteen's plaintive call of alienation: "Is there anybody alive out there?" And Elias's experience shows they may foster a broader community than we might otherwise be capable of making. It takes courage to find kinship, but these guys seem to have it dialed.

The largest of our gnomes, named Candy for the giant spiral lollipop he holds, still sits underneath the willow in our front yard. Candy presides over the commonweal, observing the adumbration of the mountains each dusk and dawn, taking delight in the piercing winter stars, bearing silent witness to passing neighbors, and comforting, by his presence, the deer, bears, and wild turkeys that wander by. If he could speak, he would cite the poet Mary Oliver: "Sometimes I need only to stand wherever I am to be blessed."

But blessedness doesn't always arrive unbidden, and like luck, sometimes you need to create your own. That's why one of my first acts as a town councilman in Basalt, Colorado, was, as mentioned earlier, to establish a Gnome Home Building Ordinance.

It gives residents permission to gather in one peaceful and beautiful place and build, out of natural materials, model homes for a special kind of creature: kindly and yet open to cross-boundary conversation, connected to place and nature, deeply rooted in community. A species that can console children, make their lives "awesome," and take care of the lonely with companionship. Gnomes are quiet, calm, and listening; some might call their ambition provincial, but their aspirations are in fact as sacred and urgent as scripture.

Of course, nothing lasts.

Elias determined that leprechauns weren't real when he found St. Patrick's Day supplies in Ellen's closet. The demise of Darby O'Gill was the domino that took out Santa, the Easter Bunny, and, in widening carnage, gnomes and even the tooth fairy.

Later, as a seventh grader, Elias didn't even like to talk about gnomes, embarrassed by his past. But who of us is not? When I bought a gnome welcome mat for my backyard office, Elias said, "It makes me feel bad."

"Really, bad?" I asked. "But gnomes are so cool."

"Not bad, weird."

I tried to explain. While gnomes may not actually come out at night and cure animals, surely there's a reason most cultures, from the Ojibwa to the Norse, have for millennia told stories of little people, spirits in the woods: tomten, pixies, tommyknockers, brownies, Nunupi. They are about something inside us.

"In that sense," I continued, as he looked past me into the near distance, "gnomes are as real as any human idea, as . . ." We are silent for a moment.

"Should we play catch?" Elias asked.

I said yes.

13

Jacob's Angel

Angel: "Let me go, for the day breaketh."

Jacob: "I will not let thee go, except thou bless me."

Genesis 32:26–37, King James Version

One of my dad's favorite stories of being a student was from an anthropology class he took at City College of New York. The professor was talking about how Neanderthals differed from modern humans, and he described the heavy brow ridge characteristic of, well, cave dwellers. "Like Schendler over there," he said.

There are many differences between prehistoric and modern humans, and not just in how we look. The archaeological record suggests that Neanderthals evolved in Asia or Europe and migrated. There was an important characteristic of their lives that defined them: when they reached big barriers, like oceans or mountain ranges, they did something sensible: they stopped.

But modern humans were different. They reached, say, the west coast of South America and saw the Pacific Ocean. And then instead of doing the sensible thing (the Neanderthal thing) and stopping, chilling, building a village or whatever, they did something insane. They built a crappy boat. And sailed off. Or at least some of them did.

"Where you going, Uncle Frank?"

"Oh, just going to see what's out there."

"What if there's nothing out there?"

Grunt.

As the Nobel Prize–winning geneticist Svante Pääbo told Elizabeth Kolbert in a *New Yorker* interview:

> It's only fully modern humans who start this thing of venturing out on the ocean where you don't see land. Part of that is technology, of course; you have to have ships to do it. But there is also, I like to think or say, some madness there. You know? How many people must have sailed out and vanished on the Pacific before you found Easter Island? I mean, it's ridiculous. And why do you do that? Is it for the glory? For immortality? For curiosity? And now we go to Mars. We never stop.[1]

Kolbert continued: "If the defining characteristic of modern humans is this sort of Faustian restlessness, then, by Pääbo's account, there must be some sort of Faustian gene. Several times, he told me that he thought it should be possible to identify the basis for this 'madness' by comparing Neanderthal and human DNA."[2]

It's hard to overstate how crazy modern humans can be, and it's worth thinking about. For starters: there are people living on Easter Island. If you look at a map, it's 2,200 miles away from the coast of Chile, or 2,500 miles from Tahiti, in the middle of the Pacific Ocean. So as Pääbo points out, some people had to have decided, probably over generations, to hop in an unbelievably crappy watercraft of some sort and go see what was out there. And when they didn't show up, the next group—crazy Uncle Frank or whoever—that person got a team together and sailed off and disappeared. And then, one day, someone made it. What drove that? Certainly, life was harder then. A part of the drive to "go and to see," as Barry Lopez called that instinct, was that perhaps anything was better than life as it was. But the known is generally preferable to the unknown for humans, so something else was at play.

It's not all that different from the kinds of things we see in mountain towns like the place I live. I have a skier friend, Chris Davenport, who found a sixty-foot cliff at Snowmass Ski Area. What did he think when he saw it? "That's scary" or "I better not accidentally ski near the edge"?

No. It was, "I think I can huck it."

And so he got photographer Tom Zuccareno to set up below to take a picture, and he launched off the cliff, landed, and skied away. Why? What was he looking for?

Something more.

This instinct, arguably, didn't just get us to Easter Island and into the record books of skiing, but it was the thing that enabled us to flourish, to thrive, to rethink the status quo, and to explore ideas, places, and pursuits that before we went "mad" were just too weird for our heavy-browed, fire-making, mammoth-spearing, meat-eating selves. It's the instinct that led to art and culture and science and technology and music and adventure and all the other "weird" and "crazy" parts of being human. It led to Picasso's Cubism and Einstein's thought experiments and Beethoven's "Ode to Joy." Maybe so-called madness created beauty. Regardless, we needed a spark to elevate our species, and madness and desire was it.

To understand the role of this special spark, think about Philippe Petit, the acrobat who tightrope-walked between the World Trade Centers in 1974 and was the subject of several famous documentaries, including *Man on Wire*, the title of which came from the police report for what they saw that day.

In order to do the unimaginable thing he wanted to do, Petit had to spend years figuring it out. Evading security. War-gaming how to string the cable between the two towers. (Petit used a bow and arrow to pull a light string, then pulled an increasingly heavy line until he was able to move the cable itself.) And then after immense time, risk, dedication, and hard work, he did the thing.

Remember, this was 1974, more or less the period described at the beginning of this book, in the heart of the dismal era I grew up in, when buildings were abandoned, Americans and Vietnamese were dying in the war, inflation was explosive, mortgage rates were climb-ing, and my neighbors were yelling at us to get off their caaaah! We desperately "needed sumfin'," as my son used to say.

Petit walked across the wire for an hour or so and did for America in 1974 what Lindbergh had done for the country fifty years earlier, when he flew across the Atlantic. As F. Scott Fitzgerald wrote then, "In the spring of '27, something bright and alien flashed across the sky. A young Minnesotan who seemed to have nothing to do with his generation did a heroic thing, and for a moment, people set down their glasses in country clubs and speakeasies and thought of their old best dreams."[3]

Petit changed how Americans viewed the world. How the world viewed America and Americans, even though he was French. He showed us what was possible out of the ruins. (He did his walk in Au-gust, no less—the absolute most oppressive time to be in New York.) He changed our understanding of the role of art in society, of the value of risk, and of how we ought to think of ourselves as a culture and people.

When he came down from the high wire, he was immediately ar-rested. But in the pictures of the police taking him away, Petit is chatting away with reporters, and the grizzled officer has an unmis-takable look of amusement.[4]

Petit was released, and as his punishment, he was required to per-form a tightrope walk for the children of New York in Central Park, demonstrating that sometimes even rigid-seeming societies recog-nize, with whimsy, the difference between disorderly conduct (Petit's charge) and a lesson in how to live.

. . .

In his masterpiece *Arctic Dreams*, Barry Lopez writes about the title banner of the *North Georgia Gazette and Winter Chronicle*, a news-paper produced aboard the ship of arctic explorer Capt. William Parry.

The Green Lantern Press, which published an annotated reprint and transcription of the original 1821 document, explains the paper's origin: "The newspaper was written aboard an English ship trapped in the Arctic. The ship's captain had the sailors produce the newspaper in order to ward off boredom." Caroline Picard, the book's editor, describes the newspaper as an "incredible existential metaphor, where, a group of people stranded in the dark, are forced to make their own meaning in order to survive the harsh conditions." Parry was twenty-nine years old at the time of the expedition.[5]

The banner, Lopez notes, was *"per freta hactenus negata*, meaning to have negotiated a strait the very existence of which has been denied. But it also suggests a continuous movement through unknown waters. It is, simultaneously, an expression of fear and of accomplishment, the cusp on which human life finds its greatest expression."[6]

We ought to see the climate problem as just this sort of opportunity, one that humans were built for down to our DNA. It is just the kind of sortie into the unknown that triggers all our best instincts, the ultimate adventure, whose outcome we can only imagine.

Earlier in this book, I described a photo taken by the Cassini spacecraft looking back at Saturn and Earth. In it, Earth is just a small point of light in the lower right quadrant, tiny below the giant rings. There are two ways to look at that picture. One is to see yourself as small, insignificant, and meaningless. The other is to be inspired: to want to do something great with your life, to make a statement worthy of the size and scale and beauty of the universe, and your own privilege to be a part of it.

I don't know how we humans ought to end up in our lives if we want fulfillment and a sense of having lived a worthy existence. We are all so different. But I know how we don't want to end up. That's best summed up by the great Joseph Conrad, the Polish-born novelist who wrote lyrical prose in his third language, English. In his short story "Youth," which my father handed to me when I was twelve, only a few years before he died at sixty-four from heart disease, Conrad writes of five men drinking Bordeaux around a mahogany table:

> And we all nodded at him: the man of finance, the man of accounts, the man of law, we all nodded at him over the polished table that like a still sheet of brown water reflected our faces, lined, wrinkled; our faces marked by toil, by deceptions, by success, by love; our weary eyes looking still, looking always, looking anxiously for something out of life, that while it is expected is already gone—has passed unseen, in a sigh, in a flash—together with the youth, with the strength, with the romance of illusions.[7]

The Long Defeat and Hope

Sometimes the road leads through dark places.
Sometimes the darkness is your friend.

—Bruce Cockburn

Each week now, different groups of the world's scientists release new reports on the threat of climate change and how to protect civilization by limiting global warming to 1.5°C.

They typically show that this critical goal is possible, but only in the same sense that it's possible that the average American could run three marathons in three days. We're going to have to want it, and even then, it will be tough.

The world would need to reduce greenhouse gas emissions about twice as fast as has ever been achieved and do it everywhere, sustained for fifty years. Northern European countries reduced emissions by about 4 or 5 percent per year in the 1970s when they went nuclear and responded to the oil crisis. We'd need around 8 or 9 percent. Every year. Every country. For half a century.[1]

In effect, we'd need to internationally diffuse the world's best climate practices—electric cars like Norway, energy efficiency like California, land protection like Costa Rica, coal bans like Europe, solar and wind power like China, beef consumption like India, bicycle use like the Netherlands.

We'd face opposition all along the way, particularly from our Goliath of a fossil fuel industry. To have a prayer of 2°C, we will need to leave most of the remaining coal, oil, and gas underground, compelling the ExxonMobil and Saudi Aramcos to forgo anticipated profits of over $33 trillion over the next twenty-five years.[2]

And while the air would almost immediately be cleaner and people healthier, the heartbreaking impacts of climate—flooded Mumbai, London, Hanoi, New York, Shanghai, Alexandria, Jakarta, and San Francisco, to touch on just one consequence—would still continue for decades.

Given the data and the challenge, cynical news headlines increasingly abound, on the order of "Scientists Agree: We're Cooked!" especially since events over the last decade—oven-like heat, dried-up rivers like the Danube and Mississippi, devastating fires from California to the arctic, massive drought—make it seem like we've crossed a threshold. To be fair, the headline writers would have a point. Solving climate is going to be harder and more improbable than winning World War II, achieving some level of civil rights, defeating bacterial infection, ending slavery, and sending Neil Armstrong to the moon, all at once.

This leads to a salient question: How do we engage in a possibly—but not probably—winnable struggle in a rigged system against great odds, the ultimate results of which we'll never see? One almost feels like saying, "Forget success. How do we even get out of bed in the morning?"

We can wring our hands and panic, or we could order Chinese and lock ourselves in the closet, but we shouldn't. Because there's good news: we're the perfect people for the job. If the human species specializes in one thing, it's taking on the impossible.

First, we are constitutionally equipped to understand the situation we're in: at the most fundamental level, we are mortal, and so our very existence is a battle against inevitable demise. We also have experience: the wicked challenges we've faced through the ages have often been unwinnable. The Black Death killed off a third of Europe in its time, a world-ending pandemic. World War II claimed more than fifty million lives. We won those battles—sort of. The truth is, we've spent our time as Homo sapiens fighting what J. R. R. Tolkien called "the long defeat."[3]

It's no wonder that our favorite moments in stories, since we began telling them, are not about victory but are about loss. There was Gilgamesh, who ultimately found that the eternal life "which you look for, you will never find." There were the three hundred outnumbered Spartans at Thermopylae. In the end of another tale, Beowulf dies fighting a dragon, leaving his people defenseless, foreseeing "enemies on the rampage, bodies in piles, slavery and abasement." *The Lord of the Rings* and *Harry Potter*, just modern versions of the same story, chronicled what theologian Charlie Trimm called, in reference to Tolkien, "a series of victories accompanied by the stubborn and incessant return of evil."[4] We've struggled and lost even in our philosophy and religion, battling nagging and unanswerable questions about the meaning of our lives on earth, about the question of theodicy, the problem of why an all-powerful God would allow evil. But these stories speak to us because they describe the nature of human life.

The poet Jorge Luis Borges put it well: "I can give you my loneliness, my darkness, the hunger of my heart; I am trying to bribe you with uncertainty, with danger, with defeat."[5]

As humans, we should say, "Sign me up! This is what we do!"

But how do we do it, especially in the face of this relatively new and all-encompassing existential crisis?

Historically, we've tackled the biggest challenge—that of meaning and the question of how to live a life—through the concept of *practice*, in the form of religion, cultural tradition, or disciplines like martial arts or tai chi. Given what climate scientists are telling us, this approach might be the most useful tool in the climate fight. Practice has value independent of outcome; it's a way of life, not a job with a clear payoff.

We need to treat the climate slog—the fact that we must be fully engaged in it, every day, even though things will only get worse in our lifetimes—more like making coffee in the morning than deploying for war. A joyful habit. The right way to live.

Such an approach will require dropping the American focus on destination over journey, releasing the concepts of winning and winners, and abandoning our goal orientation, at least in the short term. This does not in any way mean giving up or even slackening our pace.

The journalist and radical I. F. Stone famously explains: "The only kinds of fights worth fighting are those you are going to lose because somebody has to fight them and lose and lose and lose until someday, somebody who believes as you do wins. In order for somebody to win an important, major fight 100 years hence, a lot of other people have got to be willing—for the sheer fun and joy of it—to go right ahead and fight, knowing you're going to lose. You mustn't feel like a martyr. You've got to enjoy it."[6]

If Stone's notion of fighting a losing battle for fun sounds familiar, it's because he is channeling some of the greatest thinkers on the human condition. Camus wrote, "One must imagine Sisyphus happy."[7] Cormac McCarthy agreed: "All things of grace and beauty such that one holds them to one's heart have a common provenance in pain."[8]

To save civilization, most of us on earth would need to supplement our standard daily or weekly practices—for example, eating, caring for family and community, searching for meaning—with a firm, steady push on the huge institutional structures that are holding back progress; we would have to turn our focus to government, policy, social movements, and civic life. Every day, a nudge of a system. Every week, a push on power through techniques and ideas deployed by Martin Luther King Jr., Gandhi, Myles Horton, Rosa Parks, American revolutionaries, and the youth plaintiffs who, as part of the climate movement, are starting to win lawsuits against the fossil fuel industry.[9]

Such a practice starts with a deep understanding of the scale of the problem, so it means reading a little climate science, every day. It continues with an understanding of how revolutions and social change happen in society—that means reading widely in the subject, including work by Erica Chenoweth, Maria Stephan, Theda Skocpol, and the work of Extinction Rebellion. Informed by the science, our actions must be to scale but also omnipresent in our lives, in the same way that John Lewis likely never woke up without thinking about civil rights. This is absolutely not a version of focusing on small things, of saying "every little bit matters." That's not what I'm talking about here, as you've learned. This is about power. And revolution.

Real progress comes from more-difficult engagements in society: voting, running for office, getting involved in local politics, protesting in the street, writing letters and op-eds, having uncomfortable but earnest and respectful conversations with your father-in-law. Every day some science. Every day a talk. Every day a call to another elected official, a street march, a protest, a voting booth, a new volunteer position on the planning and zoning board . . . Every day a small donation to a climate nonprofit. Every month, a push in your business to wield power, drop out of obstructive trade groups, and support climate policies. A practice that is part of a broader movement, which is what has always changed society through time.

Maybe this approach doesn't seem as noble as, say, our memory of the US civil rights movement. But that era's continuous, quietly effective grinding away—when people literally wore out their shoes walking instead of taking the bus in Montgomery, Alabama—probably didn't feel all that glorious then, either. With history as our judge, though, this daily grinding seems hallowed—we're part of a long story.

And we know what happens when enough people take up a cause as practice: cultural norms change, and issues go from irrelevant to habit. Think about how people used to smoke on airplanes, and now that practice makes no sense at all. Think about chucking trash out the window of your car, now (mostly) socially taboo. Think seatbelts, automatic now, but there was carnage on the roads for decades. Think interracial marriage and then gay marriage.

There should be no shortage of motivation. Solving climate change presents humanity with an opportunity that few generations, perhaps none, have ever had: the chance to save civilization from collapse and create aspects of what King called "the beloved community."

I will end this story with the same thought with which I began it. To address and solve the climate problem would endow our lives with some of the oldest and most numinous aspirations of humankind: the desire to take care of our children; to lead a good life; to treat our neighbors well; to bless our short existence with timeless ideas like grace, dignity, respect, tolerance, love, and grounded hope. The climate struggle embodies the essence of what it means to be human, which is that we strive for the divine, an inclination that is in our blood and bones, as it was in the Uncle Franks who went sailing, skier Chris Davenport on the cliff, or Philippe Petit.

And so I say it again: perhaps the rewards of solving climate change are so compelling, so nurturing, and so natural a piece of the human soul that we can't help but do it.

We must put into practice W. H. Auden's aspiration, written in 1939, at the onset of perhaps the other darkest period in modern history: "May I, composed like them, of Eros and of dust, beleaguered by the same negation and despair, show an affirming flame."[10]

Who wouldn't sign up for that?

. . .

One autumn evening, as syrupy golden light suffuses our valley and the temperature is just perfect, I am standing, holding a cup of lapsang souchong and looking out my living room window. I see my neighbors' children Hudson and Hazel wander home from friends down the street. Hazel, five, wears her standard outfit of a pink leotard, her big baby belly sticking out, and her strawberry sunglasses up on her head, hair tied in a bow. Hudson, eight, is in camo shorts and his hands are filthy, his wispy pale arms marked with scratches and dirt and the white bionic blood-sugar-monitoring patch on his shoulder.

Like characters out of *Peanuts* or *Family Circus*, they walk an erratic line, touching sap on trees and wandering up through gaps in fences and into ditches, heads down, on a perfect random walk. They detour through my yard and stop on the uneven flagstone stairs that I built out of salvaged rock, to our front door, looking down at something and poking around in the dirt and weeds.

Hudson carries his insulin fanny pack that he always has with him. Hazel moves across the street, stopping to pirouette like the ballerina she is on the crown of the tarmac. Hudson stops to pick something up, pockets it, continues on, not to a place or in a direction but instead as part of a world of wonder and joy.

As if, to quote the poet Stanley Kunitz:

> *it didn't matter*
> *which way was home;*
> *as if he didn't know*
> *he loved the earth so much*
> *he wanted to stay forever.*[11]

How to Sue ExxonMobil for Private Nuisance

This book is partly about meaningful, large-scale solutions to climate change. None of us is successful in deploying every good idea, and I failed on probably the best one—getting corporations affected by climate change to sue the fossil fuel industry. But the idea is so good—and so potentially effective—that I'm including this briefing on how to do it, so that others might pick up the ball. It's written for a generic company, but when you're ready, just fill in the name of your company and the business you plan to sue.[1]

Executive Summary

Businesses concerned about climate change should begin exploring becoming the first corporation to sue ExxonMobil or other fossil fuel companies for "private nuisance" related to the impact of climate change on their business—impacts that were exacerbated by the fossil fuel industry's suppression of climate science over many decades. Being sued by a substantial private sector actor for injuries to its business and property would be a major shock to the fossil fuel industry and a significant development in efforts to hold it accountable for climate injuries. The goal of this action is not to win the lawsuit but instead to bring international prominence to the climate issue, to advance the climate fight with another line of attack, and to position one's business as a leader in climate advocacy. This proposal recognizes that climate change now requires far more aggressive action than ever before conceived.

Precedent for Private Lawsuits

"On Nov. 14, in an unprecedented action by private individuals in a US court, commercial fishermen in California and Oregon sued 30 oil, gas and coal companies, seeking compensation for their losses because the Dungeness crab market in the Pacific Ocean has been harmed by rising temperatures caused by burning fossil fuels."

—**Michael Hirsh**, "How Private Lawsuits Could Save the Climate," Foreign Policy, November 21, 2018

What Would the Lawsuit Achieve?

- *It would shift the political and media narrative.* The story would shift from "Radical politicians are doing this for purely political reasons" to "Private sector corporations are taking action because climate change is real and is seriously injuring their businesses."

- *It would break new ground in climate law.* Congress can eliminate public nuisance claims but cannot eliminate private nuisance claims unless the government pays "just compensation" under the Fifth Amendment's Takings Clause.

- *The act itself would be worthwhile, newsworthy, and a historically significant attack on the fossil fuel industry.* A victory could threaten the viability of the industry because it would open the floodgates to thousands of similar suits from affected parties.

- *It would position one's company as an international leader in the climate movement.*

Goal of the Lawsuit

While the intent of this action is to bring international attention to the issue of ExxonMobil's malfeasance, the specific goal of the suit in the courtroom is compensation for damages resulting from the fact that the industry has known for decades of the coming impacts of climate change but continued to promote fossil fuel consumption. That delay reaped enormous financial gains for the fossil fuel industry at the direct expense of private entities.

The Critical Nature of the Battle

Humankind is badly losing the fight against climate change. The October 2018 "Doomsday Report" by the UN Intergovernmental Panel on Climate Change explains that we are already past critical warming thresholds, and the future of any given industry is less the issue than is the future of civilization. New research on the proximity of tipping points arrives daily, and scientific, academic, and philosophical conversation is increasingly focused on the question of societal collapse, not adaptation or mitigation. A paper being circulated among climate philanthropists "is premised on the view that social collapse is now inevitable."[2]

If an issue is not in the news, the public often forgets about it. Many of Martin Luther King Jr.'s actions were designed, like this one, to elevate an issue's prominence. The public does not fully understand the substantial financial burden that climate change is imposing, and will impose, on many industries, such as snow sports, coffee and tea, beer, wine, insurance, and hospitality. Better public understanding of the threat specifically facing these beloved businesses could spark the needed social movement to create political will for change.

> ### Private Industry Precedent
>
> "Apparel maker Patagonia Inc. sued President Donald Trump over his decision to reduce the size of the Bears Ears National Monument in Utah in a case joined by conservation and preservation groups. The retailer claims Trump's Dec. 4 decision to substantially reduce the size of Bears Ears—to about 220,000 acres from 1.4 million acres—exceeds his authority under the 1906 Antiquities Act. Patagonia has been considered an 'activist company' nearly since it was started in 1973 by climber Yvon Chouinard."
>
> —**Andrew M. Harris**, "Patagonia Sues Trump over Bears Ears Monument," Bloomberg, December 7, 2017

Relief (Damages) Requested

Businesses could ask for a range of economic losses, including:

- Lost profits from climate impacts. Depending on one's business, this could include reduced snowfall, water supply, general warming, or sea-level rise.

- Increased expenditures resulting from the aforementioned issues.

- Infrastructure damage from fire and flood, plus impacts to roads, culverts, and buildings, and the cost to plan for and mitigate those impacts.

- The cost of developing an overall climate action plan.

- Equitable relief. An "unjust enrichment" claim would seek the profits ExxonMobil gained by hiding climate alteration.

Municipal Suit Precedent

"Until recently, communities suing fossil fuel companies over the costs of climate change have been located on the coasts: cities and counties in California, and New York City. But now, the litigation has jumped inland. Boulder and San Miguel Counties in Colorado, along with the city of Boulder, filed a lawsuit on Tuesday against two oil companies, ExxonMobil and Suncor Energy, the Canadian giant. The suit, filed in state court, argues that fossil fuels sold by the companies contribute to climate change, which in turn has exacerbated wildfires, droughts, severe storms and other symptoms of a warming planet that have far-ranging effects on agriculture and tourism."

—**John Schwartz**, "Climate Lawsuits, Once Limited to the Coasts, Jump Inland," *New York Times*, April 18, 2018

Risks: Impact of Legal Information Requests by ExxonMobil (aka Discovery)

Assuming one's company is able to pursue a case for damages, it would (1) have to produce evidence of financial losses to date, which will take staff time, and (2) hire experts to identify and project losses into the future. (The costs of this work would be covered by partners contractually ensured at the beginning of the process.) A business would probably also need to supply records of fossil fuel use and disclose what the business knew about climate change and when. In addition, discovery might require disclosure of how much climate change is costing the firm, including the financial data needed to make that determination. (According to counsel, that information can be kept confidential by limiting access to only the ExxonMobil legal team and its experts.)

Discovery would incur substantial time and expense, but it is far down the road. A business would file in state court, and the defendants would remove the case to federal court. The business would then have to try to remand it back to the state and then fight a motion to dismiss. Lawyers are many months into the current (Boulder) litigation with no resolution of even which court will hear the case. But on June 21, 2024, District Court Judge Robert R. Gunning denied a motion to dismiss, ruling that Boulder's "public nuisance, private nuisance, trespass, conspiracy, and unjust enrichment claims may proceed against ExxonMobil, Suncor Energy, and Suncor Sales."[3]

If the lawsuit went as far as discovery, it would be a good thing, because it would mean the case had survived and would put the plaintiff in the position of proving the dramatic impacts of climate change on its business. At that point, supporting legal teams would help to reduce the burden.

Other Risks

- *Risk of fees on motion to dismiss.* Every state is different. For example, Colorado is one of the few states that require plaintiffs to pay defendants' attorney fees and costs if the defendants succeed on a motion to dismiss. A business in Colorado has the advantage of having a similar suit—Boulder's—already in Colorado courts. If that suit is dismissed, then another wouldn't have a chance of success, and so a business would drop it before it could be dismissed.[4]

- *Valuation risk.* Convincingly arguing that climate change damages one's business runs the risk of diminishing the value of the company, and this reduced valuation could affect IPO or sale plans. That said, the impacts of climate change have long been obvious and rarely seem to affect valuation. Take Miami, Florida, as one example. That city remains a sought-after destination for home buyers and vacationers, despite bearing the assault of increasingly frequent hurricanes and other severe weather events, a direct result of climate change.

- *Retaliation.* Cases have not gotten to a stage where retaliation can be predicted. Defendants may argue that a given business's use of fossil fuels invalidates its claim. ExxonMobil has argued that local government officials in some of the California municipal cases are engaged in a "civil conspiracy" against it. The company has asserted that the jurisdictions' statements about sea-level rise in previous municipal bond disclosures contradicts statements in their complaints against ExxonMobil. There is no evidence that ExxonMobil has tried to retaliate in the Colorado case or the cases brought by New York, Baltimore, Rhode Island, and elsewhere. Nor is there a comparable approach with any company that has long publicly acknowledged the risk of climate change; and many have. According to one expert, ExxonMobil is facing so many lawsuits that the company is less likely to throw all its resources at one retaliatory suit.[5]

- *Brand risk.* There would certainly be the risk of social media and other media attacks on any company for hypocrisy. The media might complain that the plaintiff itself uses fossil fuels, that a given business is tied to or owns fossil fuel interests, and so forth. That said, the leadership and PR upside of actually suing a fossil fuel company is significant. The progressive branding benefit is likely to be far larger than the downside. Both the defending company and the plaintiff can experience these media attacks anyway, because of their positions on climate or politics. Importantly, a business would be suing ExxonMobil not because it sold fossil fuels that the business eagerly used, but rather that its intentional obfuscation of the science and capture of government regulation caused great harm. This distinction ameliorates charges of hypocrisy.

"Lots of potential here—especially as ExxonMobil comes under pressure for its hiding of data on the risks of climate change over many decades. And a case by [a recognizable business] versus ExxonMobil would be a big deal—with potential impacts beyond any legal consequences."

—**Daniel C. Esty**, Hillhouse Professor of Environmental Law and Policy, School of Forestry and Environmental Studies and Clinical Professor of Environmental Law and Policy, Yale Law School

Odds of Success

It is hard to gauge exactly what one's chances are. If a lawsuit were to stay in state court, then chances of success are 50/50. If moved to federal court, then the odds change to four-to-one against the suing business. Others are less sanguine about the state court prospects, with good reason. However, the potential success of this lawsuit is not the criterion on which to make a decision about whether to proceed, since simply filing the suit would be a success.[6]

Costs

In many cases, nonprofit support means legal costs would be fronted on contingency by third parties, and several foundations are interested in supporting this work.

Counsel

While a corporation would need to find a chief counsel, there are several top climate lawyers in the United States who would likely be eager to take on this case.[7]

NOTES

Introduction

1. Michael Herr, *Dispatches* (New York: Knopf, 1977), 18.
2. Alice McCarthy, "Research Shows That Company Modeled and Predicted Global Warming with 'Shocking Skill and Accuracy' Starting in the 1970s," *Harvard Gazette*, January 12, 2023.
3. On hiding climate science, see Neela Banerjee, Lisa Song, and David Hasemyer, "Exxon's Own Research Confirmed Fossil Fuels' Role in Global Warming Decades Ago," *Inside Climate News*, September 16, 2016; Hank Crook and Thomas Fudge, "New Book Examines Efforts to Discredit Evidence of Global Warming," *KPBS Science and Technology*, June 7, 2010. On confusion and opposing regulation, see Naomi Oreskes and Erik Conway, *Merchants of Doubt: How a Handful of Scientists Obscured the Truth on Issues from Tobacco Smoke to Global Warming* (New York: Bloomsbury, 2010).
4. US Energy Information Administration, "Wind Explained: History of Wind Power," updated April 20, 2023, https://www.eia.gov/energyexplained/wind/history -of-wind-power.php.
5. Andrew King, "Flawed Research Pumped Up ESG Investing. Now It May Speed Its Collapse," unpublished white paper and conversation with author, January 5, 2024.
6. On carbon footprint, see Rebecca Solnit, "Big Oil Coined Carbon Footprints to Blame Us for Their Greed; Keep Them on the Hook," *Guardian*, August 23, 2021. While market fundamentalism is not a focus of this book, it played a role in determining Americans' approach to environmentalism and sustainable business. That story is brilliantly told in Naomi Oreskes and Erik Conway, *The Big Myth: How American Business Taught Us to Loathe Government and Love the Free Market* (New York: Bloomsbury, 2023). Patty Limerick, *The Legacy of Conquest* (New York: W.W. Norton, 1987), disabuses the reader of the notion of frontier individualism.
7. David Schroeder, "The US Recently Has Been Averaging 20 Billion in Oil Company Subsidies," *Climate Scorecard*, May 12, 2023, https://www .climatescorecard.org/2023/05/the-us-recently-has-been-averaging-20-billion-in -oil-company-subsidies/.
8. Paul Reps, *Zen Flesh, Zen Bones* (New York: Anchor/Doubleday, 1958), 22–23.
9. Barry Lopez, *Arctic Dreams: Imagination and Desire in a Northern Landscape* (New York: Scribner, 1986), 414.

10. The Clean Air Act was passed in 1963, but as historical EPA pictures (and my own memory) show, it took some time to make an impact (US Environmental Protection Agency, "Evolution of the Clean Air Act," updated November 21, 2023, https://www.epa.gov/clean-air-act-overview/evolution-clean-air-act). The Clean Water Act passed in 1972 (US Environmental Protection Agency, "Discover the History of the Clean Water Act," updated October 17, 2023, https://www.epa.gov/laws -regulations/discover-history-clean-water-act). Am I being hyperbolic about *Blade Runner* and Jersey City? You tell me. See Andy Blair, "New Jersey in the 1970s: 26 Color Photographs Captured Urban Area of the Garden State 40 Years Ago," *Vintage Everyday*, accessed January 27, 2024, https://www.vintag.es/2016/08/new-jersey-in -1970s-26-color-photos.html.

11. Banana Republic Catalog 25, fall 1985, https://www.secretfanbase.com /banana/banana-republic-catalog-25-fall-1985/#gallery/b023e226ac306538d55cbe b04f70b359/947.

12. Bruce Springsteen, "The Promised Land," *Darkness on the Edge of Town*, Columbia Records, 1978.

13. Florence Welch and Jack Antonoff, "Free," *Dance Fever*, Florence and the Machine, Polydor, 2022.

Chapter 1

1. John Brooke, Michael Bevis, and Steve Rissing, "How Understanding the History of the Earth's Climate Can Offer Hope Amid Crisis," *Time*, September 23, 2019.

2. Cormac McCarthy, *The Road* (New York: Alfred A. Knopf, 2006), 185.

3. Meaning that, because of feedback loops, warming would accelerate, not stabilize. Kevin Anderson, "Real Clothes for the Emperor: Facing the Challenges of Climate Change," lecture given November 6. 2012, https://www.bristol.ac.uk/media -library/sites/cabot---old/migrated/documents/anderson-transcript.pdf.

4. Damian Carrington, "World Close to 'Irreversible' Climate Breakdown, Warn Major Studies," *Guardian*, October 27, 2022.

5. Barry Lopez, *Arctic Dreams: Imagination and Desire in a Northern Landscape* (New York: Scribner, 1986), 405.

6. Kurt Vonnegut Jr., *Slaughterhouse-Five* (New York: Dell Publishing, Random House, 1969), 14, 15, 19.

Chapter 2

1. Aspen Skiing Company became a subsidiary of Aspen One late in my twenty-five-year tenure there. That's the name of the company I ended up working for. Since most of the projects described in this book occurred under the aegis of Aspen Skiing Company before Aspen One was created, that's how I will refer to the company throughout.

2. Federal Reserve Bank of St. Louis, "Average Price: Electricity per Kilowatt-Hour in Seattle-Tacoma-Bellevue WA (CBSA)," FRED Economic Data, March 12, 2024, https://fred.stlouisfed.org/series/APUS49D72610.

3. On dishwashers and coal, see US Energy Administration, "Frequently Asked Questions," accessed January 27, 2024, http://tinyurl.com/3xf6wmxz. On air

pollution deaths, see Timothy Huzar, "Air Pollution May Be a Leading Global Cause of Death," *Medical News Today*, March 30, 2020, https://www.medicalnewstoday .com/articles/air-pollution-may-be-a-leading-global-cause-of-death. On the social cost of carbon, see Kevin Rennert et al., "Comprehensive Evidence Implies a Higher Social Cost of CO_2," *Nature* 610 (2022): 687–692, https://doi.org/10.1038/s41586 -022-05224-9; Coral Davenport, "Biden Administration Unleashes Powerful Regulatory Tool Aimed at Climate," *New York Times*, December 2, 2023. Regarding my own local power, the good news is that where I live, the utility is mostly getting off coal (Holy Cross Energy, "100×30: Our Journey Continues 100% Clean Energy by 2030," https://www.holycross.com/100x30/). For the story of how that happened, see chapter 6.

4. Calculate Me, "Convert Gallons of Gas to Kilowatt Hours," accessed January 27, 2024, https://www.calculateme.com/energy/gallons-of-gas/to-kilowatt -hours/. For electricity rates, see Statista, "Average Residential Sector Retail Electricity Price in the United States as of September 2023, by State," Statista, https://www .statista.com/statistics/630090/states-with-the-average-electricity-price-for-the -residential-sector-in-the-us/.

5. The long history of this idea—that environmental protection at the scale required to solve large societal problems like climate change can be achieved on the free market, without regulation—has been extensively documented by Andrew King and Ken Pucker, "The Dangerous Allure of Win-Win Strategies—11-12-2020," Institute for Business in the Global Context, the Fletcher School, Tufts University, November 12, 2020 (excerpt of article of the same title, published in *Stanford Social Innovation Review*, winter 2021), https://sites.tufts.edu/ibgc/the-dangerous-allure -of-win-win-strategies/. Also see Ted Steinberg, "Can Capitalism Save the Planet? On the Origins of Green Liberalism," *Radical History Review* 107 (spring 2010): 7–24, https://scalar.usc.edu/works/uiuc-macs410-media-information-ethics-/media /CanCapitalismSavePlanet_Steinberg.pdf, about the hegemony of markets over public policy in solving environmental problems.

Chapter 3

1. Sports Illustrated, "Foul Territory: Actually Weehawken Stadium atop the Lincoln Tunnel Is a Pretty Fair Field," *Sports Illustrated Vault*, September 5, 1994, https://vault.si.com/vault/1994/09/05/foul-territory-actually-weehawken-stadium -atop-the-lincoln-tunnel-is-a-pretty-fair-field.

2. My dad, who was sixteen years older than my mom and died of atherosclerosis at sixty-four in 1987 when I was in high school, was a quintessential New Yorker. Overwhelmed by his own curiosity and love of life, he studied for PhDs in five subjects, receiving none; attended, then dropped out of medical school in Bern, Switzerland; and was mostly unemployable over any durable time frame. He worked on a computer manual for Wang in the 1980s; edited a book on the brain; had some writing job at Citibank, from which he brought home coffee-room snacks like Oreos and crackers; and taught criminology at a prison. He spoke seven languages ("Anglish the bast," he used to joke), translated Hegel from German and Job from Hebrew, but also enjoyed watching *MacGyver*, *The Dukes of Hazzard*, and the Mets with me in the evenings. He was a flaneur, his favorite activity being walking around great cities—New York and Paris being his favorite. He was a

beautiful, creative, and spare writer, and I learned from him about simplicity, economy, and avoiding big words.

3. Kendra Pierre-Louis, "This Is What America Looked Like Before the EPA Cleaned It Up," *Popular Science*, February 25, 2017, https://www.popsci.com /america-before-epa-photos/.

4. C. Jerry Simmons, "Documerica: Snapshots of Crisis and Cure in the 1970s," *Prologue Magazine* (US National Archives) 41, no. 1 (2009), https://www.archives .gov/publications/prologue/2009/spring/documerica.html. On PCBs, see US Environmental Protection Agency, "Learn About Polychlorinated Biphenyls," updated April 2, 2024, https://www.epa.gov/pcbs/learn-about-polychlorinated-biphenyls.

5. Andrew Small, "What Cities Looked Like Before the EPA," *Bloomberg*, March 2, 2017, https://www.bloomberg.com/news/articles/2017-03-02/what-cities -looked-like-before-the-epa.

6. On the Clean Air Act, see US Environmental Protection Agency, "Evolution of the Clean Air Act," updated November 21, 2023, https://www.epa.gov /clean-air-act-overview/evolution-clean-air-act. On the Energy Policy Act, see US Department of Energy, Office of Energy Efficiency and Renewable Energy, "History and Impacts: Buildings," accessed January 27, 2024, https://www.energy.gov/eere /buildings/history-and-impacts. On enactment of the US Energy Policy Act, see Jianfeng Yu, Ting Zhang, and Jianming Qian, "The Energy Policy Act (EPAct)," in "Energy-Efficiency Technical Measures System for Electrical Motor Products," in *Electrical Motor Products* (Philadelphia: Woodhead Publishing, 2011), https://www .sciencedirect.com/topics/engineering/energy-policy-act. On the minor progress on the bill, see US Environmental Protection Agency, "Water Efficient Management Guide: Bathroom Suite," November 2017, https://www.epa.gov/sites/default/files/2017-12 /documents/ws-commercialbuildings-waterscore-bathroom-resource-guide.pdf.

7. Naomi Oreskes and Erik Conway, *The Big Myth: How American Business Taught Us to Loathe Government and Love the Free Market* (New York: Bloomsbury, 2023), 394–395.

8. Per Oreskes and Conway, *The Big Myth*, this pervasive ideology was long in the making, but it took a while to land. With the emergence and growing power of Ronald Reagan, Alan Greenspan, and Ayn Rand, it became dominant across parties, as it is today. On the market framework, see also Ted Steinberg, "Can Capitalism Save the Planet? On the Origins of Green Liberalism," *Radical History Review* 107 (spring 2010): 7–24, https://scalar.usc.edu/works/uiuc-macs410-media-information-ethics- /media/CanCapitalismSavePlanet_Steinberg.pdf.

Chapter 4

1. As I showed in my book *Getting Green Done: Hard Truths from the Front Lines of the Sustainability Revolution* (New York: PublicAffairs, 2009), while the idea made sense, it just wasn't true. Even if the potential return was huge from an efficiency project, you might have even bigger opportunities elsewhere by selling the thing you make or the service you provide. Part of the problem is that business only has so much bandwidth. So while you might be able to make money in many ways, you have to concentrate on the most lucrative. Asking the chief financial officer for $25,000 for a lighting retrofit in a garage when this executive is trying to replace roofs, remodel hotels, or replace leaky pipes will draw the flat, empty stare of a nonbeliever.

2. Nick Gromicko and Ben Gromicko, "Building Orientation for Optimum Energy," International Association of Certified Home Inspectors, accessed January 27, 2024, https://www.nachi.org/building-orientation-optimum-energy.htm.

3. You can trace the origins of the sustainable-business movement all the way back to Toyota's lean management program and work at DuPont and 3M, among other businesses. But the vision crystalized in the corporate imagination after carpet company Interface CEO Ray Anderson's "Spear in the Chest Epiphany" after reading *The Ecology of Commerce*, by Paul Hawken. That was in 1994. Anderson believed business could "do well by doing good." See Ray C. Anderson Foundation, "Ray's Life," https://www.raycandersonfoundation.org/rays-life/. On 2°C baked in, see Janet Chikofsky, "En-ROADS Updated with New Baseline Scenario," *Climate Interactive*, December 2, 2020, https://www.climateinteractive.org/blog/en-roads-updated-with -new-baseline. On hottest years and total warming, see Rebecca Lindsey and LuAnn Dahlman, "Climate Change: Global Temperature," Climate.gov (National Oceanic and Atmospheric Administration), January 18, 2024, https://www.climate.gov/news -features/understanding-climate/climate-change-global-temperature.

4. An absurdly bureaucratic third-party certification system that shows business has a commitment to "continual improvement." The problem: an ISO 140001 company that covered its property in a foot of waste oil this year could pass an ISO audit if it only had half a foot of waste oil spilled the next year . . . continual improvement.

5. Mark Kaufman, "The Carbon Footprint Sham," *Mashable*, accessed January 27, 2024, https://sea.mashable.com/science/11514/the-carbon-footprint-sham.

6. The long-form version of this story can be found in my book *Getting Green Done*.

7. Laura Sullivan, "How Big Oil Misled the Public into Believing Plastic Would Be Recycled," *Morning Edition*, NPR, September 11, 2020, https://www.npr.org /2020/09/11/897692090/how-big-oil-misled-the-public-into-believing-plastic-would -be-recycled.

8. White House, Office of the Press Secretary, "Fact Sheet: President Obama's Climate Action Plan," June 25, 2013, https://obamawhitehouse.archives .gov/the-press-office/2013/06/25/fact-sheet-president-obama-s-climate-action-plan.

9. Inquisitor, "The Crucifixion of Jesus: Capital Punishment or Noble Sacrifice?," *Medium*, March 30, 2021, https://avinashvasishth.medium.com/crucifixion-of-jesus -capital-punishment-or-nobel-sacrifice-10c92d6c05d4. Emphasis added.

10. Ben Elgin, "Little Green Lies: The Sweet Notion That Making a Company Environmentally Friendly Can Be Not Just Cost-Effective but Profitable Is Going Up in Smoke; Meet the Man Wielding the Torch," *Businessweek*, October 22, 2007.

11. Open Secrets, "David Perdue: See Data About Their Federal Congressional Candidacy," accessed January 27, 2024, https://www.opensecrets.org/members-of -congress/david-perdue/contributors?cid=N00035516&cycle=2020&recs=100&type=I. On green companies improving oil exploration, see Tim Donaghy, Caroline Henderson, and Elizabeth Jardim, "Oil in the Cloud: How Tech Companies Are Helping Big Oil Profit from Climate Destruction," Greenpeace Reports, May 19, 2020, https://www.greenpeace.org/usa/reports/oil-in-the-cloud/. On GM's climate stance, see Bloomberg, "Biden Bill Compels Barra to Put GM Before Business Roundtable," *Autoblog* (Yahoo!), August 5, 2022, https://www.autoblog .com/2022/08/05/gm-mary-barra-inflation-reduction-act-business-roundtable/.

12. Osita Nwanevu, "The Corporations Funding the End of Democracy," *New Republic*, January 26, 2021, https://newrepublic.com/article/160800/corporate-money-trump-gop-coup.

13. Open Secrets, "Procter & Gamble PAC Contributions to Federal Candidates," https://www.opensecrets.org/political-action-committees-pacs/C00257329/candidate-recipients/2016.

14. Kaufman, "Carbon Footprint Sham."

15. Kaufman, "Carbon Footprint Sham."

16. Global Footprint Network, "Our Past & Our Future," *Global Footprint Network*, accessed February 17, 2024, https://www.footprintnetwork.org/about-us/our-history/.

17. This is, of course, disproved by history and experience—the United States was created by diverse collectivism, as Patty Limerick and others have shown.

18. Jeffrey S. Cramer, interview by Steve Curwood, "Solid Seasons: The Friendship of Henry David Thoreau and Ralph Waldo Emerson," *Living on Earth*, June 7, 2019, www.loe.org/shows/segments.html?programID=19-P13-00023&segmentID=6.

19. Henry David Thoreau, "On the Duty of Civil Disobedience," 1849.

20. My work has been specific to the corporate sustainability world, but there is important thinking being done around a similarly intentional token approach to global problems by philanthropists and governments. Anand Giridharadas, a *New York Times* columnist and writer, has beautifully articulated this in his book *Winners Take All: The Elite Charade of Changing the World* (New York: Alfred A. Knopf, 2018). In short, he argues that business and "thought" leaders like those who give talks at the Aspen Institute always express concern for issues like poverty, pollution, or injustice. But their actions always fall short of a solution at scale: like changing tax policy, for example. A similar argument was made on stage at Davos by Rutger Bregman, who called out "stupid philanthropy schemes" (Guardian News, "Rutger Bregman Tells Davos to Talk About Tax: 'This Is Not Rocket Science,'" YouTube video, January 29, 2019, https://www.youtube.com/watch?v=P8ijiLqfXP0). Neither man was well received by the establishment institutions they tried to blow up.

21. Joseph Romm, "Are Carbon Offsets Unscalable, Unjust, and Unfixable—and a Threat to the Paris Climate Agreement?," white paper, Penn Center for Science, Sustainability, and the Media, University of Pennsylvania, July 7, 2023, https://bpb-us-w2.wpmucdn.com/web.sas.upenn.edu/dist/0/896/files/2023/06/OffsetPaper7.0-6-27-23-FINAL2.pdf.

22. Lynn Schenk and Danielle Kost, "COP 27: What Can Business Leaders Do to Fight Climate Change Now?," *Working Knowledge* (blog), Harvard Business School, November 9, 2022, https://hbswk.hbs.edu/item/cop27-what-can-business-leaders-do-to-fight-climate-change-now.

23. Herman Daly, quoted in Andrew C. Revkin, "'Tipping Points' and the Climate Challenge," *Dot Earth* (blog), *New York Times*, March 28, 2009.

24. Cam Simpson, Akshat Rathi, and Saijel Kishan, "The ESG Mirage," *Bloomberg*, December 10, 2021, https://www.bloomberg.com/graphics/2021-what-is-esg-investing-msci-ratings-focus-on-corporate-bottom-line.

25. Among many examples is Peter Gassmann, Casey Herman, and Colm Kelly, "Are You Ready for the ESG Revolution?," PWC, June 15, 2021, https://www.pwc.com/gx/en/issues/esg/esg-revolution.html.

26. On math errors, see Andrew A. King, "Comment and Replication: The Impact of Corporate Sustainability on Organizational Processes and Performance," *SSRN*, November 29, 2023, https://ssrn.com/abstract=4648438. On exaggerated claims, see Jitendra Aswani, Alona Bilokha, Mingying Cheng, and Benjamin M. Cole, "The Cost (and Unbenefit) of Conscious Capitalism," *SSRN*, September 3, 2022, https://ssrn .com/abstract=3926335 or http://dx.doi.org/10.2139/ssrn.3926335. On brittle findings, see Luca Berchicci and Andrew King, "Corporate Sustainability: A Model Uncertainty Analysis of Materiality," *Journal of Financial Reporting* 7, no. 2 (2022): 43–74, https://papers.ssrn.com/sol3/papers.cfm?abstract_id=3848664. On "sustainable business is good business," see "New Meta-Analysis from NYU Stern Center for Sustainable Business and Rockefeller Asset Management Finds ESG Drives Better Financial Performance," NYU Stern, February 10, 2021, https://www.stern .nyu.edu/experience-stern/faculty-research/new-meta-analysis-nyu-stern-center -sustainable-business-and-rockefeller-asset-management-finds-esg.

For the final academic report, see Ulrich Atz, Tracy Van Holt, Zongyuan Zoe Liu, and Christopher Bruno, "Does Sustainability Generate Better Financial Performance? Review, Meta-analysis, and Propositions," *S&P Global Market Intelligence*, October 6, 2020, https://papers.ssrn.com/sol3/papers.cfm?abstract_id=3708495. Andy King, conversation with author, March 17, 2024, noted: "In total, we included 238 studies as a basis to generalize to the universe of studies (1,141), for which we used binomial confidence intervals correcting for finite population size. They don't 'examine' 1,000; they sample 238. The *population* is 1,000. It's like saying we examined 350 million when you surveyed 100 US citizens." From the Atz et al. report: "In contrast with research from management and related disciplines as well as findings purported by industry reports, we did not find an outsized financial return for ESG strategies. The bulk of studies concluded that there was either no statistical difference compared to a conventional benchmark or that results were positive and negative (i.e., mixed) within a study." See also Tensie Whelan, Ulrich Atz, Tracy Van Holt, and Casey Clark, "ESG and Financial Performance: Uncovering the Relationship by Aggregating Evidence from 1,000 Plus Studies Published between 2015–2020," NYU Stern Center for Sustainable Business, accessed January 29, 2024, https://www .readkong.com/page/esg-and-financial-performance-uncovering-the-relationship -9522431.

27. Much has been written on this topic of ESG's failure, and it's worth reading the work of Tariq Fancy, "The Secret Diary of a 'Sustainable Investor': Part 1," *Medium*, August 20, 2021, https://medium.com/@sosofancy/the-secret-diary-of-a -sustainable-investor-part-1-70b6987fa139; Tom Lyon, "How a Sustainability Index Can Keep Exxon but Drop Tesla—and 3 Ways to Fix ESG Ratings to Meet Investors' Expectations," Ross School of Business, University of Michigan, May 26, 2022, https://michiganross.umich.edu/news/how-sustainability-index-can-keep-exxon -drop-tesla-and-3-ways-fix-esg-ratings-meet-investors; Kenneth P. Pucker and Andrew King, "ESG Investing Isn't Designed to Save the Planet," *Harvard Business Review*, August 1, 2022, https://hbr.org/2022/08/esg-investing-isnt -designed-to-save-the-planet.

28. Saijel Kishan, "Academics Question ESG Studies That Fueled Investment Boom," *Bloomberg*, March 11, 2024.

29. Auden Schendler and Michael W. Toffel, "The Factor Environmental Ratings Miss," *MIT Sloan Management Review*, September 21, 2011, 17–18.

30. Beth Stackpole, "Why Sustainable Business Needs Better ESG Ratings," MIT Management Sloan School, December 26, 2021, https://mitsloan.mit.edu/ideas-made-to-matter/why-sustainable-business-needs-better-esg-ratings.

31. Mark Trexler and Auden Schendler, "Science Based Carbon Targets for the Corporate World: The Ultimate Sustainability Commitment, or a Costly Distraction?," *Journal of Industrial Ecology* 19, no. 6 (December 2015): 931–933.

32. PepsiCo, "Climate Change," https://www.pepsico.com/our-impact/esg-topics-a-z/climate-change.

33. David DiMolfetta, "Climate Group Pushes Big Tech to Exit Nation's Largest Business Lobby," *Washington Post*, August 2, 2023.

34. Kate Brandt LinkedIn page, https://www.linkedin.com/posts/katebrandt_epa-honors-2022-green-power-leaders-us-activity-6976332283171545088-t9Tz/?originalSubdomain=se.

35. Bill Weihl comment on Kate Brandt LinkedIn page, https://www.linkedin.com/posts/katebrandt_lessons-from-googles-clean-energy-agenda-activity-6958547206073196544-wytb?trk.

36. A relatively new nonprofit called ClimateVoice is calling out corporations. It was founded by Bill Weihl, who used to run sustainability programs at Google and Facebook. www.climatevoice.org.

37. Including me, in my early years. I vividly remember giving a presentation to a community group about the promise of corporate sustainability and, while I was doing it, having the vague feeling I might be a fraud. On ESG defenders, see Witold Henisz, "ESG in the Crosshairs: Don't Give Up on Economics for the Sake of Ideology," *LinkedIn Pulse*, July 21, 2022, https://www.linkedin.com/pulse/esg-cross-hairs-dont-give-up-economics-sake-ideology-witold-henisz/?trackingId=PVMjBq8O%2FBV5cZQqc1pyiQ%3D%3D; Robert Eccles, "The Topology of Hate for ESG," *Forbes*, June 3, 2022, https://www.forbes.com/sites/bobeccles/2022/06/03/the-topology-of-hate-for-esg/?sh=54a701581b0a; Kassia Yanosek and David G. Victor, "How Big Business Is Taking the Lead on Climate Change," *McKinsey Insights*, March 7, 2022, https://www.mckinsey.com/capabilities/sustainability/our-insights/sustainability-blog/how-big-business-is-taking-the-lead-on-climate-change.

38. Ilana Cohen and Michael E. Mann, "Climate Research Funded by Fossil Fuel Profits Discredits Universities and Hurts the Planet," *Los Angeles Times*, April 3, 2022.

39. Benjamin Franta, quoted in Hiroko Tabuchi, "Kicking Oil Companies Out of School," *Climate Forward* (newsletter), *New York Times*, August 16, 2022, https://www.nytimes.com/2022/08/16/climate/cambridge-university-oil-gas-funding.html.

40. Benjamin Franta, "The Pernicious Influence of Big Oil on America's Universities: Stanford's Divestment Debate Shows How Effective Fossil Fuel Companies Have Been at Colonizing Academia," *New Republic*, June 8, 2020.

41. For example, as previously noted, Andy King at Boston University, Ken Pucker at Tufts University, Mark Trexler of the Climatographers, and Tom Lyon at the University of Michigan.

42. OK, Patagonia and Ben & Jerry's are exceptions. But that's like saying the exceptions to you dominating a "Guitar Hero" performance are Bruce Springsteen and Mark Knopfler. Of course they are.

43. Salesforce, "We're Bringing the Full Power of Salesforce to Accelerate the World's Journey to Net Zero," Salesforce sustainability web page, https://www.salesforce.com/company/sustainability/.

44. Alliance for Research on Corporate Sustainability, "Advancing Rigorous Academic Research on Corporate Sustainability Issues," https://corporate-sustainability.org/.

45. Pension funds in Texas, Louisiana, and South Carolina pulled $4 billion (of the $10 trillion that BlackRock manages as of March 2024) out of BlackRock funds after the firm pointed out that "climate risk is financial risk," protesting the firm's "boycott" of the fossil fuel industry. Bryan Bashur, "BlackRock Divestment Tracker," Americans for Tax Reform, June 27, 2023, https://www.atr.org/esgradar/; Jack Pitcher, "Blackrock Now Manages $10 Trillion in Assets—for the Second Time," *Wall Street Journal*, January 12, 2024, https://www.wsj.com/livecoverage/stock-market-today-dow-jones-bank-earnings-01-12-2024/card/blackrock-now-manages-10-trillion-in-assets-for-the-second-time-GL23Jawyj1lfx55YGNhg. Fink has been pilloried by the left for holding so much fossil fuel stock and for arguing for a gradual transition. Because of the divestment, BlackRock may be pulling back on its ESG investments. Silla Brush, "BlackRock, State Street Among Money Managers Closing ESG Funds," *Bloomberg*, September 21, 2023, https://www.bloomberg.com/news/articles/2023-09-21/blackrock-state-street-among-money-managers-closing-esg-funds; Catherine Clifford, "Climate Activists Criticize BlackRock CEO's Support for Slow Transition Off Oil and Natural Gas," CNBC, January 18, 2022, https://www.cnbc.com/2022/01/18/blackrock-ceo-larry-finks-support-for-fossil-fuels-criticized.html).

46. Ken Pucker, LinkedIn post, https://www.linkedin.com/posts/kenpucker_setting-the-record-straight-on-energy-investing-activity-6986019874414186496-yrvL.

47. Farhad Manjoo, "What Blackrock, Vanguard and State Street Are Doing to the Economy," *New York Times*, May 12, 2022, https://www.nytimes.com/2022/05/12/opinion/vanguard-power-blackrock-state-street.html; BlackRock, "Energy Investing: Setting the Record Straight," https://www.blackrock.com/us/individual/insights/energy-investing.

48. Felix Salmon, "BlackRock's Larry Fink Takes On Retirement Crisis in Annual Investor Letter," Axios, March 26, 2024, https://www.axios.com/2024/03/26/blackrock-larry-fink-ceo-retirement.

49. InfluenceMap, "Corporate Climate Policy Footprint," November 2021, https://influencemap.org/report/The-Carbon-Policy-Footprint-Report-2021-670f36863e7859e1ad7848ec601dda97.

50. Cormac McCarthy, *No Country for Old Men* (New York: Vintage, 1986), 45.

51. James Hansen, *Storms of My Grandchildren: The Truth About the Coming Climate Catastrophe and Our Last Chance to Save Humanity* (New York: Bloomsbury, 2010), chap. 6.

52. Hansen, *Storms of My Grandchildren*, 91.

Chapter 5

1. Although this isn't always true. Earlier in my career, I had met David Brower, the legendary mountaineer, 10th Mountain Division veteran, Sierra Club president, and activist. We had a good, if short, conversation, during which he asked me, as a rock climber, if I'd ever drill a bolt. Bolts damage the rock and become permanent features, unlike the clean climbing tools developed by Chouinard, which you place and remove. "No!" I said, knowing that Brower himself had drilled the first bolt on an American rock climb on Ship Rock.

2. Climate Change, home page, https://www.changeclimate.org/.

3. The Ur-takedown is Joe Romm, "Are Carbon Offsets Unscalable, Unjust, and Unfixable—and a Threat to the Paris Climate Agreement?," white paper, Penn Center for Science, Sustainability and the Media, University of Pennsylvania, July 7, 2023, https://bpb-us-w2.wpmucdn.com/web.sas.upenn.edu/dist/0/896/files/2023/06/OffsetPaper7.0-6-27-23-FINAL2.pdf; Ben Elgin, "Timber CEO Wants to Reform Flawed Carbon Offset Market," *Bloomberg*, March 17, 2022; Adele Peters, "Carbon Offsets Have Serious Issues. Is It Even Possible to Fix Them?" *Fast Company*, August 24, 2022; John Oliver, "Carbon Offsets," *Last Week Tonight with John Oliver*, HBO, August 21, 2022, YouTube video, https://www.youtube.com/watch?v=6p8zAbFKpW0.

4. Sam Meredith, "World's Biggest Companies Accused of Exaggerating Their Climate Actions," CNBC, February 7, 2022, https://www.cnbc.com/2022/02/07/study-worlds-biggest-firms-seen-exaggerating-their-climate-actions.html; Jocelyn Timperley, "The Truth Behind Corporate Climate Pledges," *Guardian*, July 26, 2021; Eric Rosten and Ben Elgin, "Companies' Climate Goals in Jeopardy from Flawed Energy Credits," *Bloomberg Law*, June 9, 2022.

5. Science Based Targets home page, https://sciencebasedtargets.org/.

6. Roger Voss, "Domaine Georges Roumier 2000 Le Musigny (Musigny)," *Wine Enthusiast*, had this to say about the wine and rated it 94/100: "An immediately attractive wine, with aromas of summer flowers and orange zest. Soft, sweet fruits and ripeness underline the delicious pure fruit flavors. The structure is dense but fine, the essence of a seductive Pinot Noir."

7. Ben Elgin, "Big Soda's Addiction to New Plastic Jeopardizes Climate Progress," *Bloomberg*, July 12, 2022, https://www.bloomberg.com/features/2022-coke-pepsi-plastic-recycling-climate-action/.

8. Elgin, "Big Soda's Addiction."

9. Rebecca Hughes, "Beauty Through the Ages: The History of Tanning," *Look Fantastic*, 2017, https://www.lookfantastic.com/blog/discover/beauty-through-the-ages-the-history-of-tanning/.

10. Climate Interactive, "The En-ROADS Climate Solutions Simulator," https://www.climateinteractive.org/en-roads/. On the issue of nature-based offsets, my only friendly gripe with Patagonia's approach is its disproportionate emphasis on nature-based climate solutions. We need those, but job number one, according to the models, is stopping emissions from fossil fuel combustion.

11. John Sterman, "AVIDly Seeking Carbon Offsets," white paper, Sloan School of Management, Massachusetts Institute of Technology, December 2019, revised February 2020. Also see Betsy Vereckey, "How to Choose Carbon Offsets That Actually Cut Emissions," Sloan School of Management, Massachusetts Institute of Technology, November 2, 2022, https://mitsloan.mit.edu/ideas-made-to-matter/how-to-choose-carbon-offsets-actually-cut-emissions.

12. Patrick Greenfield, Patrick. "Revealed: More than 90% of Rainforest Carbon Offsets by Biggest Certifier Are Worthless, Analysis Shows," *Guardian*, January 18, 2023, https://www.theguardian.com/environment/2023/jan/18/revealed-forest-carbon-offsets-biggest-provider-worthless-verra-aoe.

13. Romm, "Are Carbon Offsets Unscalable?"

14. Trading Economics, "EU Carbon Permits," accessed February 24, 2024, https://tradingeconomics.com/commodity/carbon.

15. Harry Bowcott, Daniel Pacthod, and Dickon Pinner, "COP26 Made Net Zero a Core Principle for Business. Here's How Leaders Can Act," *McKinsey*

Sustainability, November 12, 2021, https://www.mckinsey.com/capabilities
/sustainability/our-insights/cop26-made-net-zero-a-core-principle-for-business-heres
-how-leaders-can-act; Net Zero Tracker, "New Analysis: Half of World's Largest
Companies Are Committed to Net Zero," November 5, 2023, https://zerotracker.net
/analysis/new-analysis-half-of-worlds-largest-companies-are-committed-to-net-zero.

16. James Dyke, Robert Watson, and Wolfgang Knorr, "Climate Scientists:
Concept of Net Zero Is a Dangerous Trap," *The Conversation*, April 22, 2021.

17. "Can the Carbon Offset Market be Saved?" *Economist*, December 20, 2023,
https://www.economist.com/finance-and-economics/2023/12/20/can-the-carbon
-offset-market-be-saved.

18. Ellen Ormesher, "'There Is Too Much Impunity': Carbon Offsets Present an
Emerging Risk to Advertisers," *The Drum*, February 20, 2023, https://www.thedrum
.com/news/2023/02/20/there-too-much-impunity-carbon-offsets-present-emerging
-risk-advertisers.

19. Patrick Greenfield, "Delta Air Lines Faces Lawsuit Over $1Bn Carbon
Neutrality Claim," *Guardian*, May 30, 2023.

20. This subsection comes from an op-ed I wrote with Joe Romm, author of
the OG paper debunking offsets (Romm, "Are Carbon Offsets Unscalable?"), which
came out in 2023. The Messenger, the online news website (https://themessenger
.com) that published this op-ed, is no longer accessible; the company dissolved in
January 31, 2024. Thanks to Joe for letting me use this text.

21. Billy Gridley, "Corporate America's Silent Abdication on Climate Legislation,"
Climate and Capital Media, August 5, 2022, https://www.climateandcapitalmedia
.com/corporate-americas-silent-abdication-on-climate-legislation/.

22. InfluenceMap, "Net Zero Greenwash: The Gap Between Corporate
Commitments and Their Policy Engagement," November 2023, https://influencemap
.org/briefing/The-State-of-Net-Zero-Greenwash-24402.

Chapter 6

1. On child mortality, see Max Roser, "Mortality in the Past: Every Second Child
Died," OurWorldInData.org, April 11, 2023, https://ourworldindata.org/child
-mortality-in-the-past. Song lyrics from Bruce Springsteen, "Youngstown," *The Ghost
of Tom Joad*, Columbia Records, 1995.

2. I'm not offering a thank-you to the people from that industry who later
understood the climate impacts of coal and then supported disinformation campaigns
to prevent legislation and public understanding of the issue.

3. Holy Cross Energy, "Power Supply & Greenhouse Gas Emissions,"
https://www.holycross.com/greenhouse-gas-emissions/.

4. Power Technology, "Comanche 3 Power Station Expansion, CO, USA," *Power
Technology*, January 29, 2006, https://www.power-technology.com/projects
/comanche-3-expansion/?cf-view.

5. Here's more on Lynn and the campaign, from a Denver magazine. Her memory
of how I convinced her was a bit different from mine: Elisabeth Kwak-Hefferan,
"The Coup That Turned a Tiny Colorado Utility Company into a Clean Energy
Pioneer," *5280 (Denver's Mile High Magazine)*, July 2023, https://www.5280.com/
the-coup-that-turned-a-tiny-colorado-utility-company-into-a-clean-energy-pioneer/.

6. Scott Condon, "Holy Cross Election Heats Up," *Glenwood Springs (CO) Post
Independent*, May 20, 2008, https://www.postindependent.com/news/holy-cross
-election-heats-up/.

7. Auden Schendler, Aspen Skiing Company, to Del Worley, CEO, Holy Cross Energy, June 22, 2009, internal document at Aspen Skiing Company.

8. As it played out, Comanche 3 never worked very well as a *baseload* plant, meaning one that provided a continuous power supply. It was often down, and Xcel decided to close it early (Kevin Clark, "Poor Maintenance and Costly Breakdowns: The Troubled History of Comanche Unit 3," *Power Engineering*, September 7, 2022, https://www.power-eng.com/coal/poor-maintenance-and-costly-breakdowns-the-troubled-history-of-comanche-unit-3/#gref).

9. Scott Condon, "President of Holy Cross Board Defends Caution on Renewables," *Aspen Times*, May 21, 2009, https://www.aspentimes.com/news/president-of-holy-cross-board-defends-caution-on-renewables.

10. More than half of the company's carbon footprint comes from electricity. See Aspen Skiing Company, "Aspen Skiing Company Sustainability Report," Aspen Snowmass, 2021, https://www.aspensnowmass.com/-/media/aspen-snowmass/documents/sustainability/2021/sr2021finalsmall1122.pdf, page 34.

11. Personal communication with Jason Blevins, January 29, 2021.

12. It's not 100 percent clear that Twain said this, but it is widely attributed to him (Matt Seybold, "The Apocryphal Twain: 'The Two Most Important Days of Your Life . . . ,'" Center for Mark Twain Studies, December 6, 2016, https://marktwainstudies.com/the-apocryphal-twain-the-two-most-important-days-of-your-life/).

Chapter 7

1. Deborah Zabarenko, "Kimberly-Clark Joins Greenpeace to Protect Forests," Reuters, August 5, 2009, https://www.reuters.com/article/us-kimberlyclark/kimberly-clark-joins-greenpeace-to-protect-forests-idUSTRE5745AM20090805/.

2. Hiroko Tabuchi, "Leaks Can Make Natural Gas as Bad for the Climate as Coal, a Study Says," *New York Times*, July 13, 2023.

3. Jane Mayer, "'Kochland' Examines the Koch Brothers' Early, Crucial Role in Climate Change Denial," *New Yorker*, August 13, 2019.

4. Emily Flitter, "My Tireless Quest for a Tubeless Wipe," *New York Times*, February 28, 2020.

5. Kai Ryssdal and Amy Scott, "The Plastic Recycling Hoax," Make Me Smart, episode 993, *Marketplace*, August 29, 2023, https://www.marketplace.org/shows/make-me-smart/the-plastic-recycling-hoax/.

6. Wikipedia, s.v. "Children's Crusade (1963)," updated April 3, 2024, https://en.wikipedia.org/wiki/Children%27s_Crusade_(1963).

7. On the crab fishery lawsuit, see Erin McCormick, "Claws Out: Crab Fishermen Sue 30 Oil Firms over Climate Change," *Guardian*, November 14, 2018. On the Boulder lawsuit, see Boulder County, "Colorado Communities' Lawsuit Against Oil Giants to Continue in Local Court," Boulder Count News Archive, February 5, 2021, https://bouldercounty.gov/news/colorado-communities-lawsuit-against-oil-giants-to-continue-in-local-court/.

8. Aspen Skiing Company was the only outdoor industry business to file an amicus brief in *Mass. v. EPA*. It probably had no effect at all, but the action was the beginning of our attempt to think differently, and at a larger scale, about climate change.

Chapter 8

1. This story was most recently told by Martin Sheen, "Martin Sheen: 4 Pieces of Advice for the Next Generation," *Time*, August 26, 2019, https://time.com/4465252 /martin-sheen-we-days/. John Green describes being told the story by his spiritual adviser in his *Streetwalking with Jesus: Reaching Out in Justice and Mercy* (Huntington, IN: Our Sunday Visitor, 2011).

2. This is an intentional, gratuitous, and therefore humorous attack on snowboarders, which is a thing that's done in the ski business.

3. David Gilson, "The NRA Says It Has Five Million Members. Its Magazines Tell Another Story," *Mother Jones*, March 7, 2018.

4. Outdoor Industry Association, "2023 Outdoor Participation Trends Report," accessed March 20, 2024, https://outdoorindustry.org/resource/2023-outdoor -participation-trends-report/. On number of gun owners, see Lisa Dunn, "How Many People in the US Own Guns?" Guns & America Series, WAMU, September 18, 2020, https://wamu.org/story/20/09/18/how-many-people-in-the-u-s-own-guns/.

5. Christopher Solomon, "Lisa Murkowski Didn't Like This Ad. We Fact-Checked It," *Outside Magazine*, November 27, 2018, https://www.outsideonline.com /outdoor-adventure/environment/lisa-murkowski-environmental-record-fact-check/.

Chapter 9

1. US Securities and Exchange Commission, "SEC Proposes Rules to Enhance and Standardize Climate-Related Disclosures for Investors," press release, March 21, 2022, https://www.sec.gov/news/press-release/2022-46; Carbon Bankroll, "The Carbon Bankroll," Topo Finance, https://www.topofinance.org/carbon-bankroll-2. Per Patrick Flynn's quote on the above webpage, Salesforce, at least, didn't respond to this news with the standard corporate stonewalling or silence. To their credit, they effectively said: "Good point. We'll have to deal with that."

2. Bill McKibben, "Could Google's Carbon Emissions Have Effectively Doubled Overnight?," *New Yorker*, May 20, 2022.

Chapter 10

1. On ExxonMobil's knowledge of climate science, see Oliver Milman, "Smoking Gun Proof: Fossil Fuel Industry Knew of Carbon Danger as Early as 1954, Documents Show," *Guardian*, January 30, 2024. On global temperature spike, see Rebecca Lindsey and Luann Dahlman, "Climate Change: Global Temperature," Climate.gov, National Oceanic and Atmospheric Administration, January 18, 2024, https://www .climate.gov/news-features/understanding-climate/climate-change-global-temperature.

2. Geoffrey Supran and Naomi Oreskes, "The Forgotten Oil Ads That Told Us Climate Change Was Nothing," *Guardian*, November 18, 2021.

3. Glenn Scherer and Dailyclimate.org, "Climate Science Predictions Prove Too Conservative," *Scientific American*, December 6, 2012, https://www.scientificamerican .com/article/climate-science-predictions-prove-too-conservative/.

4. Rachel Maddow, *Blowout: Corrupted Democracy, Rogue State Russia, and the Richest, Most Destructive Industry on Earth* (New York: Crown, 2019).

5. Robert Reich, "The Real Motive Behind the GOP's 'Culture War,'" *Robert Reich* (blog), August 11, 2022, https://robertreich.org/post/692312251413168128.

6. Reich, "The Real Motive."

7. Because a gallon of gasoline, combusted, releases approximately twenty pounds of carbon dioxide, and an SUV gets, optimistically, twenty-five miles per gallon (National Aeronautics and Space Administration, "A Gallon of Gas = 20 Pounds of CO_2!," *Climate Kids*, https://climatekids.nasa.gov/review/carbon /gasoline.html.

8. Arielle Samuelson, "How to Greenwash: Propane Industry Tries to Rebrand Fuel as Renewable," *Guardian*, January 25, 2024.

9. United Nations, "Causes and Effects of Climate Change," accessed February 4, 2024, https://www.un.org/en/climatechange/science/causes-effects-climate-change.

10. Michael Thomas, "A Fossil Fuel Economy Requires 535X More Mining Than a Clean Energy Economy," *Distilled*, March 29, 2023, https://www.distilled.earth /p/a-fossil-fuel-economy-requires-535x?utm_campaign=post&utm_medium=web.

11. Bill McKibben, "Ezra Klein Interviews Bill McKibben," *Ezra Klein Show* (*New York Times*), transcript, November 15, 2022, https://www.nytimes. com/2022/11/15/podcasts/transcript-ezra-klein-interviews-bill-mckibben.html.

Chapter 11

1. Quincy Shannon, who goes by "Q," was one of a half dozen people we reached out to after George Floyd's murder to help us understand how to act in meaningful ways on issues of race, justice, and diversity. Q's story was particularly informative and almost metaphorical, and that's why I use it here. But other advisers offered us important insight and advice, including Henri Rivers, the president of the National Brotherhood of Skiers; Darnell Rose, a longtime Aspen ski instructor; Wayne Hare, of the Civil Conversations Project; Devon Joyner, then of Limelight Snowmass; and Clay Fong, now at the US Department of Justice.

2. Ben & Jerry's, "Americans Agree on Far More Than We Disagree," June 30, 2023, https://www.benjerry.com/whats-new/2022/06/americans-agree-on-issues.

3. On Microsoft's commitment, see Brad Smith, "Microsoft Will Be Carbon Negative by 2030," *Microsoft* (blog), January 16, 2020, https://blogs.microsoft .com/blog/2020/01/16/microsoft-will-be-carbon-negative-by-2030/. On Microsoft's Conference in Saudi Arabia, see Kyla Mandel, "It's Critical: Can Microsoft Make Good on Its Climate Ambitions?," *Guardian*, November 27, 2021. On Big Oil quote, see Michael Mann and Bill Weihl, "Tech's 'Inactivism' on Climate Policy Is a Big Problem," *Newsweek*, April 6, 2021.

4. Peter S. Goodman, "Big Business Pledged Gentler Capitalism. It's Not Happening in a Pandemic," *New York Times*, April 13, 2020.

5. Edelman, "2020 Annual Trust Barometer," January 19, 2020, https://www .edelman.com/trust/2020-trust-barometer.

6. Matthew T. Huber, *Climate Change as Class War: Building Socialism on a Warming Planet* (New York: Verso, 2022); Matthew T. Huber, "Ecological Politics for the Working Class," *Catalyst* 3, no. 1 (spring 2019), https://catalyst-journal .com/2019/07/ecological-politics-for-the-working-class.

7. Erik Conway and Naomi Oreskes, *The Big Myth: How Business Taught Us to Loathe Government and Love the Free Market* (New York: Bloomsbury, 2023).

8. National Academies of Sciences, "Accelerating Decarbonization in the United States: Technology, Policy and Societal Dimensions," *Consensus Study Highlights*, October 2023, https://nap.nationalacademies.org/resource/25931/interactive/. On buy-in, see Umair Irfan, "'We Risk a Yellow Vest Movement': Why the US Clean Energy Transition Must Be Equitable," *Vox*, February 4, 2021, https://www.vox .com/22264282/biden-climate-change-clean-energy-national-academies-science -transition.

9. Not only rich people support whales, according to historian Naomi Oreskes. She noted that "On whales specifically, in my ocean book, *Science on a Mission*, I talk about the public opposition to ATOC [Acoustic Thermometry, used to measure ocean temperatures], because it would harm whales. There was a huge outpouring of letters from 'ordinary' citizens against ATOC, often because people had read about it in local newspapers in California. Lots of people love whales, not just rich folks." Personal conversation with Naomi Oreskes, June 25, 2024.

10. Too many builders focus on net zero these days instead of just pure electrification, which is also net zero, just later. Focusing immediately on net zero means massive expenditures on solar panels and other features to meet the difficult standard. But electrification gets you there and allows the saved money to be spent on other things, like more electrification or, in our case, improving efficiency of existing crappy buildings. The focus should move away from net zero and toward electrification. net zero should go away.

11. Levi Sumagaysay, "Wall Street Banks Oppose Shareholder Calls for Racial Equity Audits," *Financial News*, March 18, 2021.

Chapter 12

1. Reinhold Niebuhr, *The Irony of American History* (Chicago: University of Chicago Press, 2008), 63.

2. Rarely do old-school environmentalists who oppose wind, solar, and hydro acknowledge that coal and natural gas plants, often in city downtowns, are also ugly and have the added cost of killing people with air pollution. Also, are solar panels and wind turbines not beautiful? A Harvard study, Karn Vohra et al., "Fossil Fuel Air Pollution Responsible for 1 in 5 Deaths Worldwide," T. H. Chan School of Public Health, Harvard University, February 9, 2021, https://www.hsph.harvard.edu/c -change/news/fossil-fuel-air-pollution-responsible-for-1-in-5-deaths-worldwide, showed that air pollution from fossil fuels like coal and diesel kills eight million people a year. One in five deaths can be attributed to fossil fuel pollution.

3. Auden Schendler, "Building Ghost Towns with Million Dollar Views," *Writers on the Range*, March 2, 2006.

4. Kathleen Lamp, "Making American Beautiful Again . . . Again," *Eidolon*, March 23, 2020, https://eidolon.pub/city-beautiful-9b6943bc7473.

5. Kimberly Quick, "Exclusionary Zoning Continues Racial Segregation's Ugly Work," Century Foundation, August 4, 2017, https://tcf.org/content/commentary /exclusionary-zoning-continues-racial-segregations-ugly-work/?agreed=1.

6. Dennis wrote me, after winning this fight: "This was quite the passion project toward doing the right thing. I didn't tell my family about what I was doing except my ninety-four-year-old mother. She told all of my siblings . . . They all were very excited for the outcome in the same way that I am. Even my Republican brother. It was really

special to share the experience with all of them. You, of course, were mentioned. To
wit, my mother wrote back: 'What's an Auden?'"

7. Joke: What does a snowboarder say when he gets on the ski lift with you?
Answer: "Sorry, dude."

8. Al Bartolotta, "Urban Planning in the US: Uncovering a Legacy of Racism,"
Forward Pinellas, August 13, 2020, https://forwardpinellas.org/transportation
-disadvantaged/racism-in-urban-planning/.

Chapter 13

1. Elizabeth Kolbert, "Sleeping with the Enemy," *New Yorker*, August 8, 2011.

2. Kolbert, "Sleeping with the Enemy."

3. F. Scott Fitzgerald, *Echoes of the Jazz Age* (New York: Scribner, 1931), 7.

4. Camille Sweeney and Josh Gosfield, "When Failure Is Not an Option, Typical
Career Advice Does Not Apply [Philippe Petit Part 2]," in *The Art of Doing: How
Superachievers Do What They Do and How They Do It So Well* (New York: Penguin
Group, 2013), https://theartofdoing.com/when-failure-is-not-an-option-typical-career
-advice-does-not-apply-philippe-petit-part-2/.

5. Caroline Picard, ed., *The North Georgia Gazette and Winter Chronicle*
(Chicago: Green Lantern Press, 2009).

6. Barry Lopez, *Arctic Dreams: Imagination and Desire in a Northern Landscape*
(New York: Scribner, 1986), 406.

7. Joseph Conrad, *Youth, a Narrative, and Two Other Stories*
(London: W. Blackwood and Son, 1902), 48.

Epilogue

1. Personal conversation with Andrew P. Jones of Climate Interactive based on
research behind that organization's climate models.

2. Joe Ryan, "Fossil Fuel Industry Risks Losing $33 Trillion to Climate Change,"
Bloomberg, July 11, 2016, https://www.bloomberg.com/news/articles/2016-07-11
/fossil-fuel-industry-risks-losing-33-trillion-to-climate-change.

3. "I am a Christian, and indeed a Roman Catholic," J. R. R. Tolkien writes in
one of his letters, "so that I do not expect 'history' to be anything but a 'long defeat'—
though it contains . . . some samples or glimpses of final victory." Andrew Barber,
"Tolkien and the Long Defeat," *The Gospel Coalition*, December 10, 2013.

4. Charlie Trimm, "Reflections on Tolkien's Lord of the Rings, Part One: The
Long Defeat," *The Good Book* (blog), March 21, 2016, https://www.biola.edu/blogs
/good-book-blog/2016/reflections-on-tolkien-s-lord-of-the-rings-part-one-the-long-
defeat.

5. Jorge Luis Borges, *El Otro, el Mismo* (Buenos Aires: Emecé, 1969).

6. Jon Hochschartner, "What I. F. Stone Said," Counterpunch, June 1, 2023,
https://www.counterpunch.org/2023/06/01/what-i-f-stone-said/.

7. Albert Camus, *The Myth of Sisyphus*, translated by Justin O'Brien (New York:
Vintage Books, 1955), 91.

8. Cormac McCarthy, *The Road* (New York: Alfred A. Knopf, 2006), 54.

9. Mike Baker and David Gelles, "Judge Rules in Favor of Montana Youths in a
Landmark Climate Case," *New York Times*, August 14, 2023.

10. W. H. Auden, *Another Time* (New York: Random House, 1940).

11. Stanley Kunitz, *The Collected Poems* (New York: Norton, 2003).

Appendix

1. Suing a fossil fuel company is the big leagues, so you'll want to have good legal counsel and move carefully.

2. On losing the fight, see David Wallace-Wells, "Time to Panic: The Planet Is Getting Warmer in Catastrophic Ways. And Fear May Be the Only Thing That Saves Us," *New York Times*, February 16, 2019. On tipping points, see Holly Evarts, "Climate Change Tipping Point Could Be Coming Sooner Than We Think," Columbia Engineering, Columbia University, New York, press release, January 23, 2019, https://engineering.columbia.edu/press-releases/climate-change-tipping-point. On the inevitability of social collapse, see Jem Bendell, "Deep Adaptation: A Map for Navigating Climate Tragedy," Initiative for Leadership and Sustainability (IFLAS), University of Cumbria, UK, occasional paper 2, July 27, 2018; revised July 27, 2020, https://www.lifeworth.com/deepadaptation.pdf.

3. Robert R. Gunning, "Order Re: Defendants' Motion to Dismiss," June 21, 2024. Board of County Commissioners of Boulder County; City of Boulder v. Suncor Energy (U.S.A.), Inc.; Suncor Energy Sales, Inc.; Suncor Energy Inc.; ExxonMobil Corporation, 2018CV30349 (Boulder County District Court).

4. Suing ExxonMobil requires filing in a state where the business operates. That's why Colorado works, because ExxonMobil is involved in gas drilling there. Another good state to target would be New Jersey.

5. Gina McCarthy (former EPA administrator in Obama administration), discussion with author, January 16, 2019.

6. The true odds of success in federal court are likely closer to zero because of the makeup of the Supreme Court and the fact that the Clean Air Act is the tool used to regulate pollutants at the federal level.

7. I spoke with various lawyers about this issue in January 2019.

INDEX

CREDITS

Portions of this work were originally published in different form in other media. Chapter 4: Auden Schendler, "The Complicity of Corporate Sustainability," *Stanford Social Innovation Review*, April 7, 2021, and Auden Schendler, "Worrying About Your Carbon Footprint Is Exactly What Big Oil Wants You to Do," *New York Times*, August 31, 2021. Chapter 5 came from my article "The False Promise of Corporate Carbon Neutrality," *Stanford Social Innovation Review*, October 4, 2022, and an op-ed Joe Romm and I wrote together but didn't publish, and from a column in the online journal *The Messenger*, which is now defunct. Thanks to Joe Romm for permission to use this work. Chapter 6: Auden Schendler's letter to Holy Cross CEO Del Worley reprinted with Aspen One's permission. Chapter 8: "Give a Flake" postcard reprinted with Aspen One's permission. Chapter 9: Auden Schendler, "How Businesses Can Hold Their Banks Accountable on Climate Change," hbr.org, June 30, 2022; the letter to Del Worley of Holy Cross Energy is reprinted with permission from Aspen Skiing Company. Chapter 11: Auden Schendler, "The Climate-Equity Connection," hbr.org, May 13, 2021. Portions of chapter 12: Auden Schendler, "How to Fix the Mountain Town Housing Crisis," Outsideonline.com, January 25, 2018. Epilogue: Auden Schendler and Andrew (Drew) P. Jones, "Stopping Climate Change Is Hopeless. Let's Do It," *New York Times*, October 6, 2018. Much of the epilogue was originally conceived of and written with Drew Jones and is used with his permission.

The interludes at the ends of the chapters were essays I wrote and previously published elsewhere. Chapter 1's interlude first appeared as "On Hatteras, Putting Ourselves, and the World, Back Together" in *Huffington Post*. Chapter 2's interlude appeared as "How I Tried to Patch Together a Disintegrating World," in *High Country News*. Chapter 3: "Journeys We Take at Home," *Baltimore Sun* and, later, *High Country News*. Chapter 4: "When a Scientist Becomes an Activist," *High Country News*. Chapter 5: "Floating Past Ghosts on the Green River," *High Country News*. Chapter 6: "With a Grin and a Wink, Adam Palmer Had Missions in Life Far Beyond Himself," *Big Pivots* e-magazine. Chapter 7: "In Small Town Baseball, a Wider World," *High Country News*. Chapter 8: "Debris Huts and Other Skills," *Mountain Gazette*. Chapter 9: "Love, Loneliness, and How to Treat Each Other," *Your Teen* magazine as "My Middle School Daughter Has No Friends at School." Chapter 10: "A Lifetime of Service on the North Dakota Plains," *High Country News*. Chapter 11: "Childhood's End," *High Country News*. Chapter 12: "Gnomes and the Meaning of Life: Connecting with My Son," *Your Teen* magazine.

ACKNOWLEDGMENTS

It's hard to publish a book these days, so I'll start with the people who made it happen. First is a writer of the highest caliber, Charles Fishman, who has been unerringly supportive since my first book, which he also helped make possible. He's also viciously frank. After failing to get any traction with publishers, I read my pitch to Charles, telling him I was talking to Harvard Business Review Press the next week. When I finished, there was a silence. "Auden," he said. "You have Covid. Call the editor, tell him you're sick, and give yourself another week to buff this out. And here's what you need to do . . . " I did exactly what he suggested. And, as it turned out, the guy I pitched to ultimately became my editor, Jeff Kehoe. Jeff had been introduced to me by my old friend and *Harvard Business Review* editor Eben Harrell, who said this about him: "He's a calm, kind, wonderful 'mensch' of a man. Very active in local politics in his town. A former Marine, so there's grit under the gentle exterior. Been with HBR for donkey's years so he's very savvy about the business and the editorial side. I think you'll like him very much." Eben was right. Jeff understood what I was doing even better than I did. "Is this a memoir?" he asked me early on, when I'd never even considered that possibility. There's little in life more gratifying than finding someone who understands the complicated idea you're trying to convey better than you do, and this was true of Jeff because he's a thinking, caring, and careful person. But he's also scrupulously honest: one of his editorial comments was "Come on. This is juvenile." Or "Let's cut the snark."

I loved it. If this book had never made it into print but gave me the chance to work with Jeff Kehoe, it would have been worth it.

Others who helped me think through the book's concept, title, and strategy and encouraged me forward include my very old friends and brothers in arms Joe Romm and Drew Jones. Drew often seemed more excited about the book than I was. His visceral happiness for a friend is a unique and rare human trait. Florence Williams, one of my first editors, helped me bang around titles. It was Michael Miracle at Aspen One, a formidable writer in his own right, who came into my office after I'd told him another crazy story about my kids and life and family, and said, "I wonder if you could combine that with your climate work into a book?" And Hannah Berman, also from Aspen One, bugged and encouraged me for years: "When's your next book?" (My typical answer: "I only have one in me.") Both participated in the thinking and doing that's in the final product.

My grouchy old men's club (which includes women), the apostates in the sustainability business world, are part of the book's intellectual foundation. They include Adam Rome, Ken Pucker, Andy King, who was invaluable in reviewing and contributing to the ESG thinking in chapter 4, Naomi Oreskes, Kelly Eskew, and Steven Kreft. Ken, Adam, and Steven offered early comments on the first draft that were invaluable and generous. Thanks to Mario Molina for his work at POW, and Yasmin Bhan for her expert digital marketing. My brother-in-law Paul Freedman, also a professor, was both encouraging and a thought partner on many of the questions in the book. And of course, my mother-in-law, Fran, already thinks this is the best book in the world, and I the best son-in-law. Back at her.

Thanks to Chris Lotspeich for wanting it all, and trying to get it, in that little cubicle with me at RMI.

Thanks to Ryan and Bonnie Slack and their wonderful kids, Hudson and Hazel, for letting me use part of their family story to end this book and for showing me what it means to be a good neighbor.

My family, Ellen, Willa, and Elias, were the people who over many years lived what became my notion of "Terrible Beauty."

They remain, well, terribly beautiful. Ellen tolerates, even abets, my post-coffee rants and is a partner without whom I would be barely functional and less than the human I aspire to be. I am so lucky to have found her. Elias and Willa's wicked humor means that I can often say dark, absurd, even incomprehensible things that they will understand right away—and fire back. Both "get" the nature of the world I describe in this book. How did these kids become the rare and offbeat people I have long admired? My love for all three is the foundation of my climate work.

I also want to express my gratitude to those mentors and friends who, to quote Stanley Kunitz, "fell along the way": my father, David Schendler, Ed Marston, Randy Udall, Dave Bellack, and Ted Smith—all helpfully incorrigible and contrary in their own ways. Kunitz again: ". . . their manic dust bitterly stings my face," in a good way. They helped me realize that my job was not to mourn them, but to take on the role they played for me, and offer it to others—I'm the elder now.

My mom, Mary Jo, who possesses a North Dakota matter-of-factness and durability as well as a joy of life and a sense of humor, still guides me through life. My sister, Rachel, and her children Gabriel, May, and Isaiah, while far away, have been touchstones too.

Lib and Roger Smith helped create my worldview as surrogate parents for many, many summers, even to this day, in Montana. Their offspring, including Theo, and Catherine and Chris Filardi, their kids Wren and Leo, and my oldest friend and cousin Topher, his wife Julie, and their kids have been constants in parenting and adventure and now middle age.

My "men's drinking and vice society" friends are the personification of the decades-long Harvard happiness study. They include Jamie Ames, Mark Thomas, Peter Mueller, Matt (and Jenny) Jones, John Rigney, and Chris Lane, brothers from another mother all. Also friends and technical engineering masters, Dave Houghton and Peter Rumsey, and poet and most erudite of all people Mark Scott. Mark Trexler has always been willing to dig as deeply as necessary into any climate topic, and his wealth of knowledge and experience is vast.

Thanks to the Crown family for providing my livelihood for twenty-five years and for letting the leash out dangerously far. Pat O'Donnell originally empowered me, and Mike Kaplan let me run. Later, Dave Tanner understood what I was doing, and did me a solid by reviewing this book under deadline.

The writings of Barry Lopez, Cormac McCarthy, Marilynne Robinson, and Jack Kerouac deeply affected my thinking and writing. Bill McKibben has been an inspiration and a kind and generous friend, as have Tom Friedman, Gina McCarthy, Conrad Anker, Casey Sheahan, Naomi Oreskes, and Annie Leonard. Greg Williams, Penn Newhard, and the team at Backbone Media have been generous with their time and expertise and have taught me a great deal about modern marketing and media. Matt Hamilton has been a valuable sounding board for years. Thanks to Bill Weihl for his courage and vision, and to Joel Makower for publishing my ideas over many years. Betsy Marston's influence as an editor, writer, and life force has been profound.

The Udall clan, with their humor and backcountry companionship, have been part of my family's life since I was twenty-two.

Thanks to Chris Conway for being all-in on my writing and my ideas and for paying attention to and publishing my work in the *New York Times* despite overwhelming pressures in that crazy job of his.

Wayne Hare, Q Shannon, Darnell Rose, and Clay Fong are friends—some of them for several decades—who also helped me think about race and justice in America.

Thanks also to the production, editing, and design experts at Harvard Business Review Press: Jennifer Waring, Cheyenne Paterson, Felicia Sinusas, design director Stephani Finks (who, along with Alissa Dinallo, nailed the cover), Jon Shipley, Julie Devoll, Lindsey Dietrich, Jordan Concannon, Alex Kephart, Sally Ashworth, Bill Gallagher, Rick Emanuel, Ed Domina, copy editors

Patricia Boyd and Karen Palmer, my wonderful fact-checkers, and the rest of this exceptional team.

Thanks to all the foot soldiers in the trenches of the sustainable-business movement, mostly young, who have contacted me over the years and themselves strived for a bigger vision and impact, asking the question from *Mad Max: Fury Road:* "Where are we to go, we who wander this wasteland in search of our better selves?" This book is, in part, for all of you.

ABOUT THE AUTHOR

Auden Schendler spent twenty-five years running sustainability programs at Aspen One, which operates ski resorts, hotels, restaurants, and retail stores. He focuses on scale solutions to climate change, including clean-energy development, policy, advocacy, movement building, and activism. Along with Protect Our Winters, where he served on the board for a decade, he is working to mobilize the outdoor industry as a political force. Previously a research associate at Rocky Mountain Institute (RMI), he is the author of the book *Getting Green Done: Hard Truths from the Front Lines of the Sustainability Revolution*, which climatologist James Hansen called "an antidote to greenwash." He was named a "climate innovator" by *Time* magazine and a "climate saver" by the EPA. Auden served on Colorado's Air Quality Control Commission, where he developed state climate policy, and between 2016 and 2020 he was elected to the town council of Basalt, Colorado. An avid outdoorsman and "dirtbag," he has climbed Denali, North America's highest peak; kayaked the Grand Canyon in winter; and twice ascended Mount Rainier's Liberty Ridge: the first time terrified, the second competently. He has worked as a burger flipper, Bobcat driver, medic on a rural ambulance service, a Forest Service goose-nest island builder in Alaska, auction junk sorter, gas station attendant, Outward Bound instructor, high school English and math teacher, ski instructor, and low-income housing weatherization technician. A graduate of Stuyvesant High School and Bowdoin College, he lives in Basalt, Colorado, with his wife, Ellen, and children, Willa and Elias. Additional writing, podcasts, and interviews can be found at Audenschendler.com.